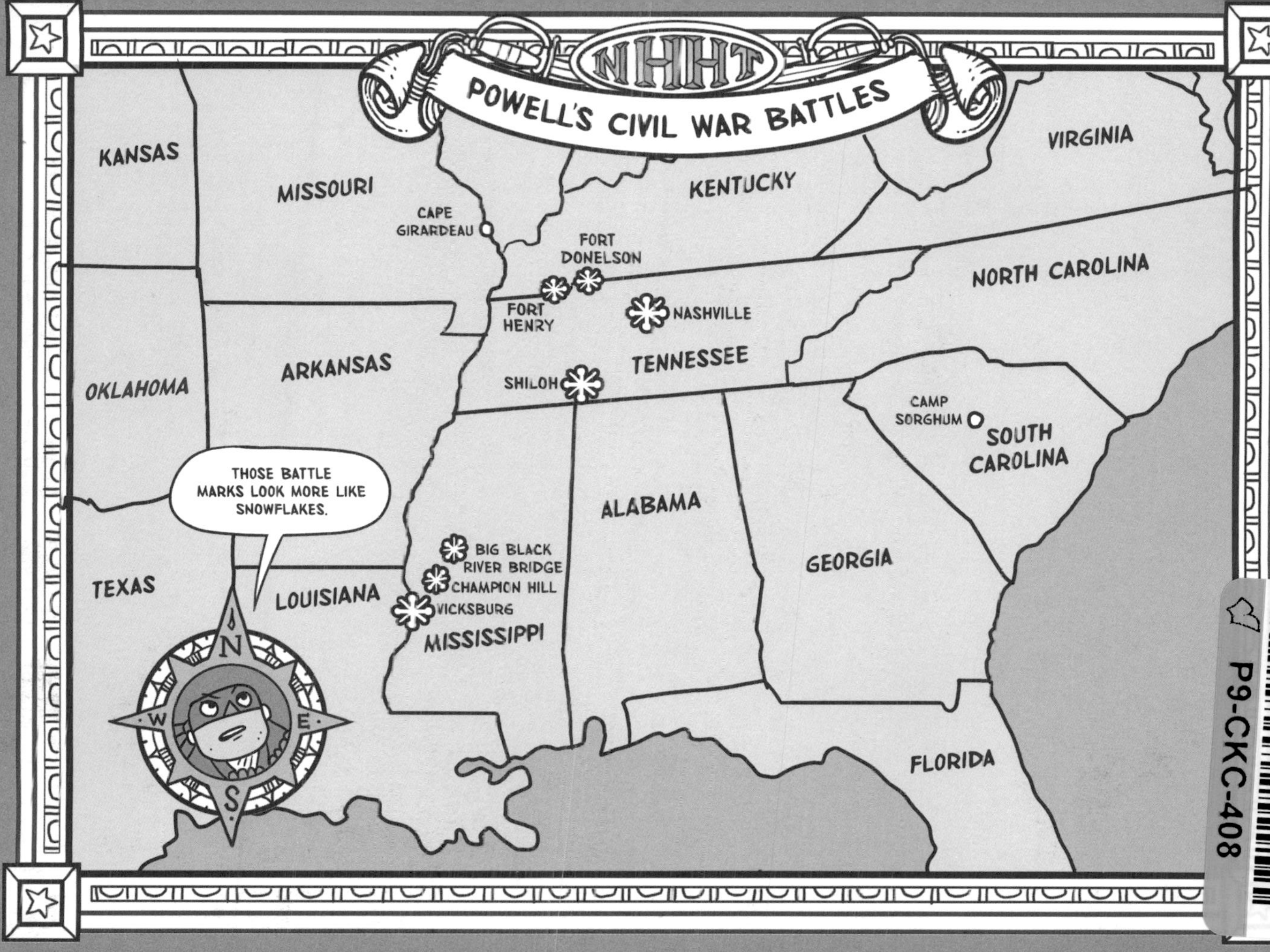
NHHT
POWELL'S CIVIL WAR BATTLES
KANSAS
MISSOURI
CAPE GIRARDEAU
KENTUCKY
VIRGINIA
FORT DONELSON
FORT HENRY
NASHVILLE
NORTH CAROLINA
TENNESSEE
ARKANSAS
OKLAHOMA
SHILOH
CAMP SORGHUM
SOUTH CAROLINA
THOSE BATTLE MARKS LOOK MORE LIKE SNOWFLAKES.
ALABAMA
BIG BLACK RIVER BRIDGE
CHAMPION HILL
VICKSBURG
GEORGIA
TEXAS
LOUISIANA
MISSISSIPPI
N
W
E
S
FLORIDA

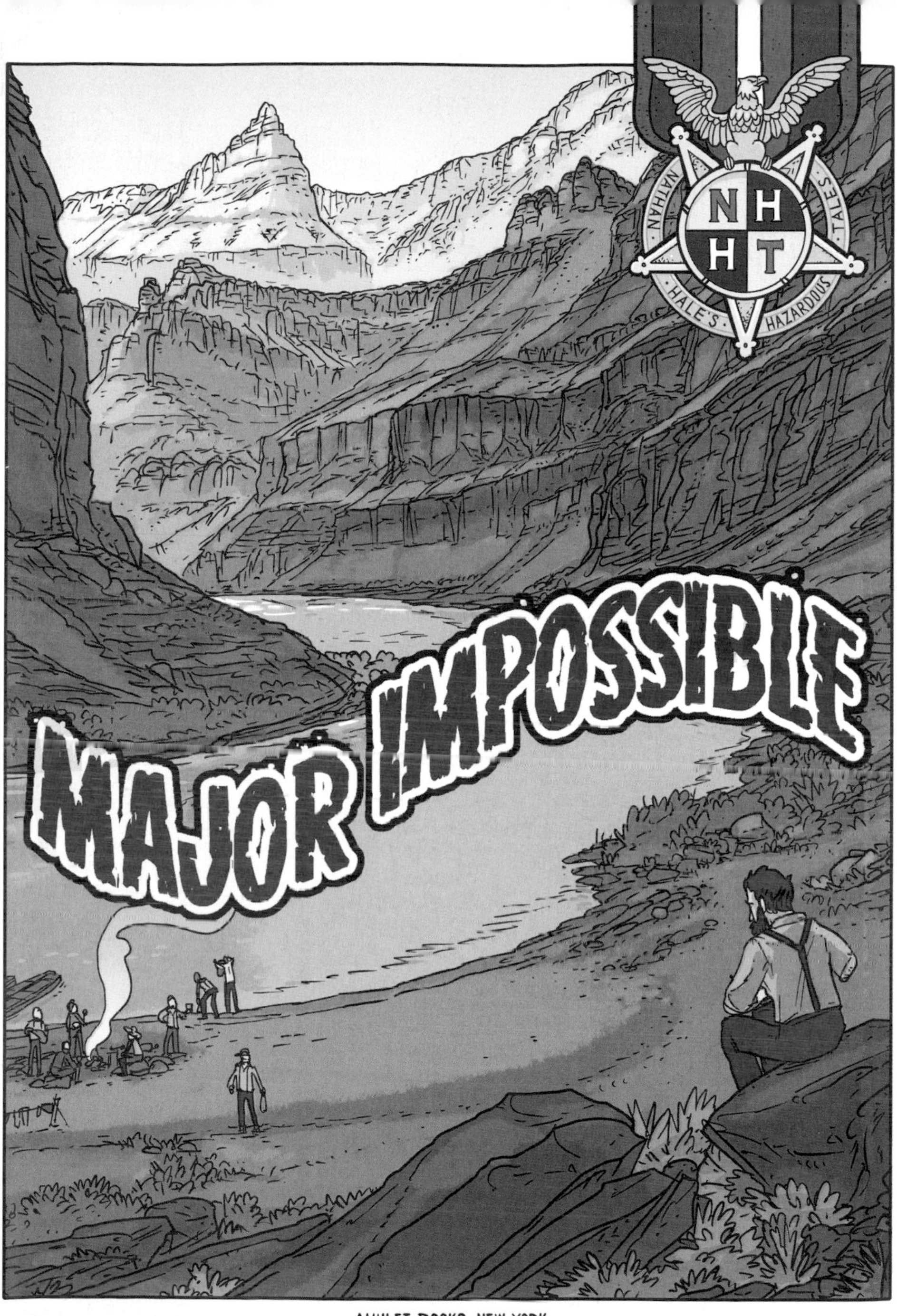
NATHAN HALE'S HAZARDOUS TALES
NH
HT
MAJOR IMPOSSIBLE

AMULET BOOKS, NEW YORK

CATALOGING--IN--PUBLICATION DATA HAS BEEN APPLIED FOR
AND MAY BE OBTAINED FROM THE LIBRARY OF CONGRESS.

ISBN 978--1--4197--3708--4

TEXT AND ILLUSTRATIONS COPYRIGHT © 2019 NATHAN HALE
BOOK DESIGN BY NATHAN HALE AND MAX TEMESCU

PRINTED AND BOUND IN U.S.A.
10 9 8 7 6 5 4 3 2

AMULET BOOKS ARE AVAILABLE AT SPECIAL DISCOUNTS WHEN
PURCHASED IN QUANTITY FOR PREMIUMS AND PROMOTIONS
AS WELL AS FUNDRAISING OR EDUCATIONAL USE. SPECIAL
EDITIONS CAN ALSO BE CREATED TO SPECIFICATION. FOR
DETAILS, CONTACT SPECIALSALES@ABRAMSBOOKS.COM OR
THE ADDRESS BELOW.

AMULET BOOKS® IS A REGISTERED TRADEMARK OF
HARRY N. ABRAMS, INC.

ABRAMS The Art of Books
195 Broadway, New York, NY 10007
abramsbooks.com

TO NEWTY, LEIGH,
LUTKE, WREN, KELLY, JOEL, BEN,
WILEY, JOE, MICKELL, JOHNNY,
AND LINDSAY--GUIDES
ON THE GRAND

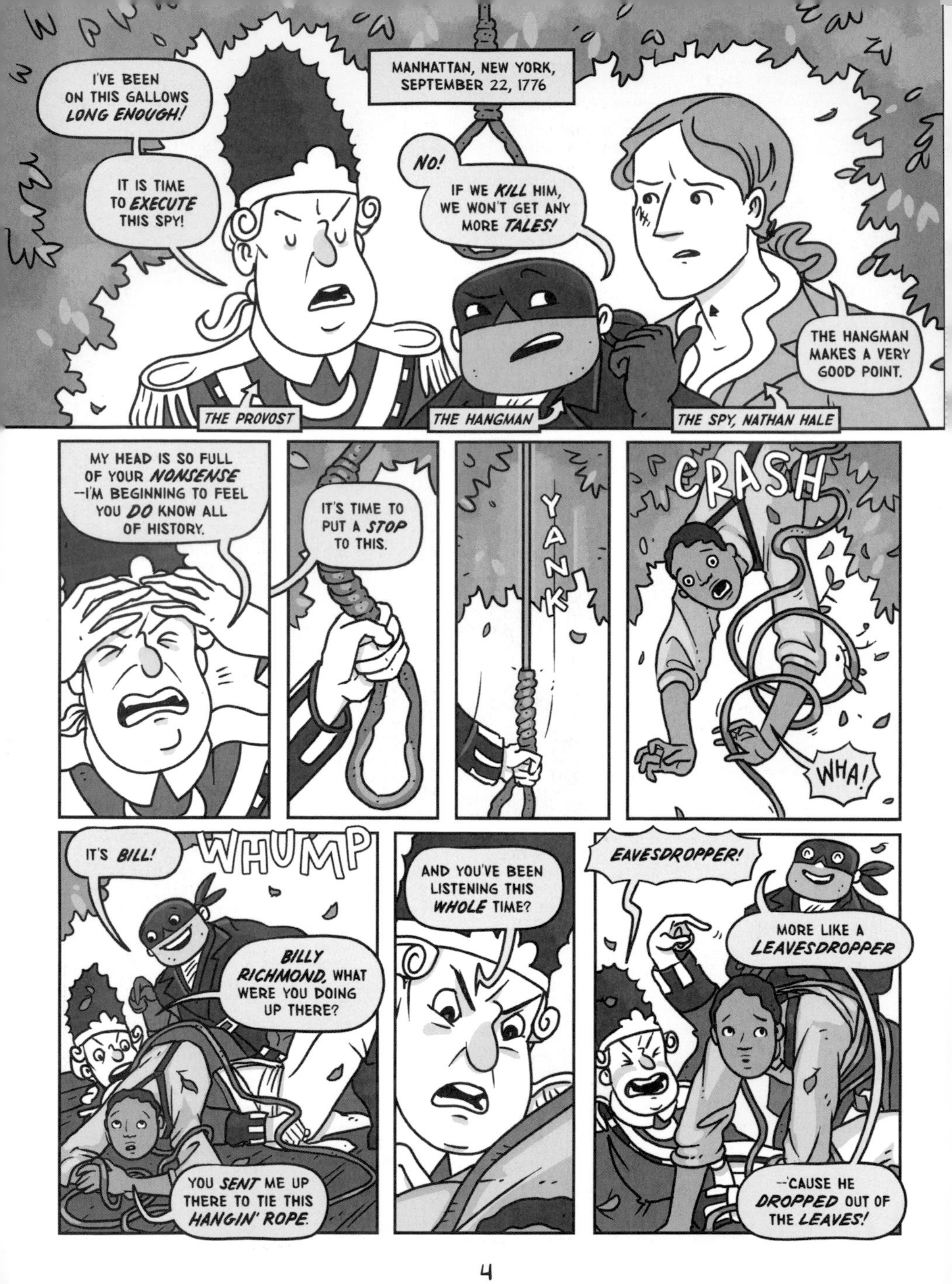
MANHATTAN, NEW YORK, SEPTEMBER 22, 1776
I'VE BEEN ON THIS GALLOWS LONG ENOUGH!
IT IS TIME TO EXECUTE THIS SPY!
NO!
IF WE KILL HIM, WE WON'T GET ANY MORE TALES!
THE HANGMAN MAKES A VERY GOOD POINT.
THE PROVOST
THE HANGMAN
THE SPY, NATHAN HALE
MY HEAD IS SO FULL OF YOUR NONSENSE —I'M BEGINNING TO FEEL YOU DO KNOW ALL OF HISTORY.
IT'S TIME TO PUT A STOP TO THIS.
YANK
CRASH
WHA!
IT'S BILL!
WHUMP
BILLY RICHMOND, WHAT WERE YOU DOING UP THERE?
YOU SENT ME UP THERE TO TIE THIS HANGIN' ROPE.
AND YOU'VE BEEN LISTENING THIS WHOLE TIME?
EAVESDROPPER!
MORE LIKE A LEAVESDROPPER
—'CAUSE HE DROPPED OUT OF THE LEAVES!

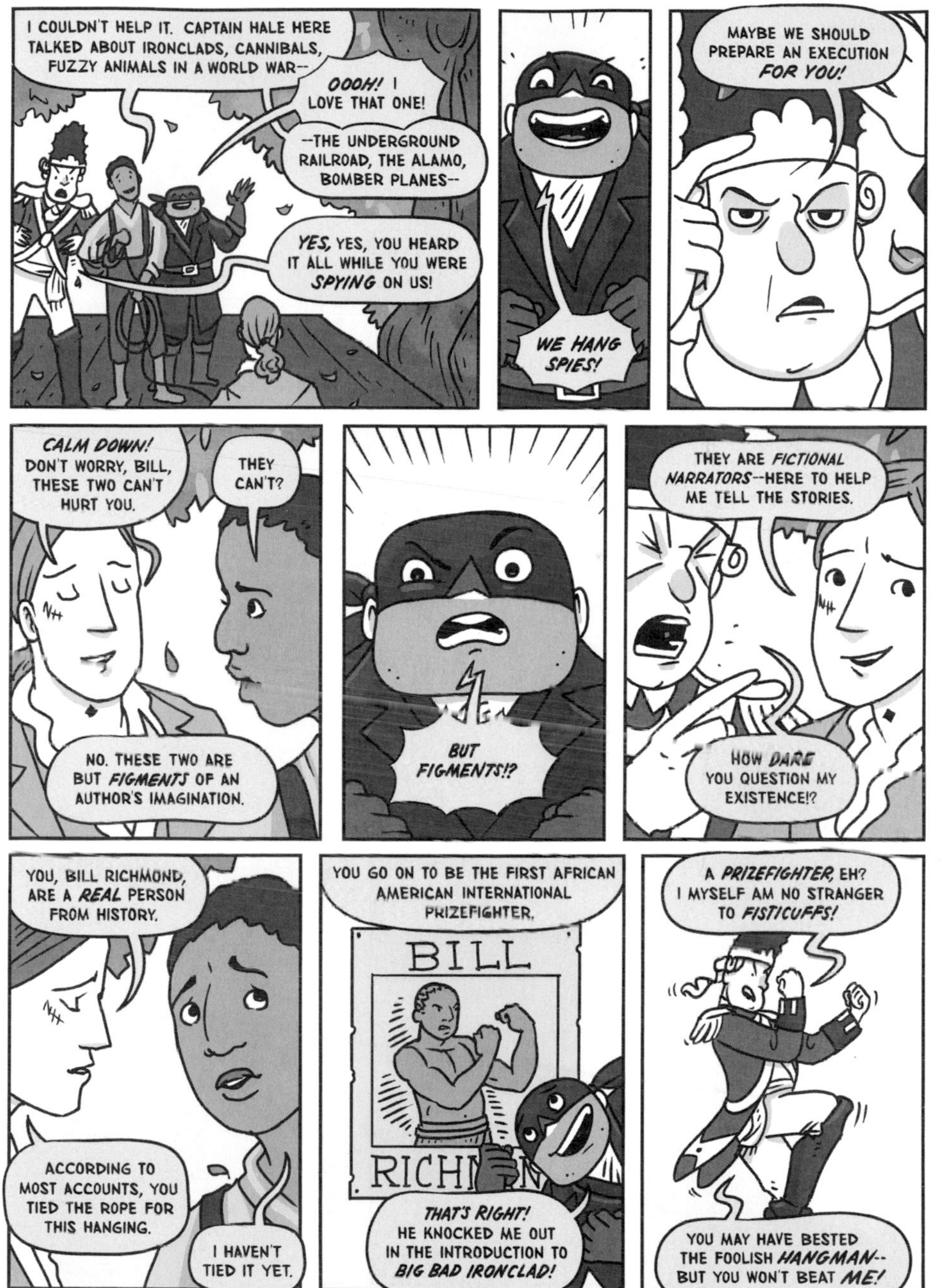
I COULDN'T HELP IT. CAPTAIN HALE HERE TALKED ABOUT IRONCLADS, CANNIBALS, FUZZY ANIMALS IN A WORLD WAR--
OOOH! I LOVE THAT ONE!
--THE UNDERGROUND RAILROAD, THE ALAMO, BOMBER PLANES--
YES, YES, YOU HEARD IT ALL WHILE YOU WERE SPYING ON US!
WE HANG SPIES!
MAYBE WE SHOULD PREPARE AN EXECUTION FOR YOU!
CALM DOWN! DON'T WORRY, BILL, THESE TWO CAN'T HURT YOU.
THEY CAN'T?
NO. THESE TWO ARE BUT FIGMENTS OF AN AUTHOR'S IMAGINATION.
BUT FIGMENTS!?
THEY ARE FICTIONAL NARRATORS--HERE TO HELP ME TELL THE STORIES.
HOW DARE YOU QUESTION MY EXISTENCE!?
YOU, BILL RICHMOND, ARE A REAL PERSON FROM HISTORY.
ACCORDING TO MOST ACCOUNTS, YOU TIED THE ROPE FOR THIS HANGING.
I HAVEN'T TIED IT YET.
YOU GO ON TO BE THE FIRST AFRICAN AMERICAN INTERNATIONAL PRIZEFIGHTER.
BILL
RICHM
THAT'S RIGHT! HE KNOCKED ME OUT IN THE INTRODUCTION TO BIG BAD IRONCLAD!
A PRIZEFIGHTER, EH? I MYSELF AM NO STRANGER TO FISTICUFFS!
YOU MAY HAVE BESTED THE FOOLISH HANGMAN--BUT YOU WON'T BEAT ME!

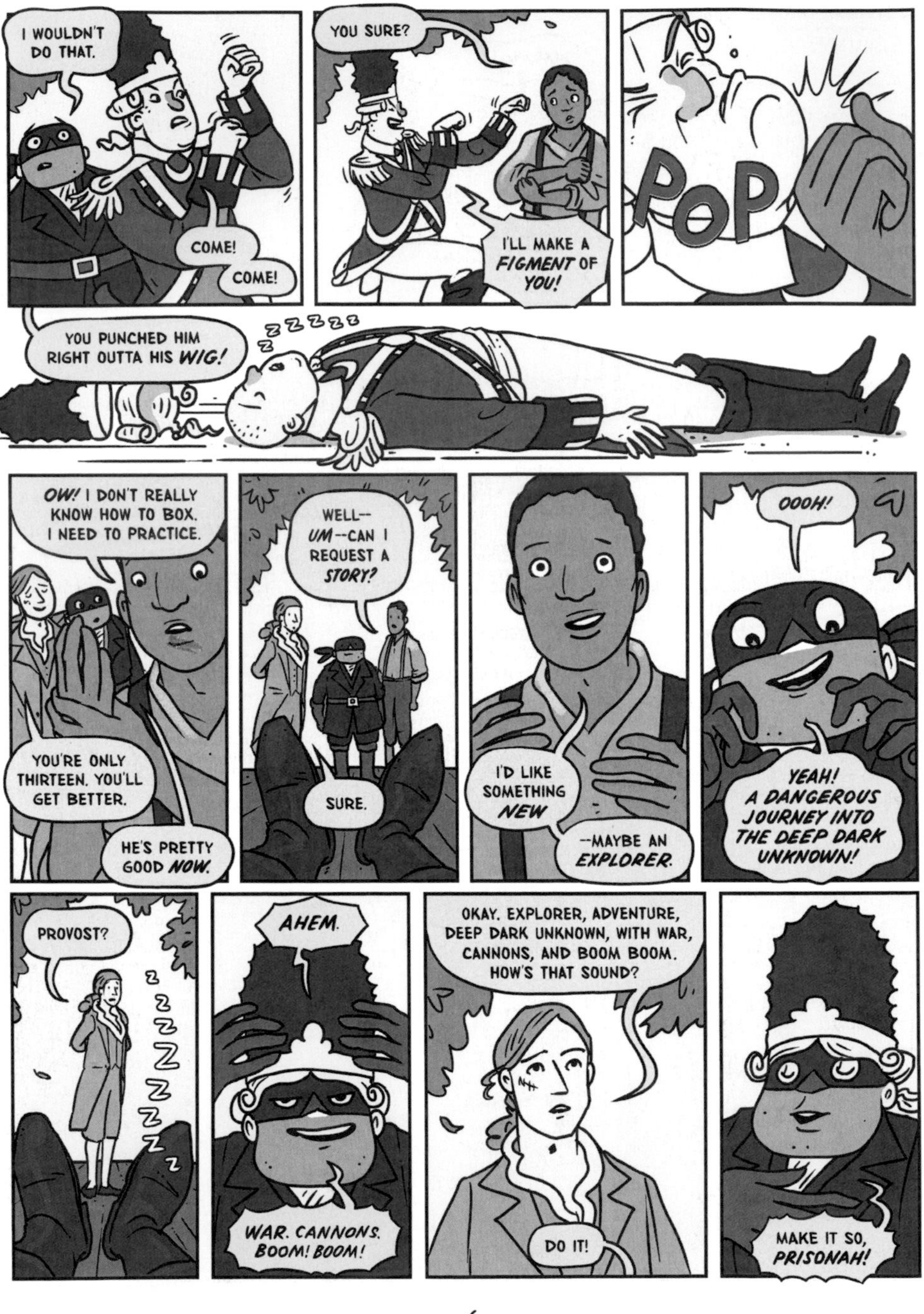
I WOULDN'T DO THAT.
COME!
COME!
YOU SURE?
I'LL MAKE A *FIGMENT* OF *YOU!*
POP
YOU PUNCHED HIM RIGHT OUTTA HIS *WIG!*
ZZZZZZ
OW! I DON'T REALLY KNOW HOW TO BOX. I NEED TO PRACTICE.
YOU'RE ONLY THIRTEEN. YOU'LL GET BETTER.
HE'S PRETTY GOOD *NOW.*
WELL-- *UM*--CAN I REQUEST A *STORY?*
SURE.
I'D LIKE SOMETHING *NEW*
--MAYBE AN *EXPLORER.*
OOOH!
YEAH! A DANGEROUS JOURNEY INTO THE DEEP DARK UNKNOWN!
PROVOST?
Z Z Z Z Z Z Z Z
AHEM.
WAR. CANNONS. BOOM! BOOM!
OKAY. EXPLORER, ADVENTURE, DEEP DARK UNKNOWN, WITH WAR, CANNONS, AND BOOM BOOM. HOW'S THAT SOUND?
DO IT!
MAKE IT SO, *PRISONAH!*

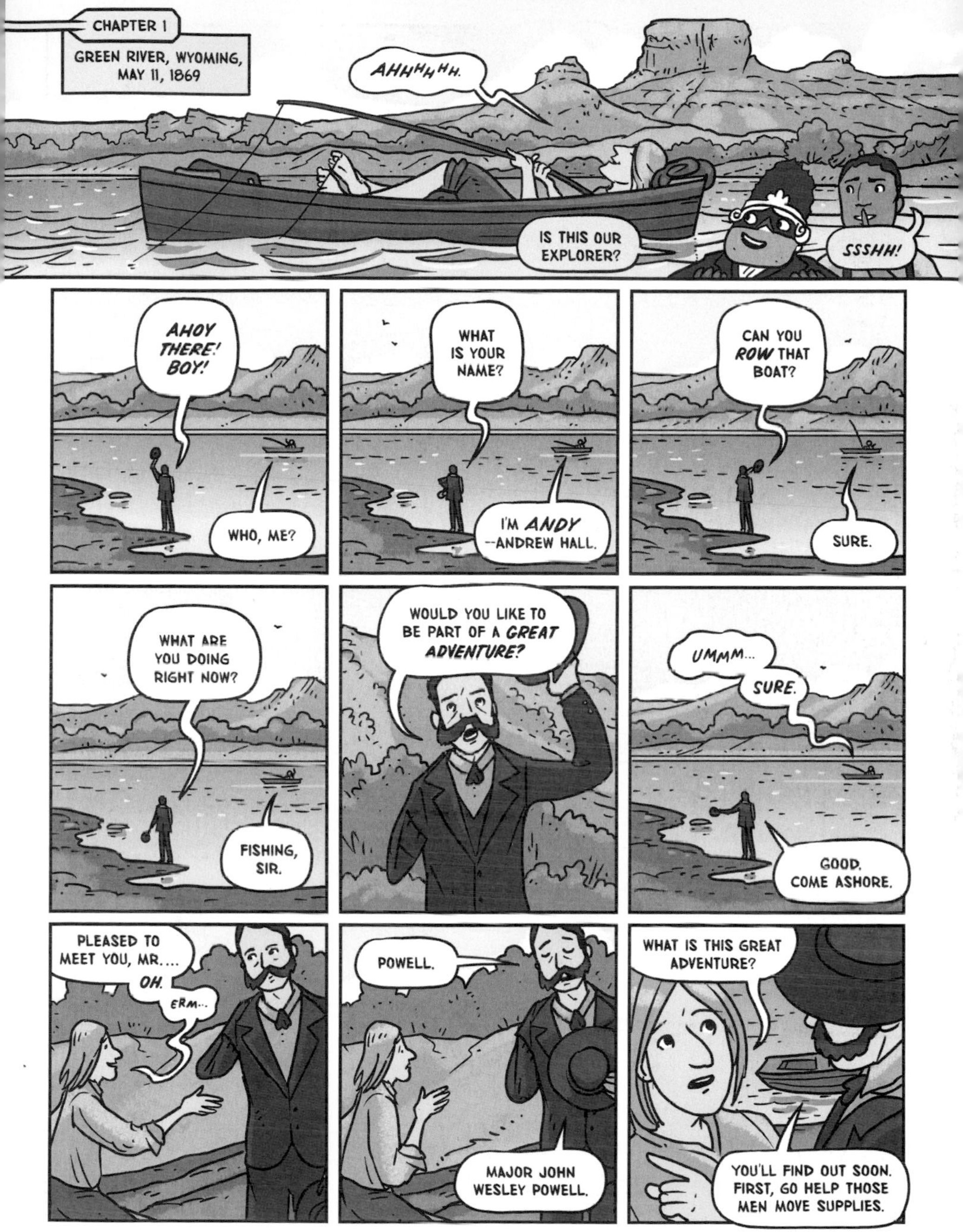
CHAPTER 1
GREEN RIVER, WYOMING, MAY 11, 1869
AHHHHHH.
IS THIS OUR EXPLORER?
SSSHH!
AHOY THERE! BOY!
WHO, ME?
WHAT IS YOUR NAME?
I'M ANDY --ANDREW HALL.
CAN YOU ROW THAT BOAT?
SURE.
WHAT ARE YOU DOING RIGHT NOW?
FISHING, SIR.
WOULD YOU LIKE TO BE PART OF A GREAT ADVENTURE?
UMMM...
SURE.
GOOD. COME ASHORE.
PLEASED TO MEET YOU, MR....
OH.
ERM...
POWELL.
MAJOR JOHN WESLEY POWELL.
WHAT IS THIS GREAT ADVENTURE?
YOU'LL FIND OUT SOON. FIRST, GO HELP THOSE MEN MOVE SUPPLIES.

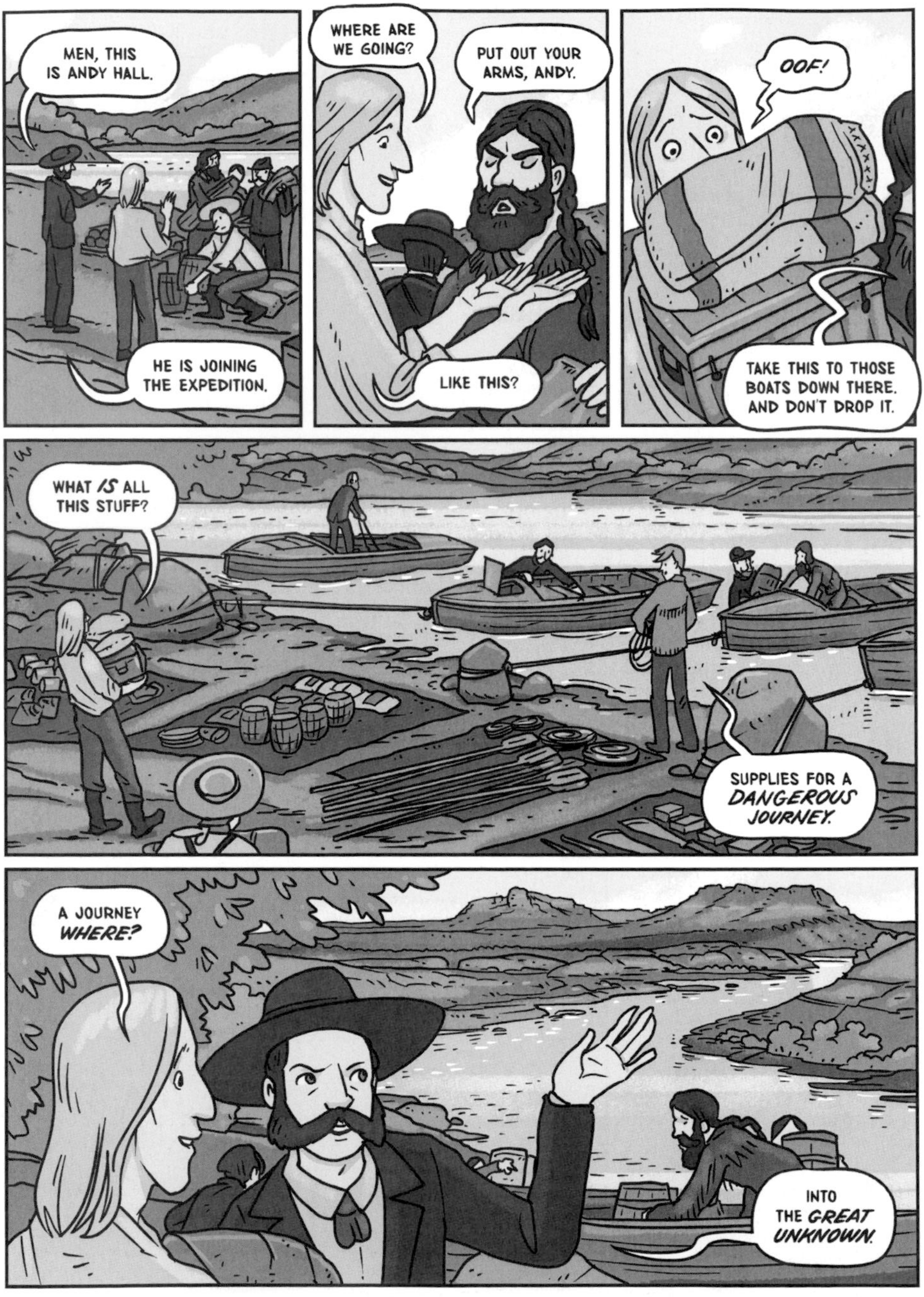
MEN, THIS IS ANDY HALL.
HE IS JOINING THE EXPEDITION.
WHERE ARE WE GOING?
PUT OUT YOUR ARMS, ANDY.
LIKE THIS?
OOF!
TAKE THIS TO THOSE BOATS DOWN THERE. AND DON'T DROP IT.
WHAT IS ALL THIS STUFF?
SUPPLIES FOR A DANGEROUS JOURNEY.
A JOURNEY WHERE?
INTO THE GREAT UNKNOWN.

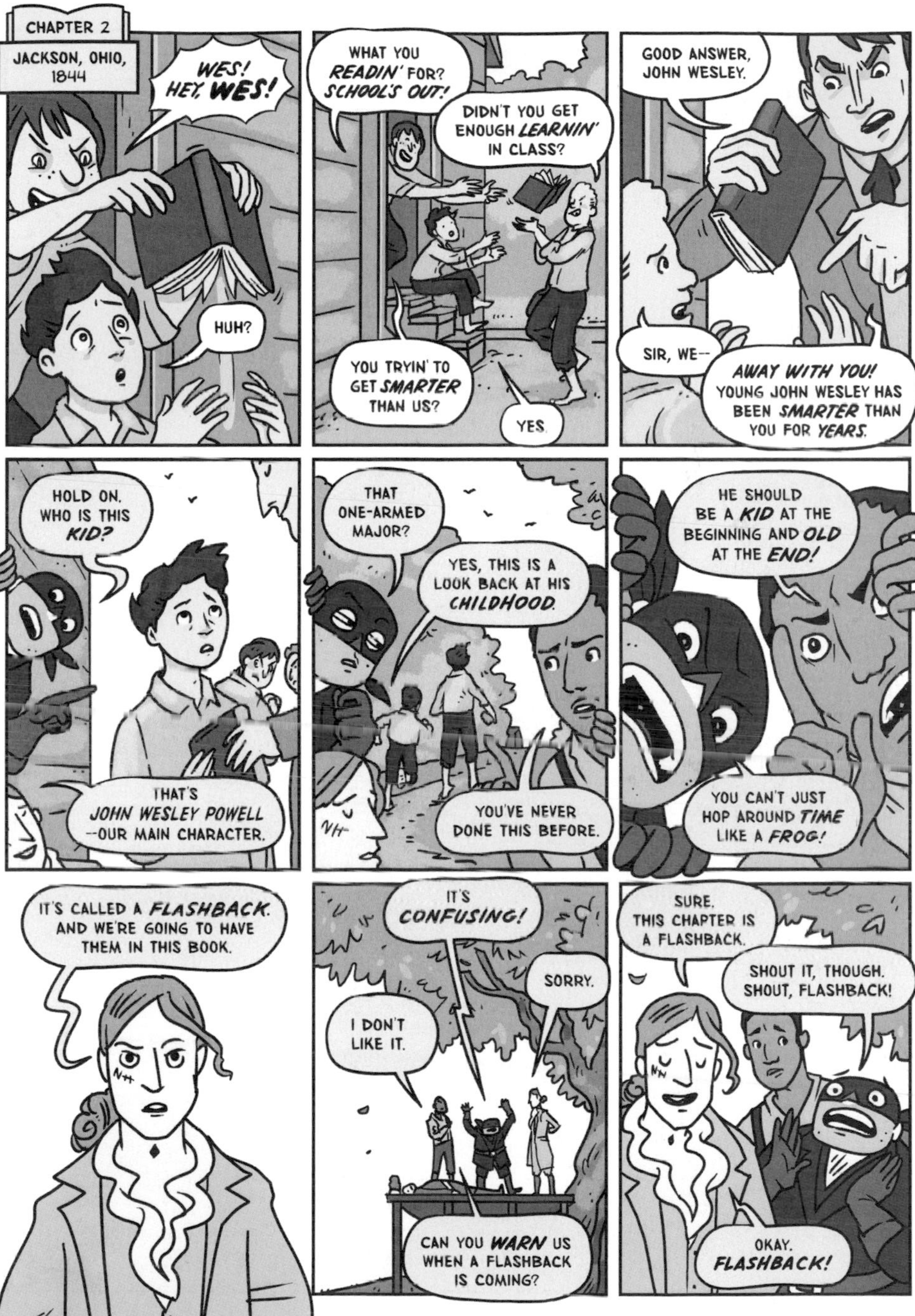

CHAPTER 2
JACKSON, OHIO, 1844
WES! HEY, WES!
HUH?
WHAT YOU READIN' FOR? SCHOOL'S OUT!
DIDN'T YOU GET ENOUGH LEARNIN' IN CLASS?
YOU TRYIN' TO GET SMARTER THAN US?
YES.
GOOD ANSWER, JOHN WESLEY.
SIR, WE--
AWAY WITH YOU! YOUNG JOHN WESLEY HAS BEEN SMARTER THAN YOU FOR YEARS.
HOLD ON. WHO IS THIS KID?
THAT'S JOHN WESLEY POWELL --OUR MAIN CHARACTER.
THAT ONE-ARMED MAJOR?
YES, THIS IS A LOOK BACK AT HIS CHILDHOOD.
YOU'VE NEVER DONE THIS BEFORE.
HE SHOULD BE A KID AT THE BEGINNING AND OLD AT THE END!
YOU CAN'T JUST HOP AROUND TIME LIKE A FROG!
IT'S CALLED A FLASHBACK. AND WE'RE GOING TO HAVE THEM IN THIS BOOK.
IT'S CONFUSING!
I DON'T LIKE IT.
SORRY.
CAN YOU WARN US WHEN A FLASHBACK IS COMING?
SURE. THIS CHAPTER IS A FLASHBACK.
SHOUT IT, THOUGH. SHOUT, FLASHBACK!
OKAY. FLASHBACK!

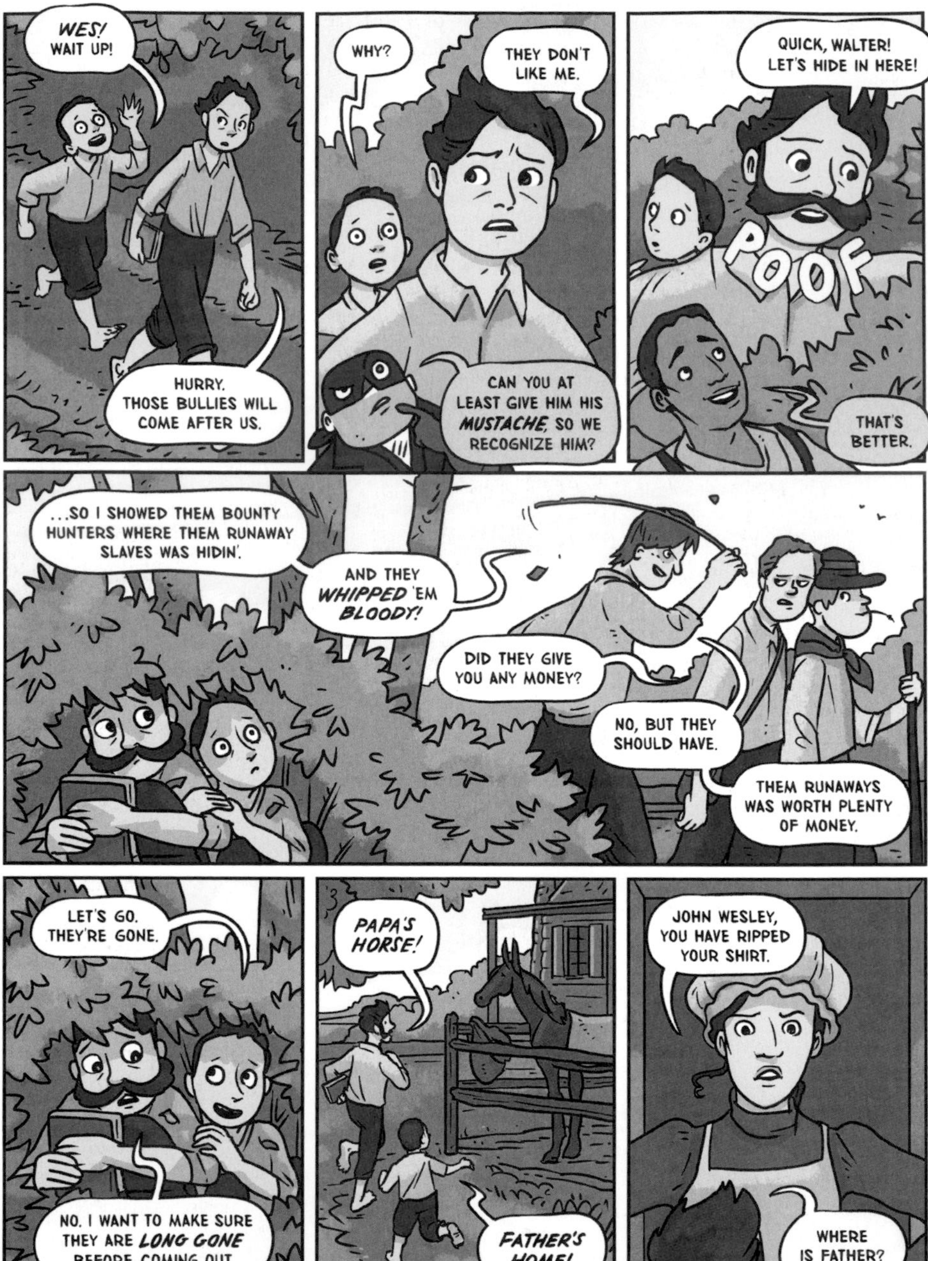
WES! WAIT UP!
HURRY. THOSE BULLIES WILL COME AFTER US.
WHY?
THEY DON'T LIKE ME.
CAN YOU AT LEAST GIVE HIM HIS MUSTACHE, SO WE RECOGNIZE HIM?
QUICK, WALTER! LET'S HIDE IN HERE!
POOF
THAT'S BETTER.
...SO I SHOWED THEM BOUNTY HUNTERS WHERE THEM RUNAWAY SLAVES WAS HIDIN'.
AND THEY WHIPPED 'EM BLOODY!
DID THEY GIVE YOU ANY MONEY?
NO, BUT THEY SHOULD HAVE.
THEM RUNAWAYS WAS WORTH PLENTY OF MONEY.
LET'S GO. THEY'RE GONE.
NO. I WANT TO MAKE SURE THEY ARE LONG GONE BEFORE COMING OUT.
PAPA'S HORSE!
FATHER'S HOME!
JOHN WESLEY, YOU HAVE RIPPED YOUR SHIRT.
WHERE IS FATHER?

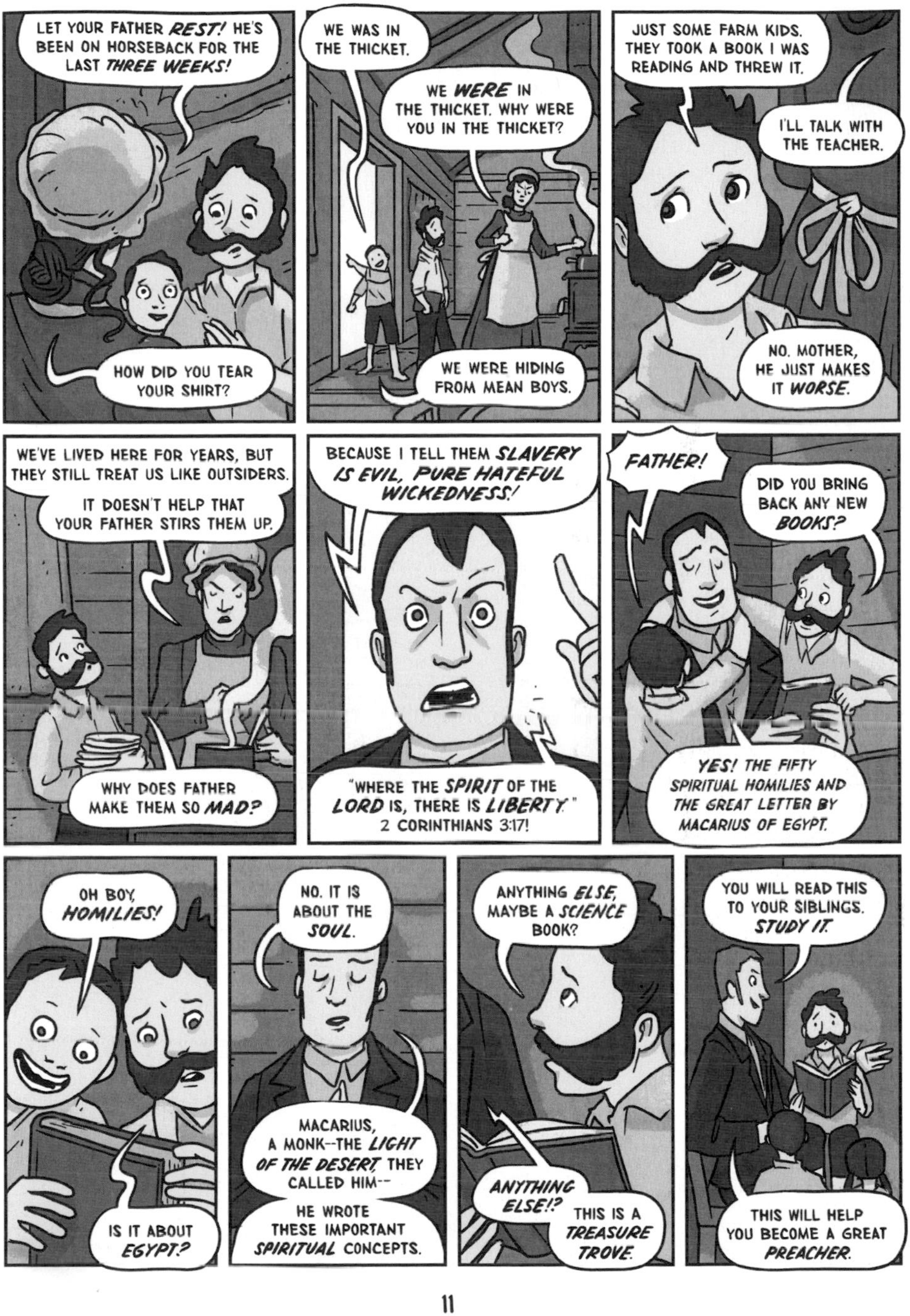
LET YOUR FATHER REST! HE'S BEEN ON HORSEBACK FOR THE LAST THREE WEEKS!
HOW DID YOU TEAR YOUR SHIRT?
WE WAS IN THE THICKET.
WE WERE IN THE THICKET. WHY WERE YOU IN THE THICKET?
WE WERE HIDING FROM MEAN BOYS.
JUST SOME FARM KIDS. THEY TOOK A BOOK I WAS READING AND THREW IT.
I'LL TALK WITH THE TEACHER.
NO, MOTHER, HE JUST MAKES IT WORSE.
WE'VE LIVED HERE FOR YEARS, BUT THEY STILL TREAT US LIKE OUTSIDERS.
IT DOESN'T HELP THAT YOUR FATHER STIRS THEM UP.
WHY DOES FATHER MAKE THEM SO MAD?
BECAUSE I TELL THEM SLAVERY IS EVIL, PURE HATEFUL WICKEDNESS!
"WHERE THE SPIRIT OF THE LORD IS, THERE IS LIBERTY." 2 CORINTHIANS 3:17!
FATHER!
DID YOU BRING BACK ANY NEW BOOKS?
YES! THE FIFTY SPIRITUAL HOMILIES AND THE GREAT LETTER BY MACARIUS OF EGYPT.
OH BOY, HOMILIES!
IS IT ABOUT EGYPT?
NO. IT IS ABOUT THE SOUL.
MACARIUS, A MONK--THE LIGHT OF THE DESERT, THEY CALLED HIM--
HE WROTE THESE IMPORTANT SPIRITUAL CONCEPTS.
ANYTHING ELSE, MAYBE A SCIENCE BOOK?
ANYTHING ELSE!?
THIS IS A TREASURE TROVE.
YOU WILL READ THIS TO YOUR SIBLINGS. STUDY IT.
THIS WILL HELP YOU BECOME A GREAT PREACHER.

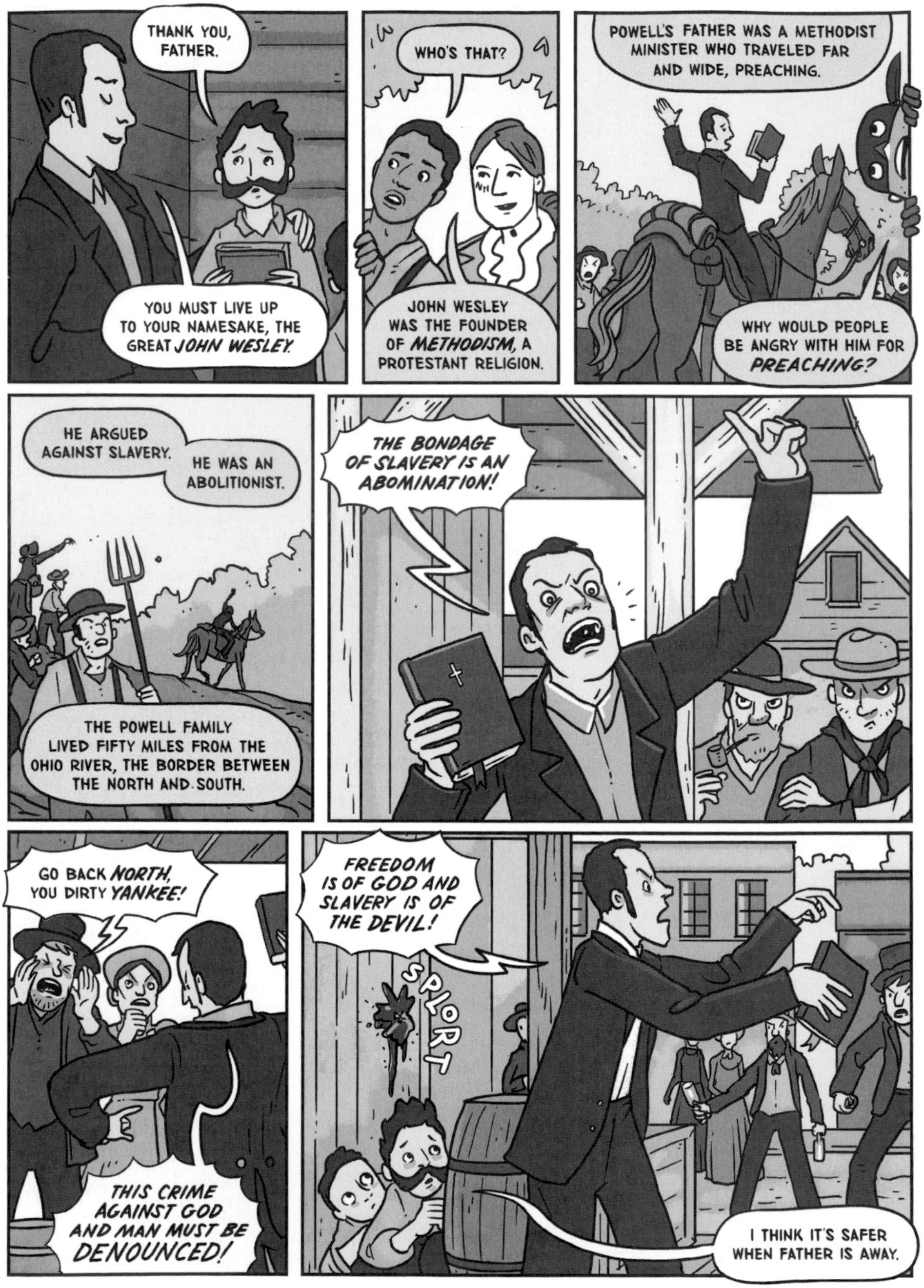

THANK YOU, FATHER.
YOU MUST LIVE UP TO YOUR NAMESAKE, THE GREAT JOHN WESLEY.
WHO'S THAT?
JOHN WESLEY WAS THE FOUNDER OF METHODISM, A PROTESTANT RELIGION.
POWELL'S FATHER WAS A METHODIST MINISTER WHO TRAVELED FAR AND WIDE, PREACHING.
WHY WOULD PEOPLE BE ANGRY WITH HIM FOR PREACHING?
HE ARGUED AGAINST SLAVERY.
HE WAS AN ABOLITIONIST.
THE POWELL FAMILY LIVED FIFTY MILES FROM THE OHIO RIVER, THE BORDER BETWEEN THE NORTH AND SOUTH.
THE BONDAGE OF SLAVERY IS AN ABOMINATION!
GO BACK NORTH, YOU DIRTY YANKEE!
THIS CRIME AGAINST GOD AND MAN MUST BE DENOUNCED!
FREEDOM IS OF GOD AND SLAVERY IS OF THE DEVIL!
SPLORT
I THINK IT'S SAFER WHEN FATHER IS AWAY.

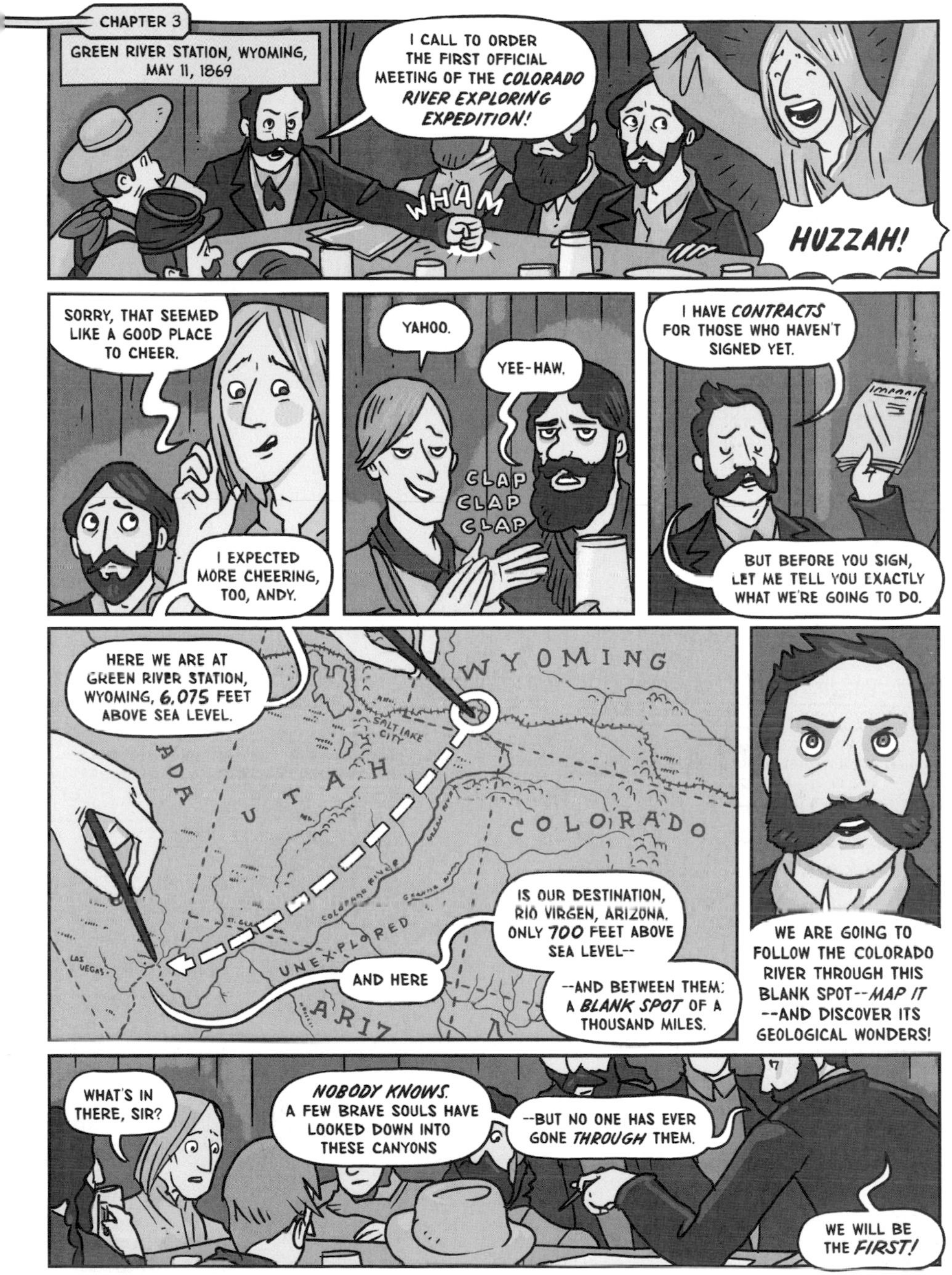
CHAPTER 3
GREEN RIVER STATION, WYOMING, MAY 11, 1869
I CALL TO ORDER THE FIRST OFFICIAL MEETING OF THE *COLORADO RIVER EXPLORING EXPEDITION!*
WHAM
HUZZAH!
SORRY, THAT SEEMED LIKE A GOOD PLACE TO CHEER.
I EXPECTED MORE CHEERING, TOO, ANDY.
YAHOO.
YEE-HAW.
CLAP CLAP CLAP
I HAVE *CONTRACTS* FOR THOSE WHO HAVEN'T SIGNED YET.
BUT BEFORE YOU SIGN, LET ME TELL YOU EXACTLY WHAT WE'RE GOING TO DO.
HERE WE ARE AT GREEN RIVER STATION, WYOMING, *6,075* FEET ABOVE SEA LEVEL.
WYOMING
SALT LAKE CITY
UTAH
COLORADO
UNEXPLORED
LAS VEGAS
ARIZ
AND HERE
IS OUR DESTINATION, RIO VIRGEN, ARIZONA, ONLY *700* FEET ABOVE SEA LEVEL--
--AND BETWEEN THEM: A *BLANK SPOT* OF A THOUSAND MILES.
WE ARE GOING TO FOLLOW THE COLORADO RIVER THROUGH THIS BLANK SPOT--*MAP IT* --AND DISCOVER ITS GEOLOGICAL WONDERS!
WHAT'S IN THERE, SIR?
NOBODY KNOWS. A FEW BRAVE SOULS HAVE LOOKED DOWN INTO THESE CANYONS
--BUT NO ONE HAS EVER GONE *THROUGH* THEM.
WE WILL BE THE *FIRST!*

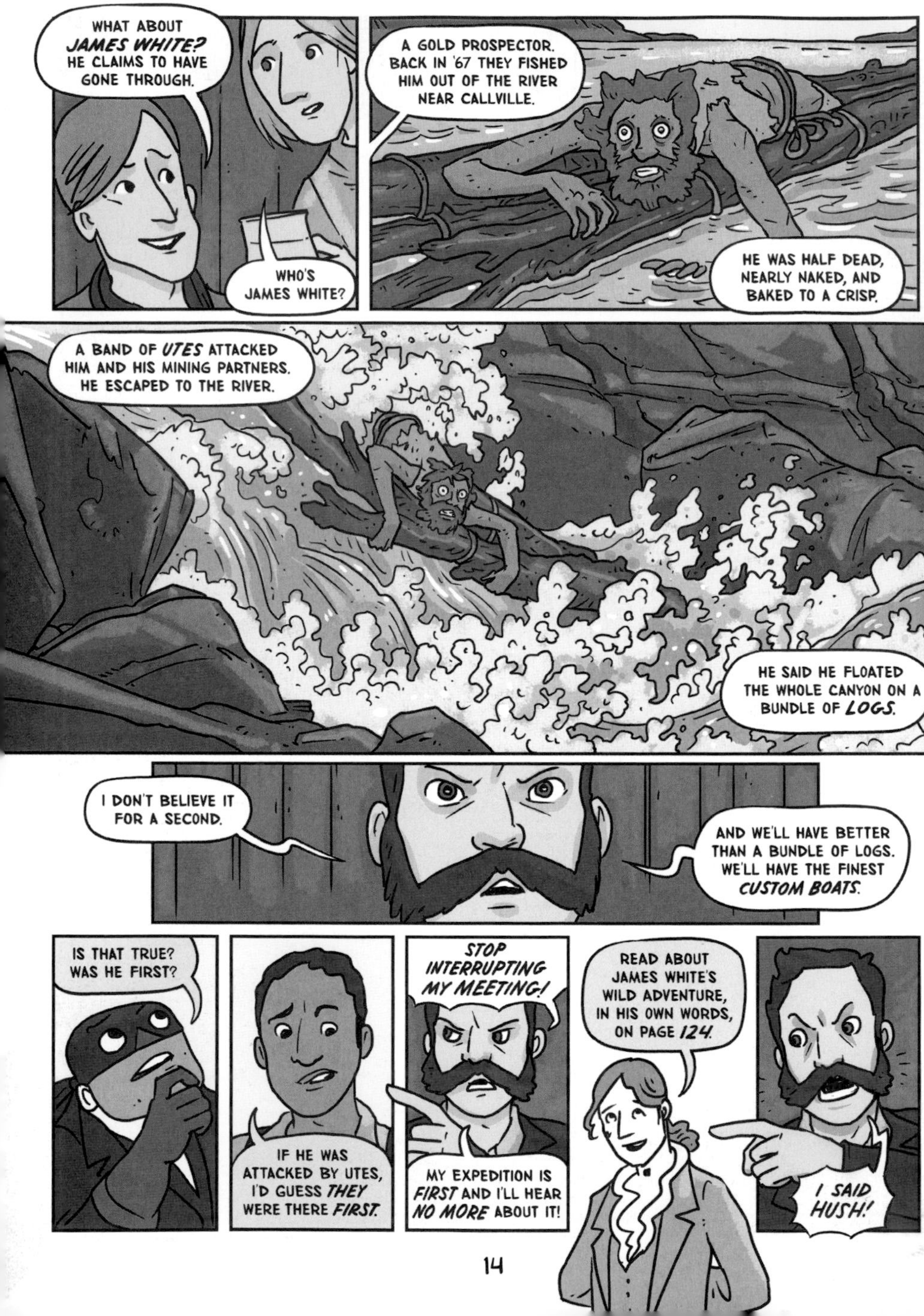
WHAT ABOUT *JAMES WHITE?* HE CLAIMS TO HAVE GONE THROUGH.
WHO'S JAMES WHITE?
A GOLD PROSPECTOR. BACK IN '67 THEY FISHED HIM OUT OF THE RIVER NEAR CALLVILLE.
HE WAS HALF DEAD, NEARLY NAKED, AND BAKED TO A CRISP.
A BAND OF *UTES* ATTACKED HIM AND HIS MINING PARTNERS. HE ESCAPED TO THE RIVER.
HE SAID HE FLOATED THE WHOLE CANYON ON A BUNDLE OF *LOGS*.
I DON'T BELIEVE IT FOR A SECOND.
AND WE'LL HAVE BETTER THAN A BUNDLE OF LOGS. WE'LL HAVE THE FINEST *CUSTOM BOATS*.
IS THAT TRUE? WAS HE FIRST?
IF HE WAS ATTACKED BY UTES, I'D GUESS *THEY* WERE THERE *FIRST*.
STOP INTERRUPTING MY MEETING!
MY EXPEDITION IS *FIRST* AND I'LL HEAR *NO MORE* ABOUT IT!
READ ABOUT JAMES WHITE'S WILD ADVENTURE, IN HIS OWN WORDS, ON PAGE *124*.
I SAID HUSH!

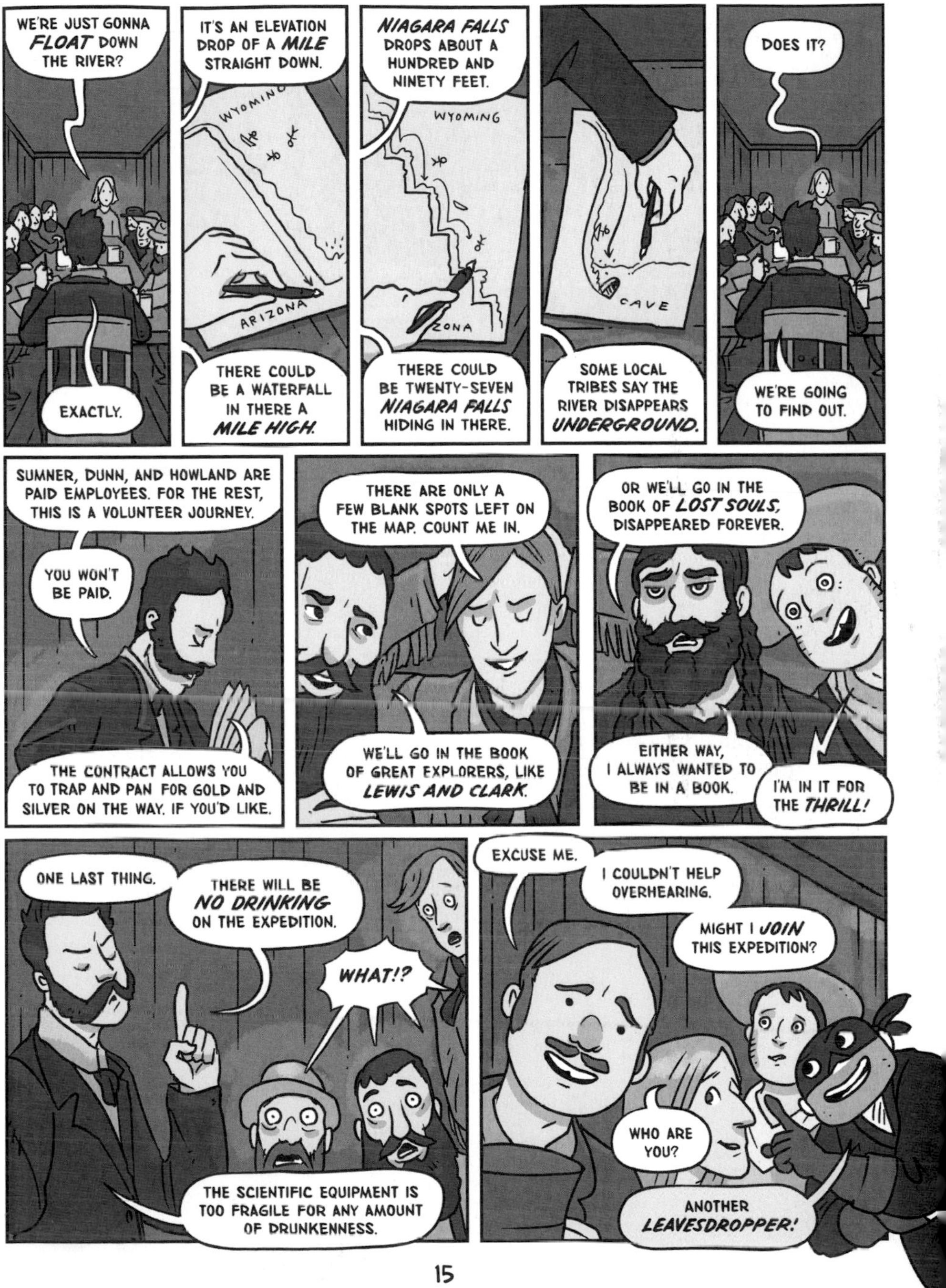

WE'RE JUST GONNA FLOAT DOWN THE RIVER?
EXACTLY.
IT'S AN ELEVATION DROP OF A MILE STRAIGHT DOWN.
WYOMING
ARIZONA
THERE COULD BE A WATERFALL IN THERE A MILE HIGH.
NIAGARA FALLS DROPS ABOUT A HUNDRED AND NINETY FEET.
WYOMING
ZONA
THERE COULD BE TWENTY-SEVEN NIAGARA FALLS HIDING IN THERE.
CAVE
SOME LOCAL TRIBES SAY THE RIVER DISAPPEARS UNDERGROUND.
DOES IT?
WE'RE GOING TO FIND OUT.
SUMNER, DUNN, AND HOWLAND ARE PAID EMPLOYEES. FOR THE REST, THIS IS A VOLUNTEER JOURNEY.
YOU WON'T BE PAID.
THE CONTRACT ALLOWS YOU TO TRAP AND PAN FOR GOLD AND SILVER ON THE WAY, IF YOU'D LIKE.
THERE ARE ONLY A FEW BLANK SPOTS LEFT ON THE MAP. COUNT ME IN.
WE'LL GO IN THE BOOK OF GREAT EXPLORERS, LIKE LEWIS AND CLARK.
OR WE'LL GO IN THE BOOK OF LOST SOULS, DISAPPEARED FOREVER.
EITHER WAY, I ALWAYS WANTED TO BE IN A BOOK.
I'M IN IT FOR THE THRILL!
ONE LAST THING.
THERE WILL BE NO DRINKING ON THE EXPEDITION.
WHAT!?
THE SCIENTIFIC EQUIPMENT IS TOO FRAGILE FOR ANY AMOUNT OF DRUNKENNESS.
EXCUSE ME.
I COULDN'T HELP OVERHEARING.
MIGHT I JOIN THIS EXPEDITION?
WHO ARE YOU?
ANOTHER LEAVESDROPPER!

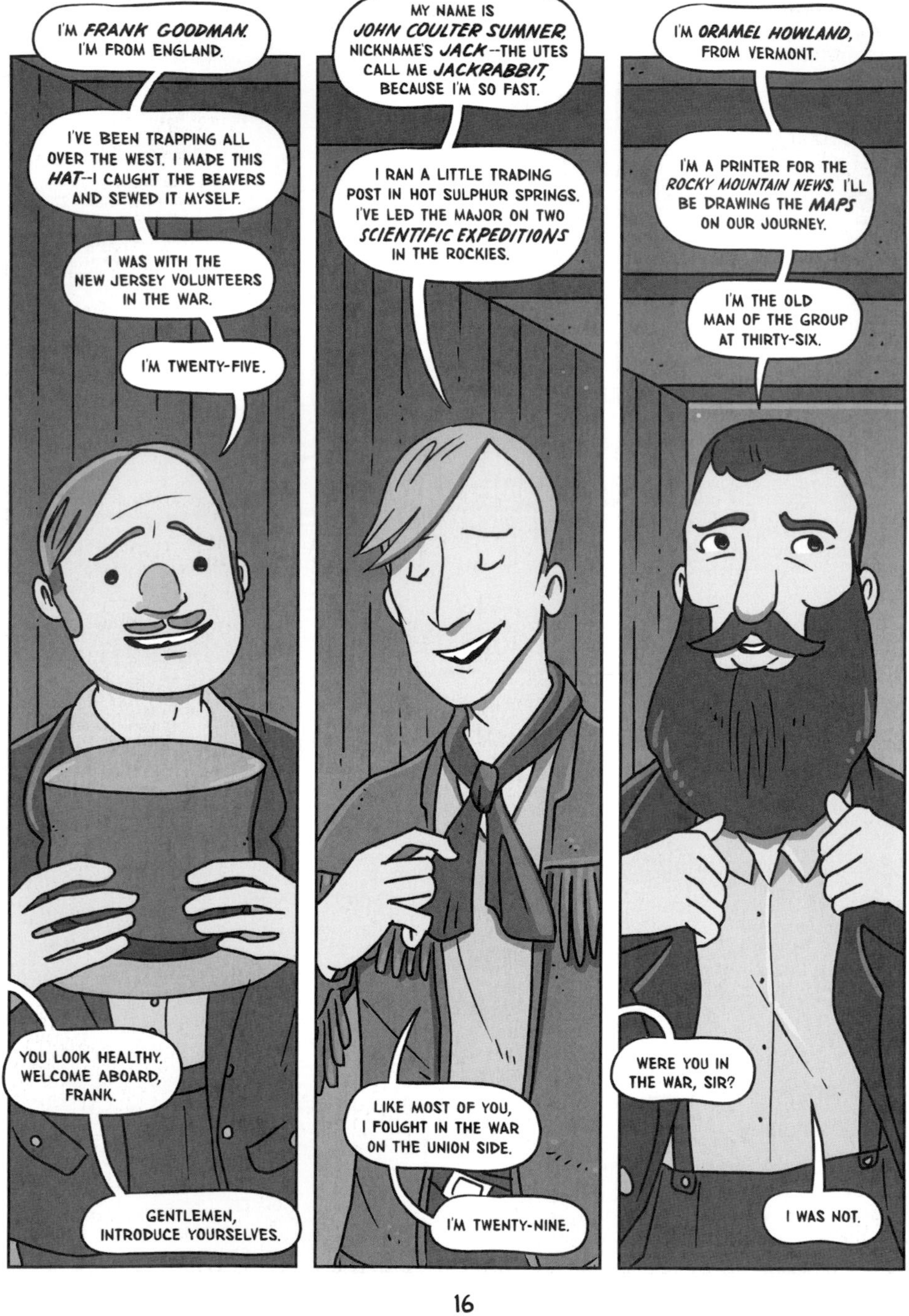

I'M FRANK GOODMAN. I'M FROM ENGLAND.
I'VE BEEN TRAPPING ALL OVER THE WEST. I MADE THIS HAT--I CAUGHT THE BEAVERS AND SEWED IT MYSELF.
I WAS WITH THE NEW JERSEY VOLUNTEERS IN THE WAR.
I'M TWENTY-FIVE.
GENTLEMEN, INTRODUCE YOURSELVES.
YOU LOOK HEALTHY. WELCOME ABOARD, FRANK.
MY NAME IS JOHN COULTER SUMNER. NICKNAME'S JACK--THE UTES CALL ME JACKRABBIT, BECAUSE I'M SO FAST.
I RAN A LITTLE TRADING POST IN HOT SULPHUR SPRINGS. I'VE LED THE MAJOR ON TWO SCIENTIFIC EXPEDITIONS IN THE ROCKIES.
LIKE MOST OF YOU, I FOUGHT IN THE WAR ON THE UNION SIDE.
I'M TWENTY-NINE.
I'M ORAMEL HOWLAND, FROM VERMONT.
I'M A PRINTER FOR THE ROCKY MOUNTAIN NEWS. I'LL BE DRAWING THE MAPS ON OUR JOURNEY.
I'M THE OLD MAN OF THE GROUP AT THIRTY-SIX.
WERE YOU IN THE WAR, SIR?
I WAS NOT.

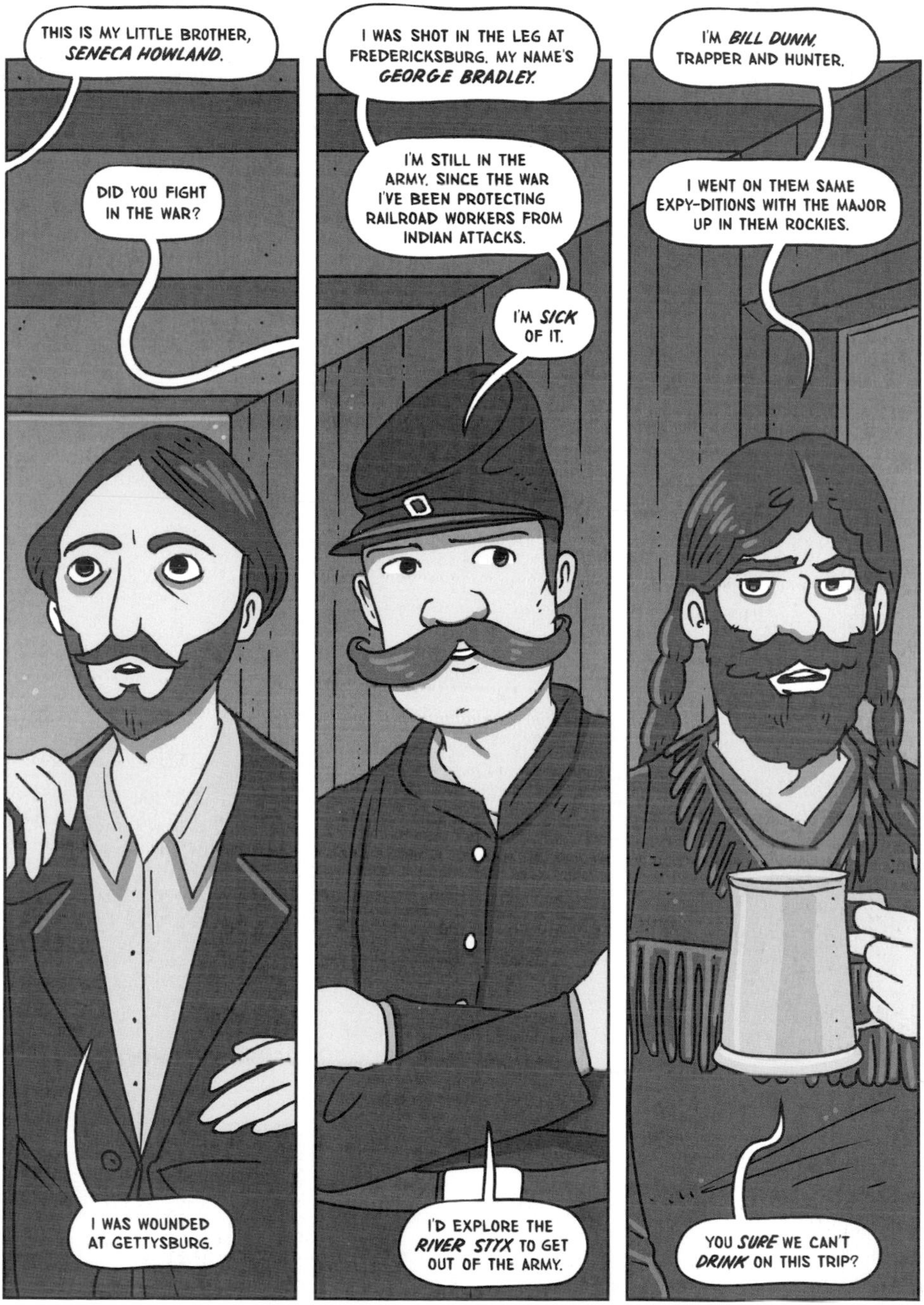
THIS IS MY LITTLE BROTHER, SENECA HOWLAND.
DID YOU FIGHT IN THE WAR?
I WAS WOUNDED AT GETTYSBURG.
I WAS SHOT IN THE LEG AT FREDERICKSBURG. MY NAME'S GEORGE BRADLEY.
I'M STILL IN THE ARMY. SINCE THE WAR I'VE BEEN PROTECTING RAILROAD WORKERS FROM INDIAN ATTACKS.
I'M SICK OF IT.
I'D EXPLORE THE RIVER STYX TO GET OUT OF THE ARMY.
I'M BILL DUNN, TRAPPER AND HUNTER.
I WENT ON THEM SAME EXPY-DITIONS WITH THE MAJOR UP IN THEM ROCKIES.
YOU SURE WE CAN'T DRINK ON THIS TRIP?

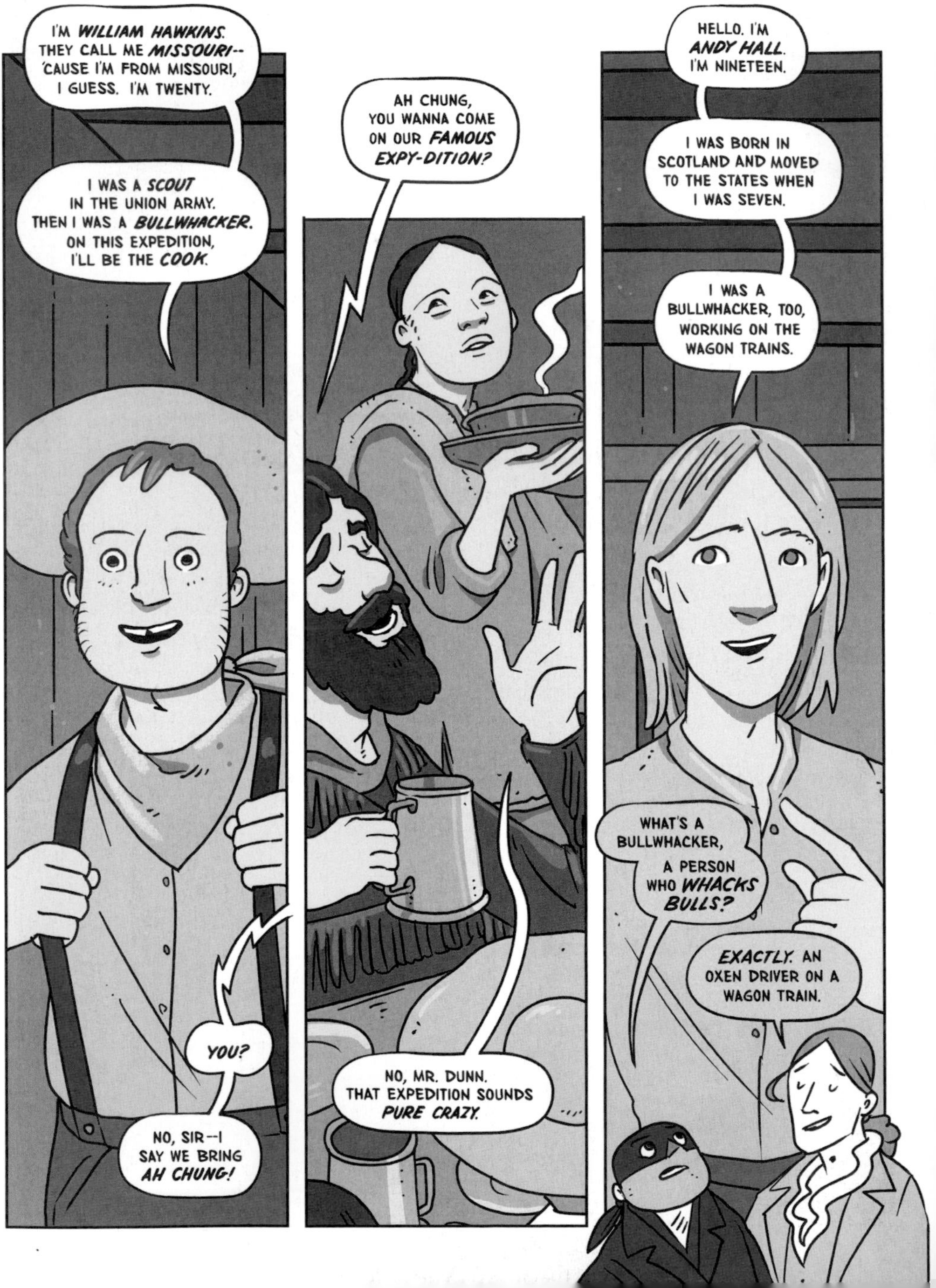
I'M WILLIAM HAWKINS. THEY CALL ME MISSOURI-- 'CAUSE I'M FROM MISSOURI, I GUESS. I'M TWENTY.
I WAS A SCOUT IN THE UNION ARMY. THEN I WAS A BULLWHACKER. ON THIS EXPEDITION, I'LL BE THE COOK.
YOU?
NO, SIR--I SAY WE BRING AH CHUNG!
AH CHUNG, YOU WANNA COME ON OUR FAMOUS EXPY-DITION?
NO, MR. DUNN. THAT EXPEDITION SOUNDS PURE CRAZY.
HELLO. I'M ANDY HALL. I'M NINETEEN.
I WAS BORN IN SCOTLAND AND MOVED TO THE STATES WHEN I WAS SEVEN.
I WAS A BULLWHACKER, TOO, WORKING ON THE WAGON TRAINS.
WHAT'S A BULLWHACKER, A PERSON WHO WHACKS BULLS?
EXACTLY. AN OXEN DRIVER ON A WAGON TRAIN.

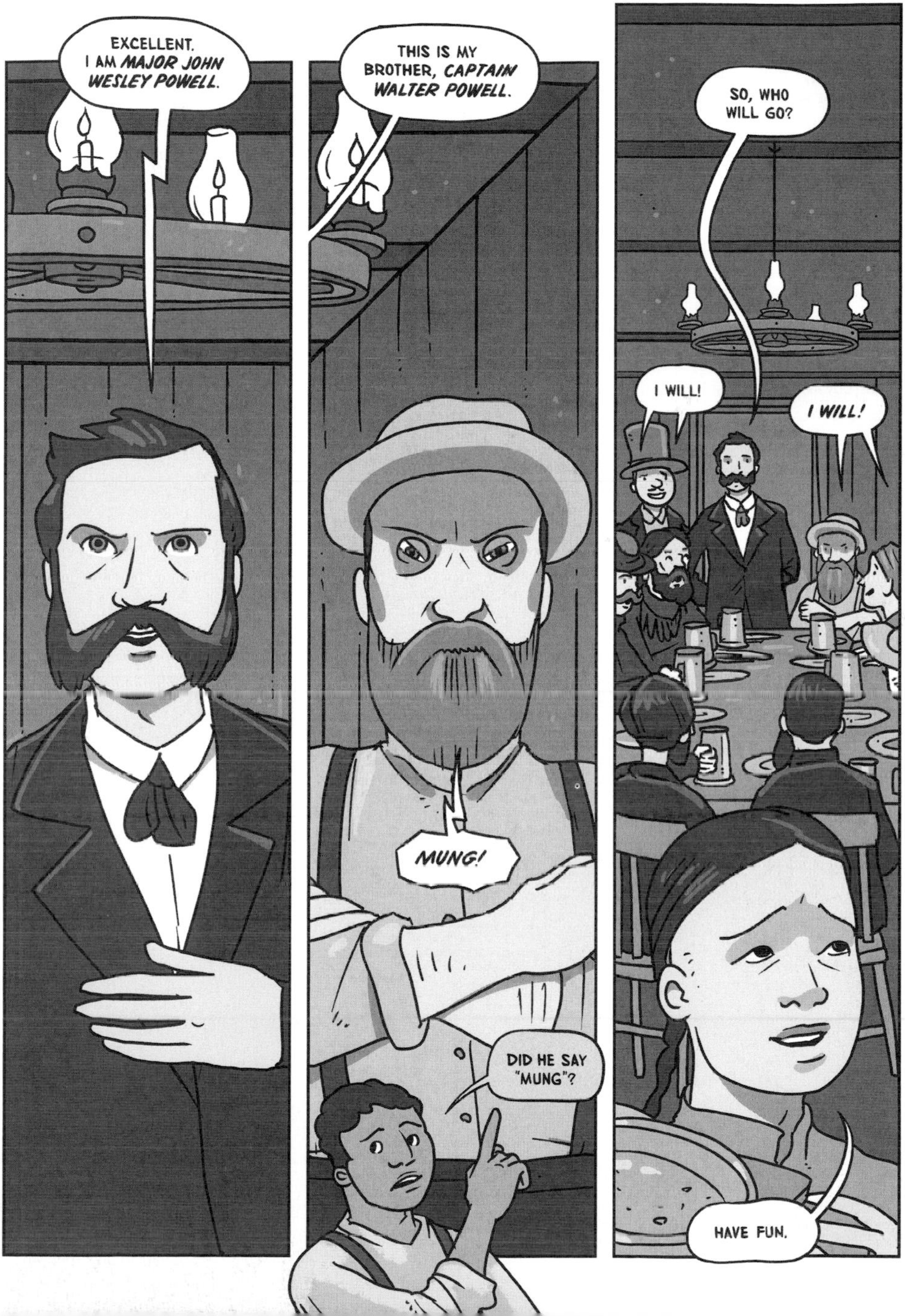

EXCELLENT. I AM MAJOR JOHN WESLEY POWELL.
THIS IS MY BROTHER, CAPTAIN WALTER POWELL.
MUNG!
DID HE SAY "MUNG"?
SO, WHO WILL GO?
I WILL!
I WILL!
HAVE FUN.

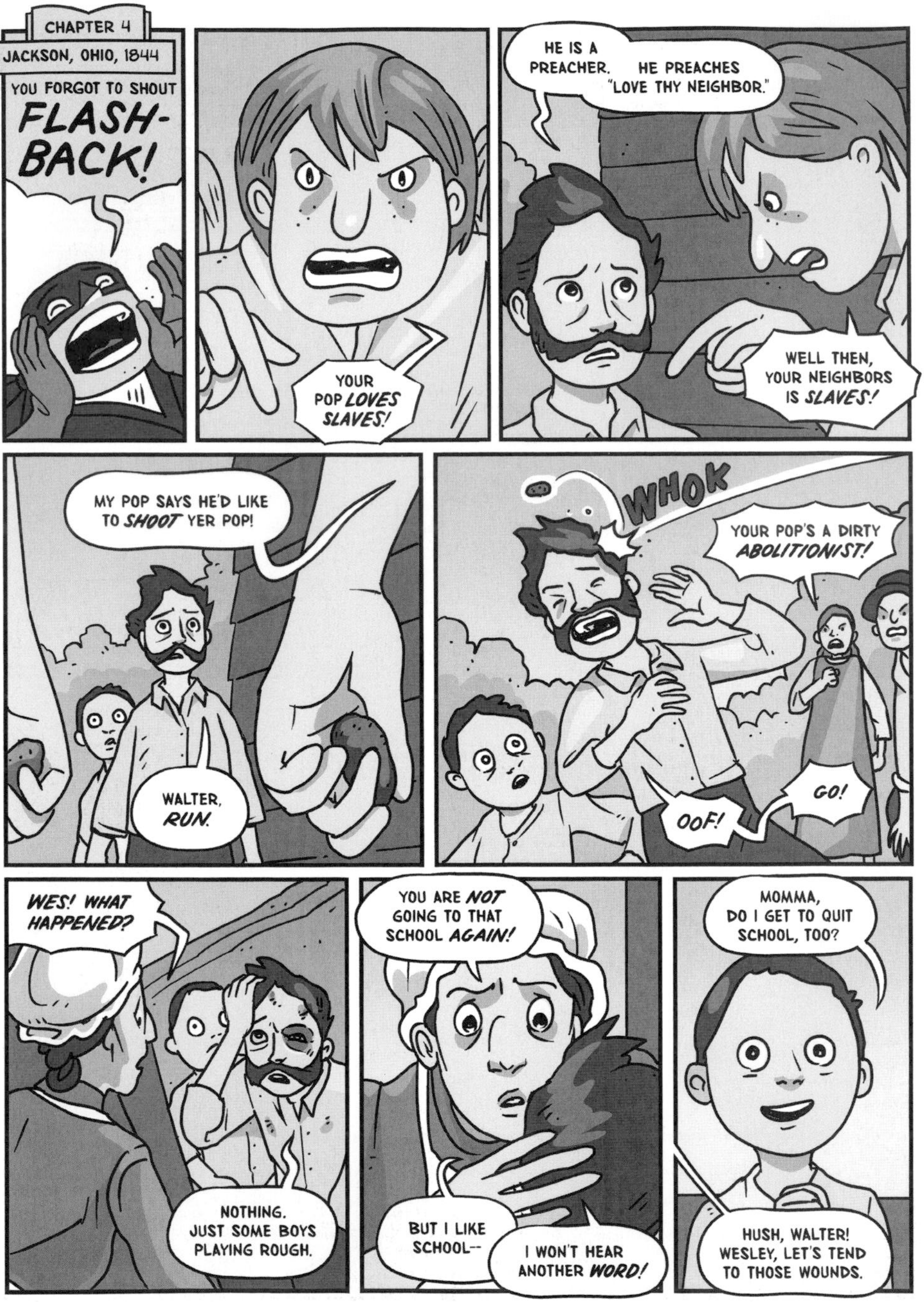
CHAPTER 4
JACKSON, OHIO, 1844
YOU FORGOT TO SHOUT FLASH-BACK!
YOUR POP LOVES SLAVES!
HE IS A PREACHER. HE PREACHES "LOVE THY NEIGHBOR."
WELL THEN, YOUR NEIGHBORS IS SLAVES!
MY POP SAYS HE'D LIKE TO SHOOT YER POP!
WALTER, RUN.
WHOK
YOUR POP'S A DIRTY ABOLITIONIST!
OOF!
GO!
WES! WHAT HAPPENED?
NOTHING. JUST SOME BOYS PLAYING ROUGH.
YOU ARE NOT GOING TO THAT SCHOOL AGAIN!
BUT I LIKE SCHOOL--
I WON'T HEAR ANOTHER WORD!
MOMMA, DO I GET TO QUIT SCHOOL, TOO?
HUSH, WALTER! WESLEY, LET'S TEND TO THOSE WOUNDS.

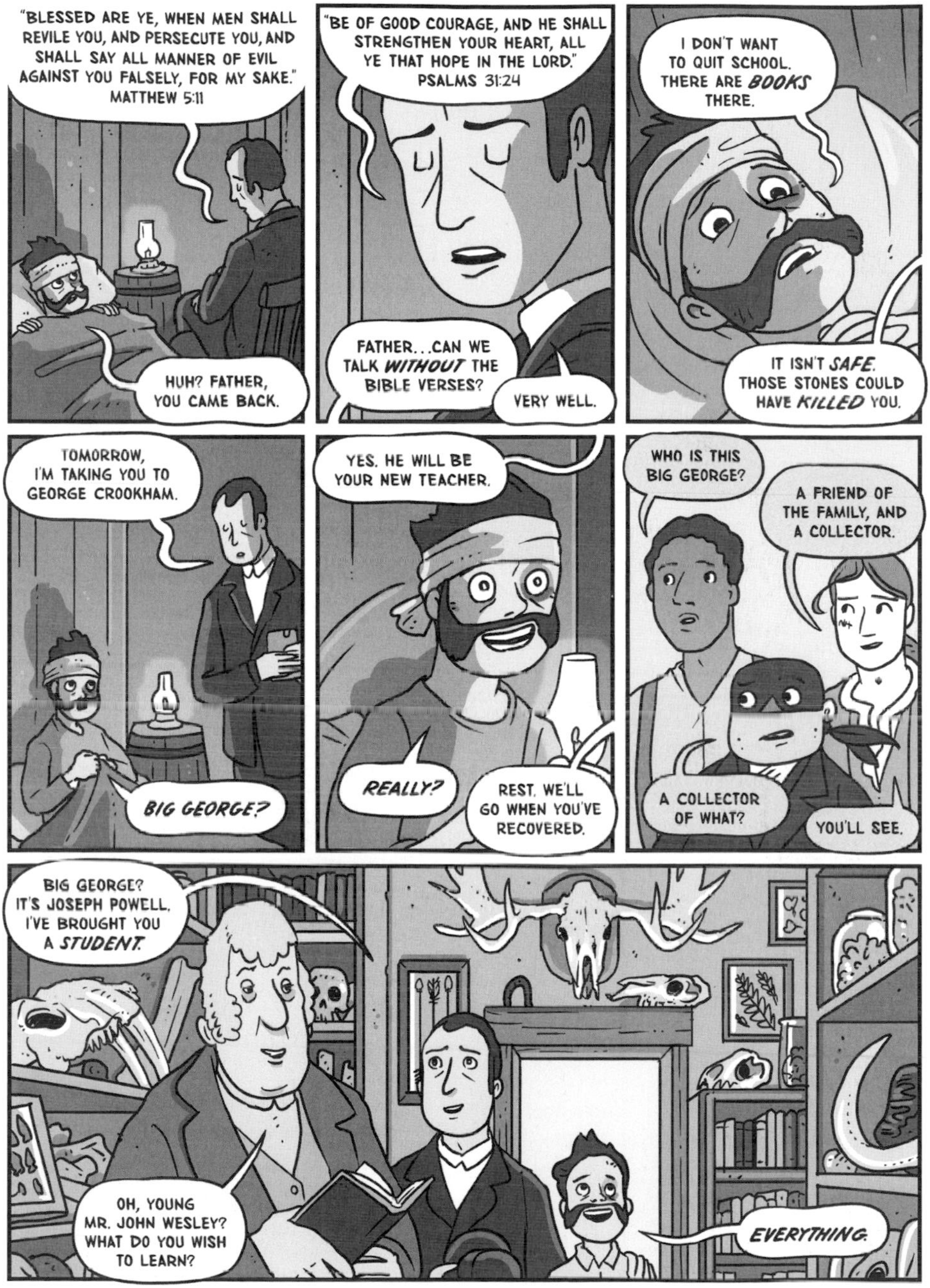

"BLESSED ARE YE, WHEN MEN SHALL REVILE YOU, AND PERSECUTE YOU, AND SHALL SAY ALL MANNER OF EVIL AGAINST YOU FALSELY, FOR MY SAKE." MATTHEW 5:11
HUH? FATHER, YOU CAME BACK.
"BE OF GOOD COURAGE, AND HE SHALL STRENGTHEN YOUR HEART, ALL YE THAT HOPE IN THE LORD." PSALMS 31:24
FATHER...CAN WE TALK *WITHOUT* THE BIBLE VERSES?
VERY WELL.
I DON'T WANT TO QUIT SCHOOL. THERE ARE *BOOKS* THERE.
IT ISN'T *SAFE*. THOSE STONES COULD HAVE *KILLED* YOU.
TOMORROW, I'M TAKING YOU TO GEORGE CROOKHAM.
BIG GEORGE?
YES. HE WILL BE YOUR NEW TEACHER.
REALLY?
REST. WE'LL GO WHEN YOU'VE RECOVERED.
WHO IS THIS BIG GEORGE?
A FRIEND OF THE FAMILY, AND A COLLECTOR.
A COLLECTOR OF WHAT?
YOU'LL SEE.
BIG GEORGE? IT'S JOSEPH POWELL. I'VE BROUGHT YOU A *STUDENT*.
OH, YOUNG MR. JOHN WESLEY? WHAT DO YOU WISH TO LEARN?
EVERYTHING.

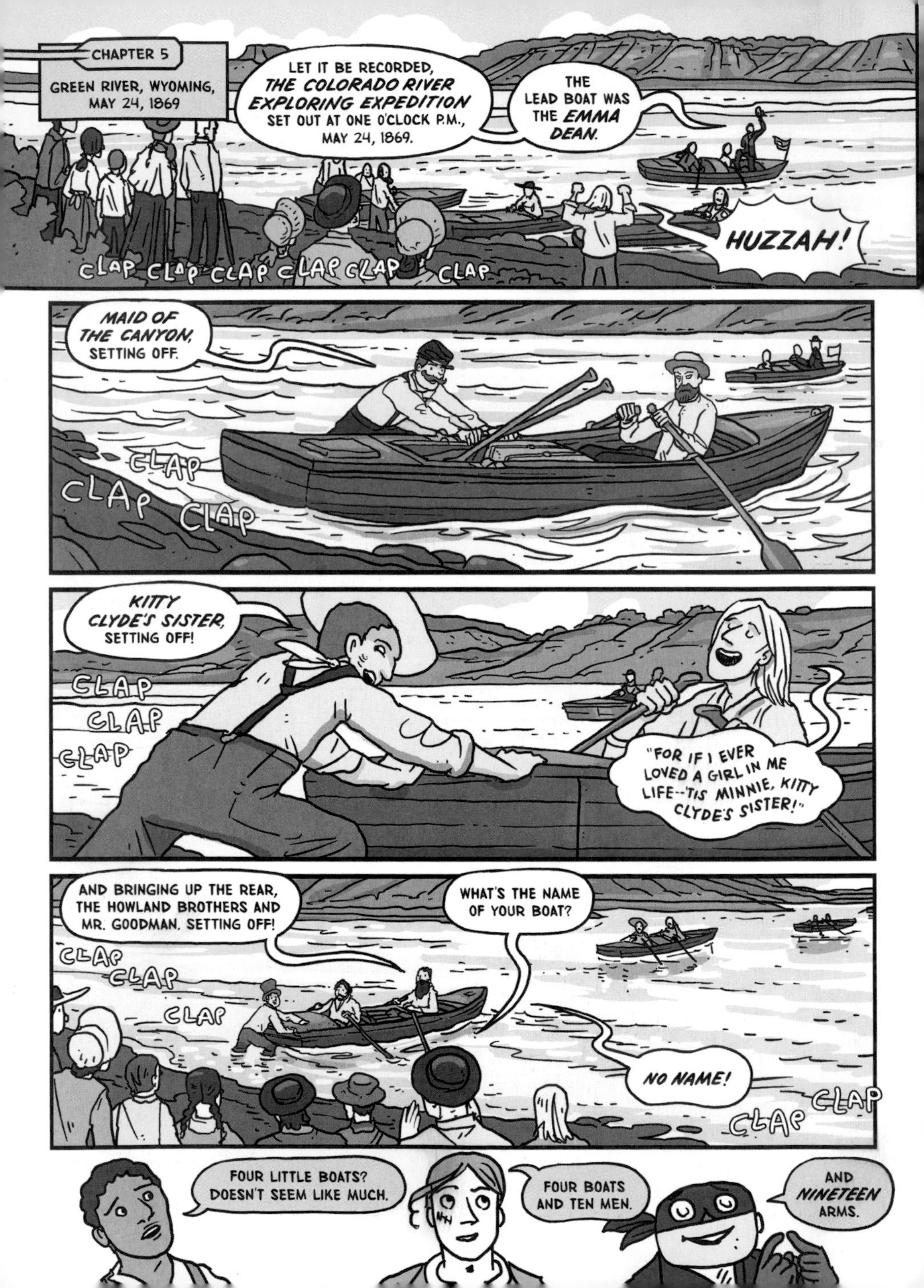
CHAPTER 5
GREEN RIVER, WYOMING, MAY 24, 1869
LET IT BE RECORDED, THE COLORADO RIVER EXPLORING EXPEDITION SET OUT AT ONE O'CLOCK P.M., MAY 24, 1869.
THE LEAD BOAT WAS THE EMMA DEAN.
HUZZAH!
CLAP CLAP CLAP CLAP CLAP CLAP
MAID OF THE CANYON, SETTING OFF.
CLAP CLAP CLAP
KITTY CLYDE'S SISTER, SETTING OFF!
CLAP CLAP CLAP
"FOR IF I EVER LOVED A GIRL IN ME LIFE--'TIS MINNIE, KITTY CLYDE'S SISTER!"
AND BRINGING UP THE REAR, THE HOWLAND BROTHERS AND MR. GOODMAN. SETTING OFF!
WHAT'S THE NAME OF YOUR BOAT?
CLAP CLAP CLAP
NO NAME!
CLAP CLAP
FOUR LITTLE BOATS? DOESN'T SEEM LIKE MUCH.
FOUR BOATS AND TEN MEN.
AND NINETEEN ARMS.

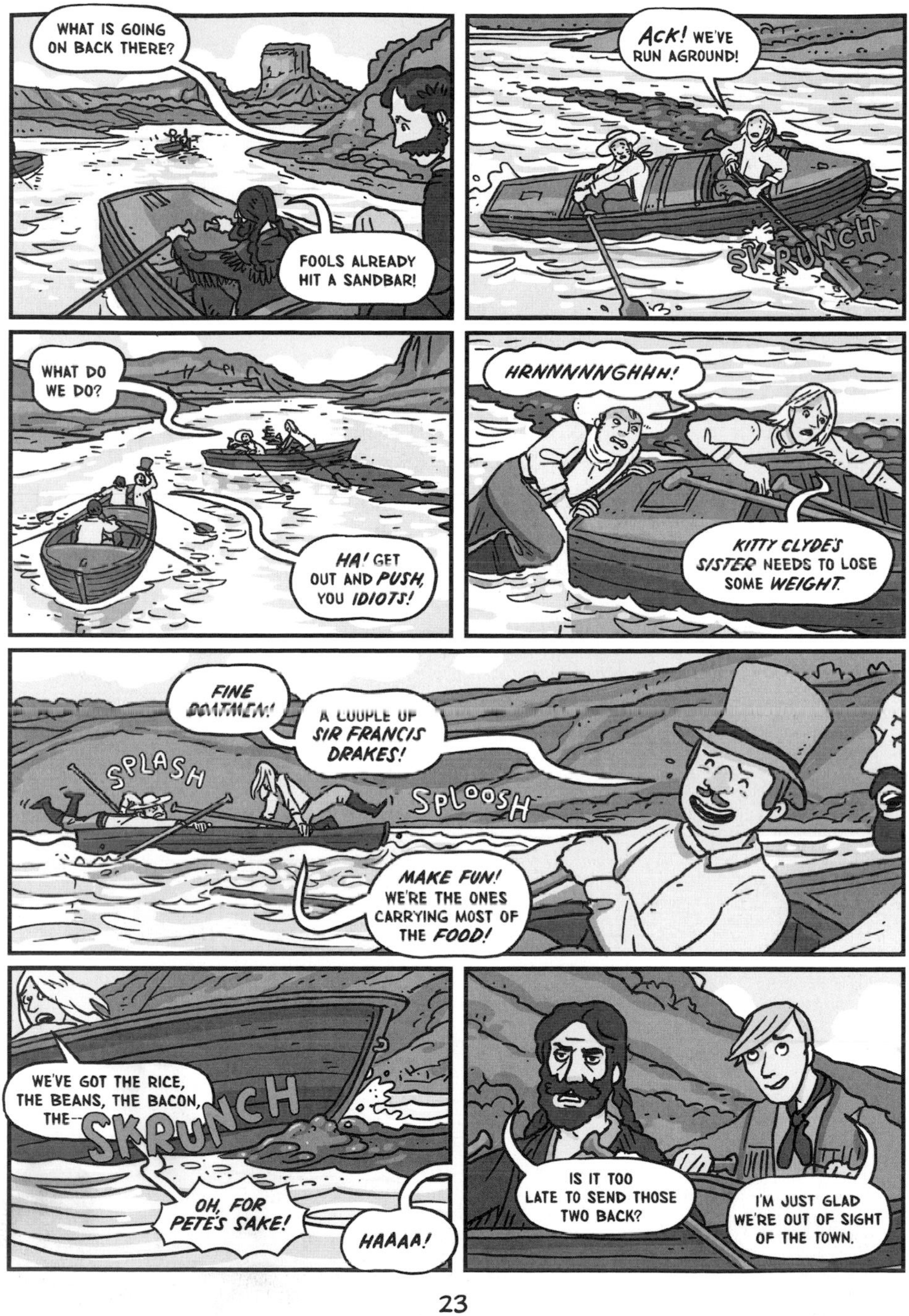
WHAT IS GOING ON BACK THERE?
FOOLS ALREADY HIT A SANDBAR!
ACK! WE'VE RUN AGROUND!
SKRUNCH
WHAT DO WE DO?
HA! GET OUT AND PUSH, YOU IDIOTS!
HRNNNNNGHHH!
KITTY CLYDE'S SISTER NEEDS TO LOSE SOME WEIGHT.
FINE BOATMEN!
A COUPLE OF SIR FRANCIS DRAKES!
SPLASH
SPLOOSH
MAKE FUN! WE'RE THE ONES CARRYING MOST OF THE FOOD!
WE'VE GOT THE RICE, THE BEANS, THE BACON, THE--
SKRUNCH
OH, FOR PETE'S SAKE!
HAAAA!
IS IT TOO LATE TO SEND THOSE TWO BACK?
I'M JUST GLAD WE'RE OUT OF SIGHT OF THE TOWN.

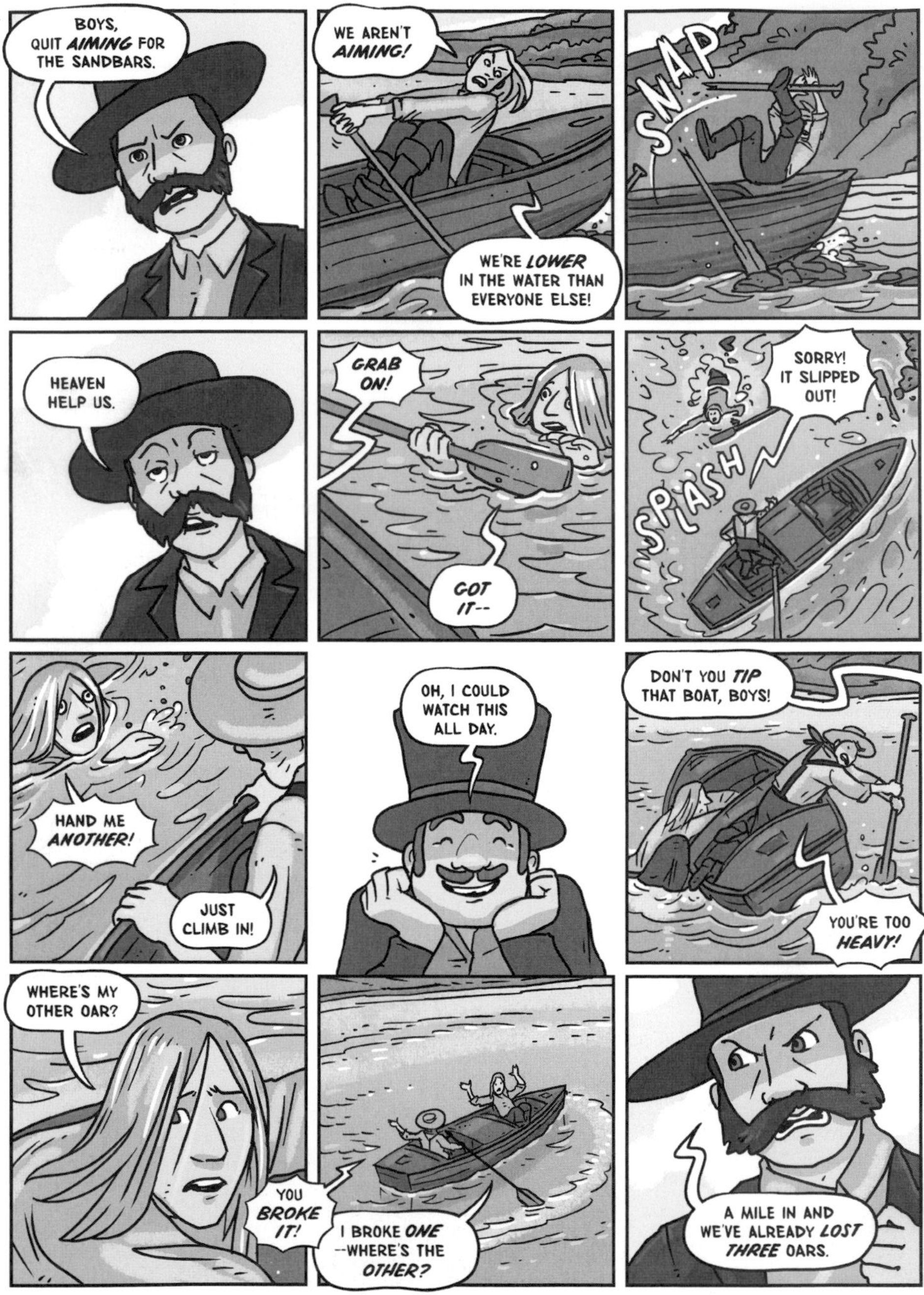

BOYS, QUIT *AIMING* FOR THE SANDBARS.
WE AREN'T *AIMING!*
WE'RE *LOWER* IN THE WATER THAN EVERYONE ELSE!
SNAP
HEAVEN HELP US.
GRAB ON!
GOT IT--
SPLASH
SORRY! IT SLIPPED OUT!
HAND ME *ANOTHER!*
JUST CLIMB IN!
OH, I COULD WATCH THIS ALL DAY.
DON'T YOU *TIP* THAT BOAT, BOYS!
YOU'RE TOO *HEAVY!*
WHERE'S MY OTHER OAR?
YOU BROKE IT!
I BROKE *ONE* --WHERE'S THE *OTHER?*
A MILE IN AND WE'VE ALREADY *LOST THREE* OARS.

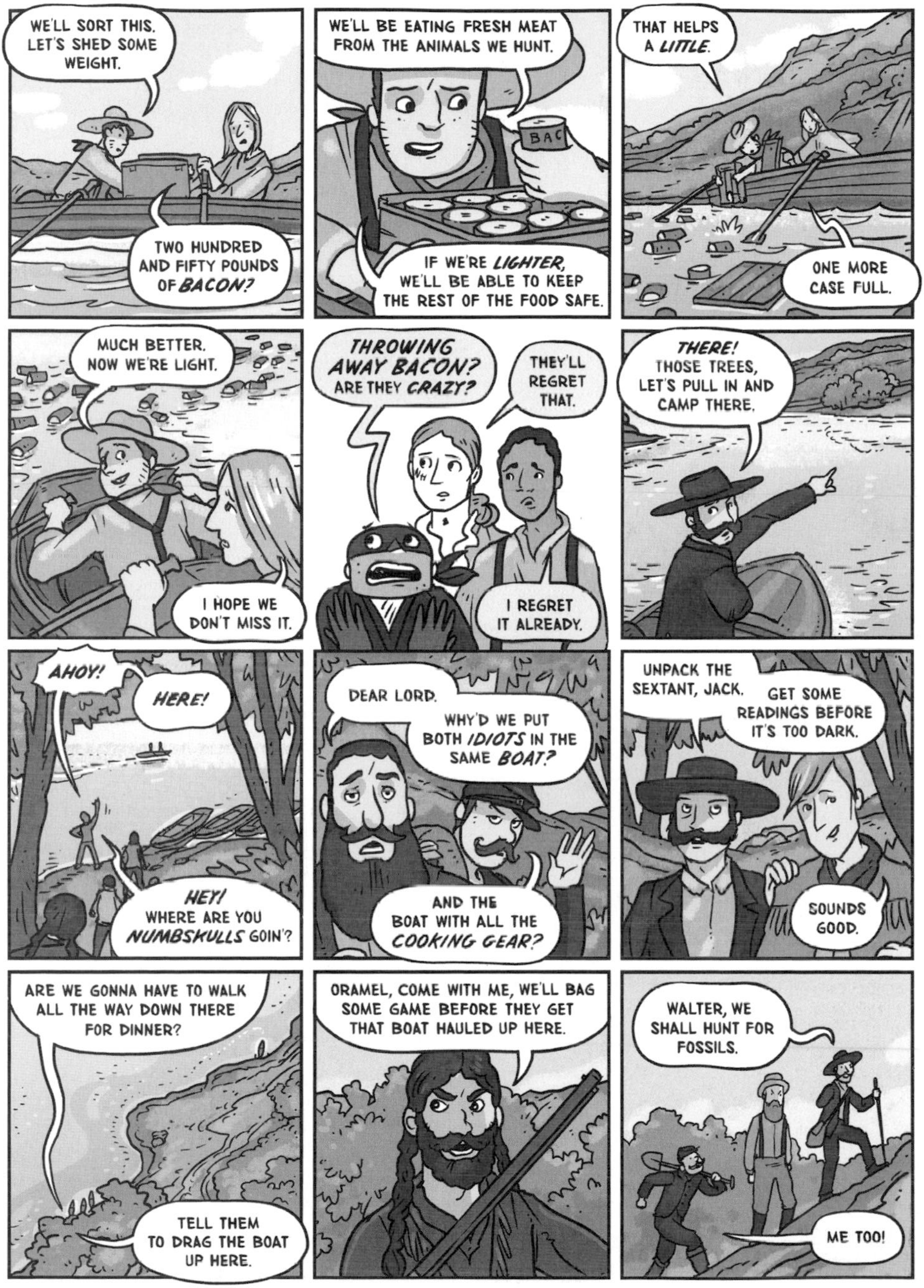
WE'LL SORT THIS. LET'S SHED SOME WEIGHT.
TWO HUNDRED AND FIFTY POUNDS OF BACON?
WE'LL BE EATING FRESH MEAT FROM THE ANIMALS WE HUNT.
BAC
IF WE'RE LIGHTER, WE'LL BE ABLE TO KEEP THE REST OF THE FOOD SAFE.
THAT HELPS A LITTLE.
ONE MORE CASE FULL.
MUCH BETTER. NOW WE'RE LIGHT.
I HOPE WE DON'T MISS IT.
THROWING AWAY BACON? ARE THEY CRAZY?
THEY'LL REGRET THAT.
I REGRET IT ALREADY.
THERE! THOSE TREES, LET'S PULL IN AND CAMP THERE.
AHOY!
HERE!
HEY! WHERE ARE YOU NUMBSKULLS GOIN'?
DEAR LORD.
WHY'D WE PUT BOTH IDIOTS IN THE SAME BOAT?
AND THE BOAT WITH ALL THE COOKING GEAR?
UNPACK THE SEXTANT, JACK.
GET SOME READINGS BEFORE IT'S TOO DARK.
SOUNDS GOOD.
ARE WE GONNA HAVE TO WALK ALL THE WAY DOWN THERE FOR DINNER?
TELL THEM TO DRAG THE BOAT UP HERE.
ORAMEL, COME WITH ME, WE'LL BAG SOME GAME BEFORE THEY GET THAT BOAT HAULED UP HERE.
WALTER, WE SHALL HUNT FOR FOSSILS.
ME TOO!

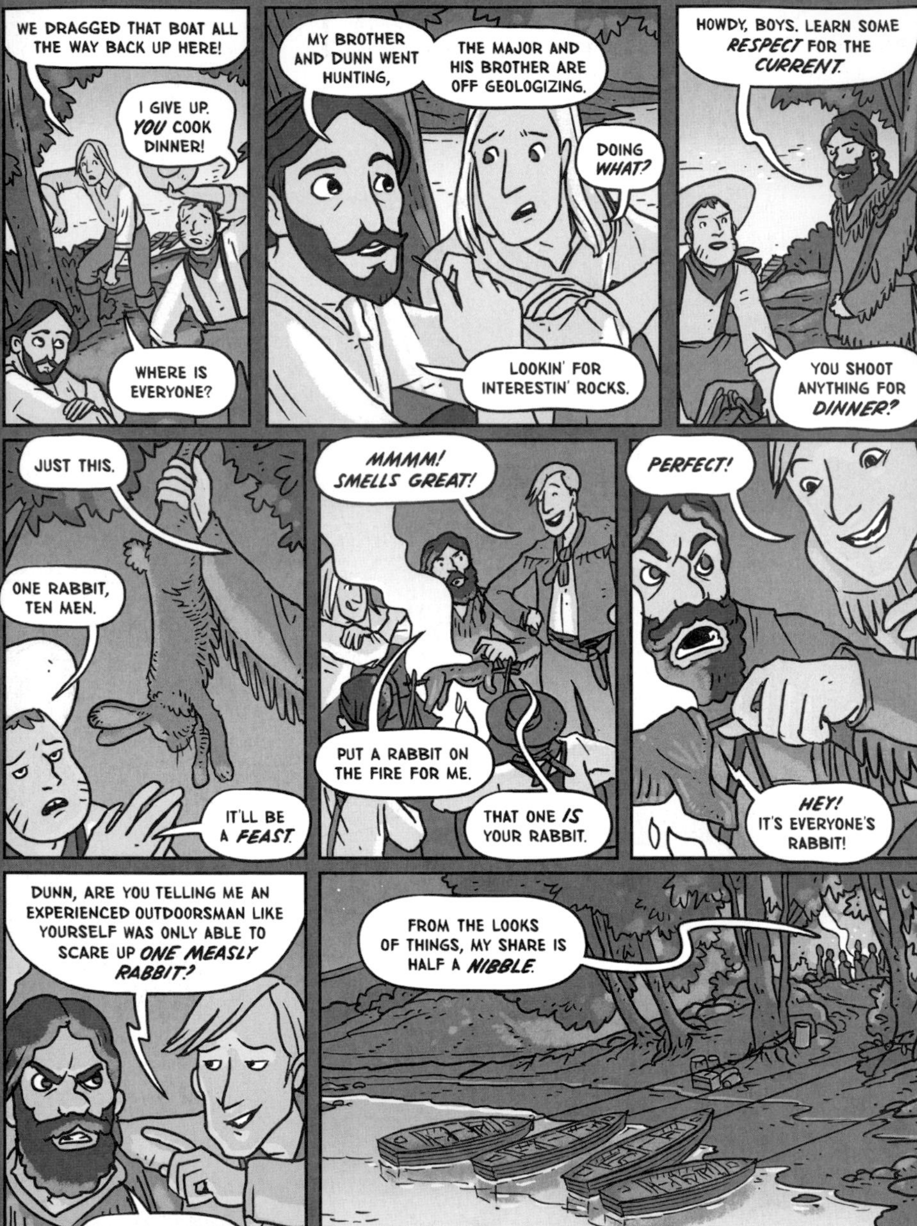

WE DRAGGED THAT BOAT ALL THE WAY BACK UP HERE!
I GIVE UP. *YOU* COOK DINNER!
WHERE IS EVERYONE?
MY BROTHER AND DUNN WENT HUNTING,
THE MAJOR AND HIS BROTHER ARE OFF GEOLOGIZING.
DOING *WHAT?*
LOOKIN' FOR INTERESTIN' ROCKS.
HOWDY, BOYS. LEARN SOME *RESPECT* FOR THE *CURRENT.*
YOU SHOOT ANYTHING FOR *DINNER?*
JUST THIS.
ONE RABBIT, TEN MEN.
IT'LL BE A *FEAST.*
MMMM! SMELLS GREAT!
PUT A RABBIT ON THE FIRE FOR ME.
THAT ONE *IS* YOUR RABBIT.
PERFECT!
HEY! IT'S EVERYONE'S RABBIT!
DUNN, ARE YOU TELLING ME AN EXPERIENCED OUTDOORSMAN LIKE YOURSELF WAS ONLY ABLE TO SCARE UP *ONE MEASLY RABBIT?*
KEEP IT UP, JACK, YOU'LL LOSE YOUR SHARE.
FROM THE LOOKS OF THINGS, MY SHARE IS HALF A *NIBBLE.*

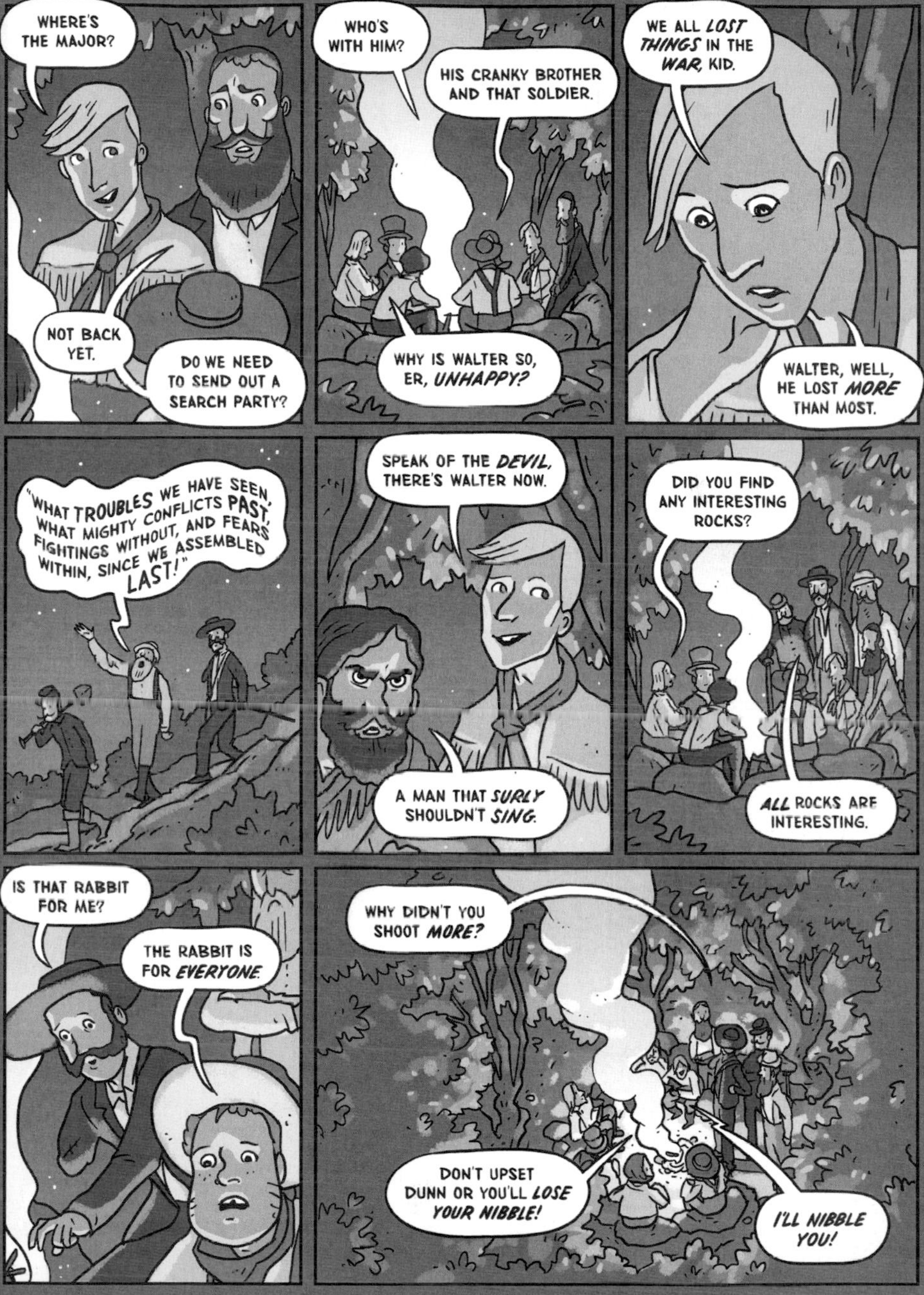
WHERE'S THE MAJOR?
NOT BACK YET.
DO WE NEED TO SEND OUT A SEARCH PARTY?
WHO'S WITH HIM?
HIS CRANKY BROTHER AND THAT SOLDIER.
WHY IS WALTER SO, ER, UNHAPPY?
WE ALL LOST THINGS IN THE WAR, KID.
WALTER, WELL, HE LOST MORE THAN MOST.
"WHAT TROUBLES WE HAVE SEEN, WHAT MIGHTY CONFLICTS PAST, FIGHTINGS WITHOUT, AND FEARS WITHIN, SINCE WE ASSEMBLED LAST!"
SPEAK OF THE DEVIL, THERE'S WALTER NOW.
A MAN THAT SURLY SHOULDN'T SING.
DID YOU FIND ANY INTERESTING ROCKS?
ALL ROCKS ARE INTERESTING.
IS THAT RABBIT FOR ME?
THE RABBIT IS FOR EVERYONE.
WHY DIDN'T YOU SHOOT MORE?
DON'T UPSET DUNN OR YOU'LL LOSE YOUR NIBBLE!
I'LL NIBBLE YOU!

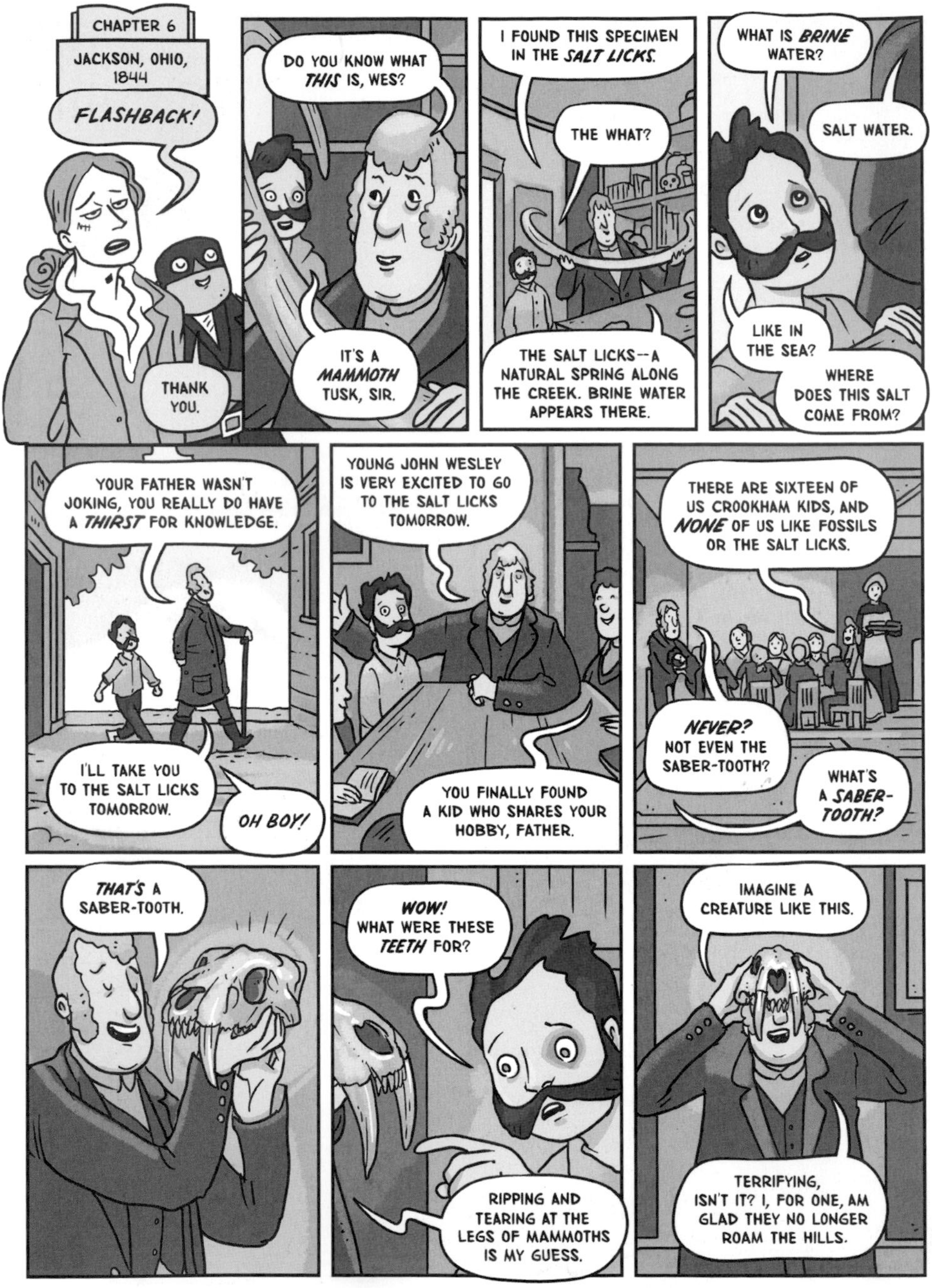
CHAPTER 6
JACKSON, OHIO, 1844
FLASHBACK!
THANK YOU.
DO YOU KNOW WHAT THIS IS, WES?
IT'S A MAMMOTH TUSK, SIR.
I FOUND THIS SPECIMEN IN THE SALT LICKS.
THE WHAT?
THE SALT LICKS--A NATURAL SPRING ALONG THE CREEK. BRINE WATER APPEARS THERE.
WHAT IS BRINE WATER?
SALT WATER.
LIKE IN THE SEA?
WHERE DOES THIS SALT COME FROM?
YOUR FATHER WASN'T JOKING, YOU REALLY DO HAVE A THIRST FOR KNOWLEDGE.
I'LL TAKE YOU TO THE SALT LICKS TOMORROW.
OH BOY!
YOUNG JOHN WESLEY IS VERY EXCITED TO GO TO THE SALT LICKS TOMORROW.
YOU FINALLY FOUND A KID WHO SHARES YOUR HOBBY, FATHER.
THERE ARE SIXTEEN OF US CROOKHAM KIDS, AND NONE OF US LIKE FOSSILS OR THE SALT LICKS.
NEVER? NOT EVEN THE SABER-TOOTH?
WHAT'S A SABER-TOOTH?
THAT'S A SABER-TOOTH.
WOW! WHAT WERE THESE TEETH FOR?
RIPPING AND TEARING AT THE LEGS OF MAMMOTHS IS MY GUESS.
IMAGINE A CREATURE LIKE THIS.
TERRIFYING, ISN'T IT? I, FOR ONE, AM GLAD THEY NO LONGER ROAM THE HILLS.

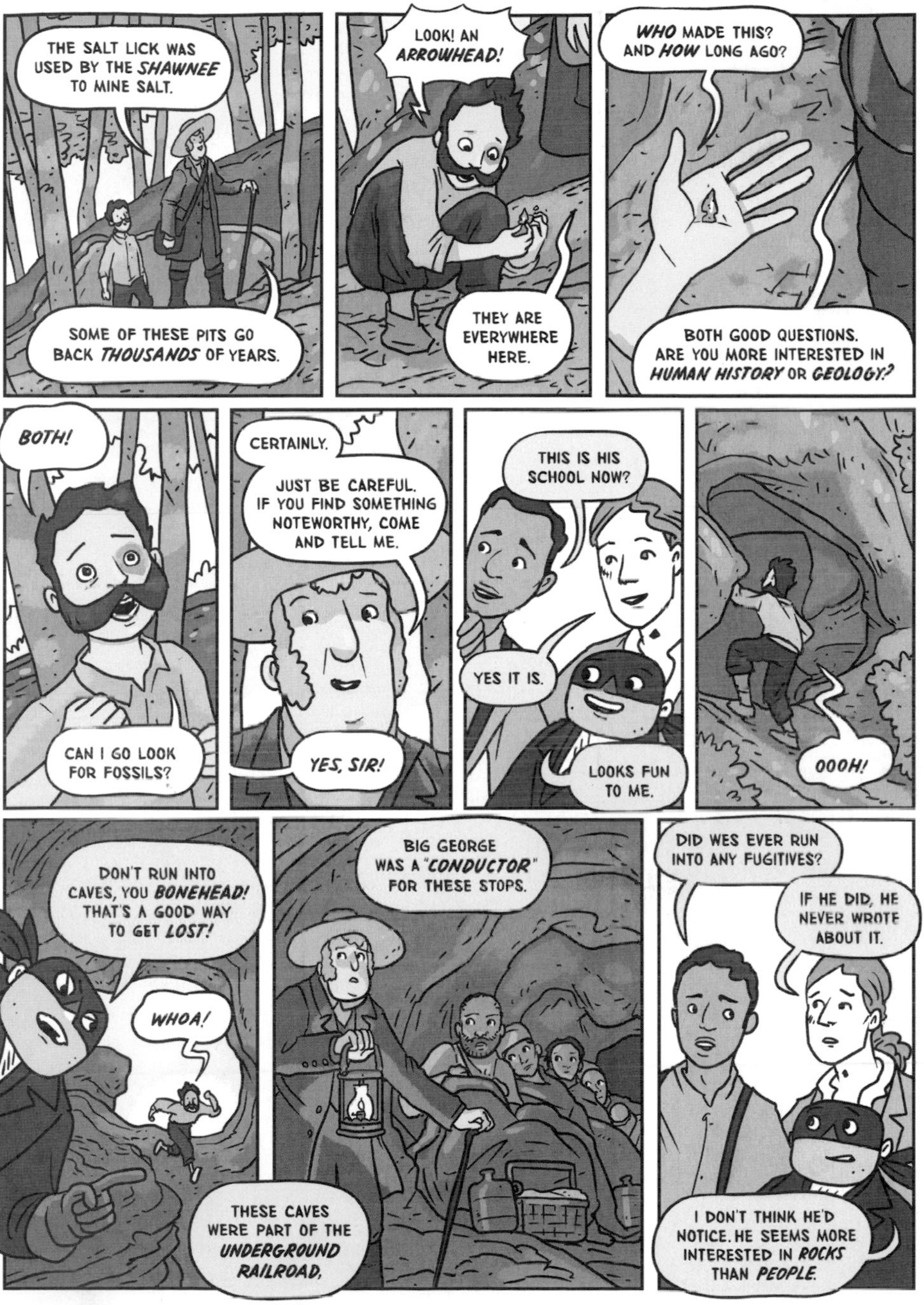
THE SALT LICK WAS USED BY THE SHAWNEE TO MINE SALT.
SOME OF THESE PITS GO BACK THOUSANDS OF YEARS.
LOOK! AN ARROWHEAD!
THEY ARE EVERYWHERE HERE.
WHO MADE THIS? AND HOW LONG AGO?
BOTH GOOD QUESTIONS. ARE YOU MORE INTERESTED IN HUMAN HISTORY OR GEOLOGY?
BOTH!
CAN I GO LOOK FOR FOSSILS?
CERTAINLY.
JUST BE CAREFUL. IF YOU FIND SOMETHING NOTEWORTHY, COME AND TELL ME.
YES, SIR!
THIS IS HIS SCHOOL NOW?
YES IT IS.
LOOKS FUN TO ME.
OOOH!
DON'T RUN INTO CAVES, YOU BONEHEAD! THAT'S A GOOD WAY TO GET LOST!
WHOA!
BIG GEORGE WAS A "CONDUCTOR" FOR THESE STOPS.
THESE CAVES WERE PART OF THE UNDERGROUND RAILROAD.
DID WES EVER RUN INTO ANY FUGITIVES?
IF HE DID, HE NEVER WROTE ABOUT IT.
I DON'T THINK HE'D NOTICE. HE SEEMS MORE INTERESTED IN ROCKS THAN PEOPLE.

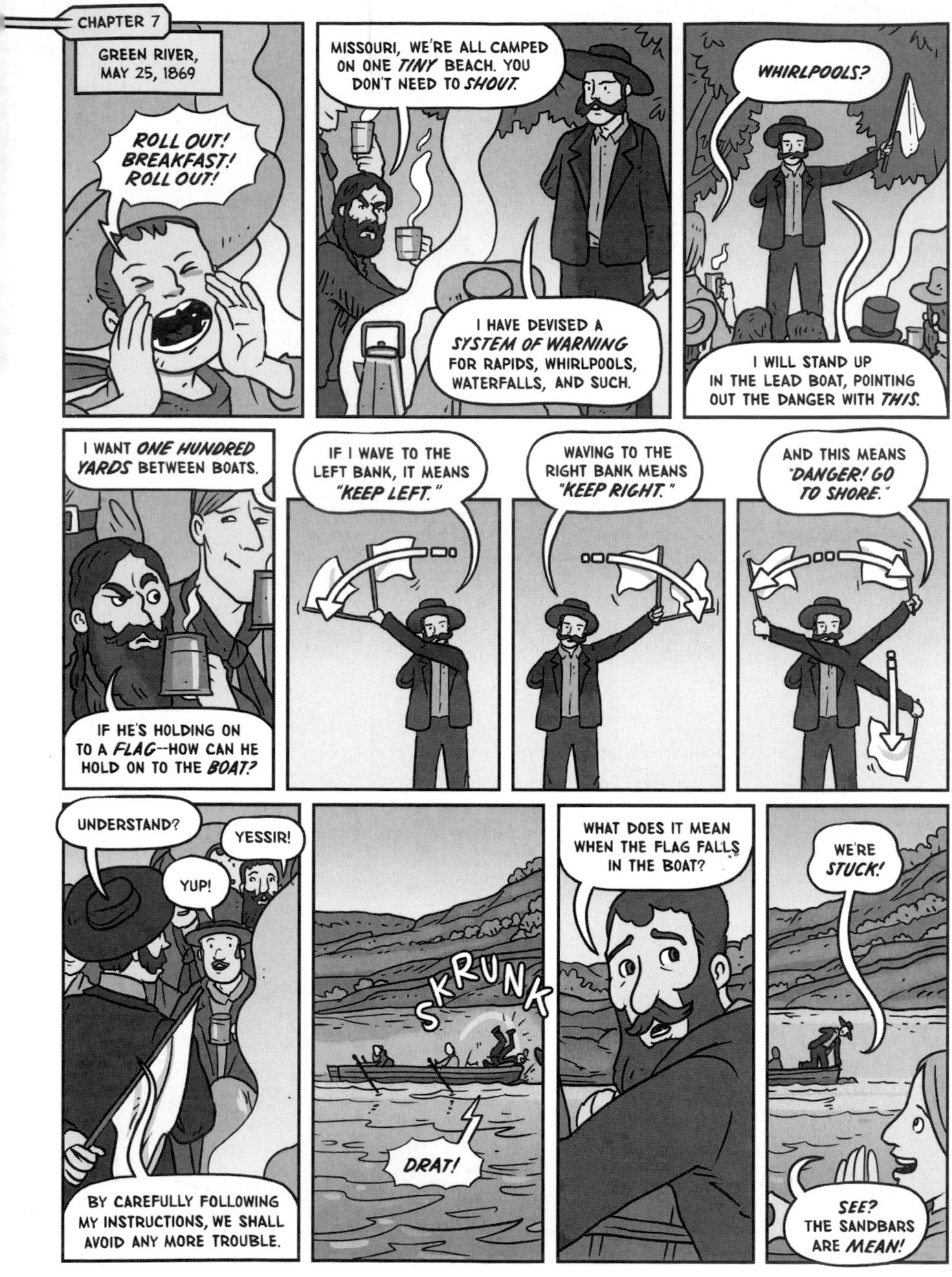
CHAPTER 7
GREEN RIVER, MAY 25, 1869
ROLL OUT! BREAKFAST! ROLL OUT!
MISSOURI, WE'RE ALL CAMPED ON ONE TINY BEACH. YOU DON'T NEED TO SHOUT.
I HAVE DEVISED A SYSTEM OF WARNING FOR RAPIDS, WHIRLPOOLS, WATERFALLS, AND SUCH.
WHIRLPOOLS?
I WILL STAND UP IN THE LEAD BOAT, POINTING OUT THE DANGER WITH THIS.
I WANT ONE HUNDRED YARDS BETWEEN BOATS.
IF HE'S HOLDING ON TO A FLAG--HOW CAN HE HOLD ON TO THE BOAT?
IF I WAVE TO THE LEFT BANK, IT MEANS "KEEP LEFT."
WAVING TO THE RIGHT BANK MEANS "KEEP RIGHT."
AND THIS MEANS "DANGER! GO TO SHORE."
UNDERSTAND?
YESSIR!
YUP!
BY CAREFULLY FOLLOWING MY INSTRUCTIONS, WE SHALL AVOID ANY MORE TROUBLE.
SKRUNK
DRAT!
WHAT DOES IT MEAN WHEN THE FLAG FALLS IN THE BOAT?
WE'RE STUCK!
SEE? THE SANDBARS ARE MEAN!

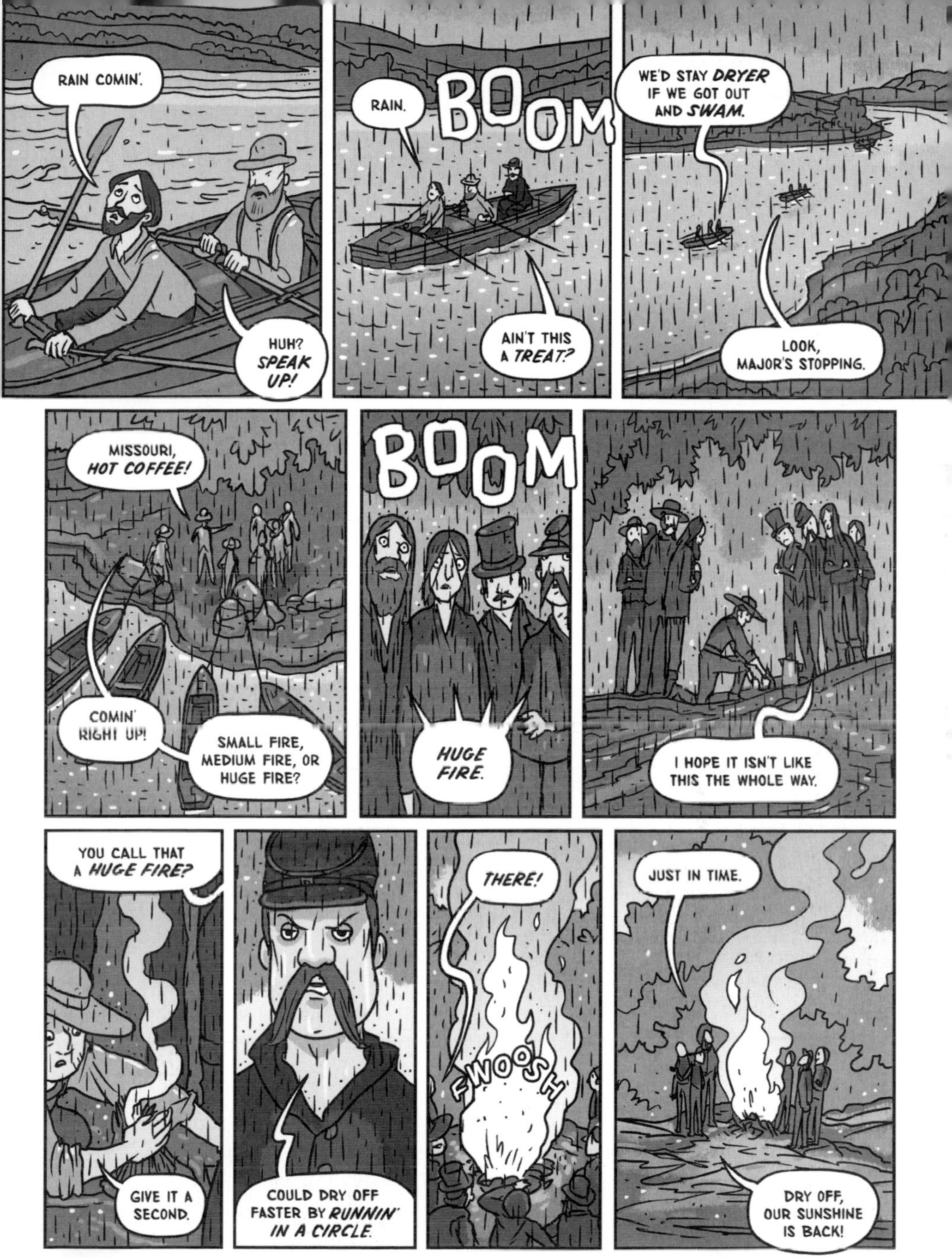
RAIN COMIN'.
HUH? SPEAK UP!
RAIN.
BOOM
AIN'T THIS A TREAT?
WE'D STAY DRYER IF WE GOT OUT AND SWAM.
LOOK, MAJOR'S STOPPING.
MISSOURI, HOT COFFEE!
COMIN' RIGHT UP!
SMALL FIRE, MEDIUM FIRE, OR HUGE FIRE?
BOOM
HUGE FIRE.
I HOPE IT ISN'T LIKE THIS THE WHOLE WAY.
YOU CALL THAT A HUGE FIRE?
GIVE IT A SECOND.
COULD DRY OFF FASTER BY RUNNIN' IN A CIRCLE.
THERE!
FWOOSH
JUST IN TIME.
DRY OFF, OUR SUNSHINE IS BACK!

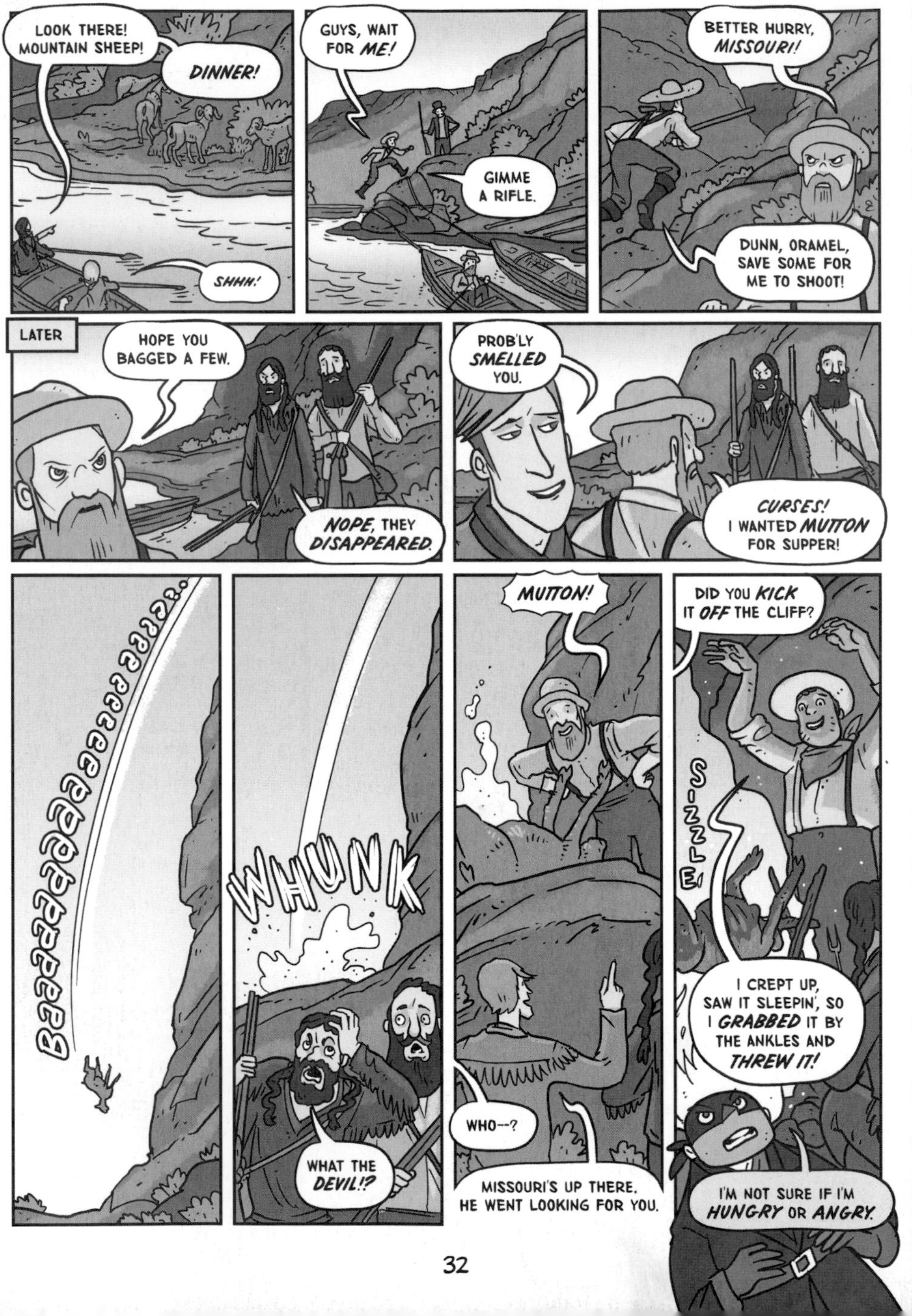
LOOK THERE! MOUNTAIN SHEEP!
DINNER!
SHHH!
GUYS, WAIT FOR ME!
GIMME A RIFLE.
BETTER HURRY, MISSOURI!
DUNN, ORAMEL, SAVE SOME FOR ME TO SHOOT!
LATER
HOPE YOU BAGGED A FEW.
NOPE, THEY DISAPPEARED.
PROB'LY SMELLED YOU.
CURSES! I WANTED MUTTON FOR SUPPER!
BAAAAAAAAEEEEEEEEEEEE?..
WHUNK
WHAT THE DEVIL!?
MUTTON!
WHO--?
MISSOURI'S UP THERE. HE WENT LOOKING FOR YOU.
DID YOU KICK IT OFF THE CLIFF?
SIZZLE
I CREPT UP, SAW IT SLEEPIN', SO I GRABBED IT BY THE ANKLES AND THREW IT!
I'M NOT SURE IF I'M HUNGRY OR ANGRY.

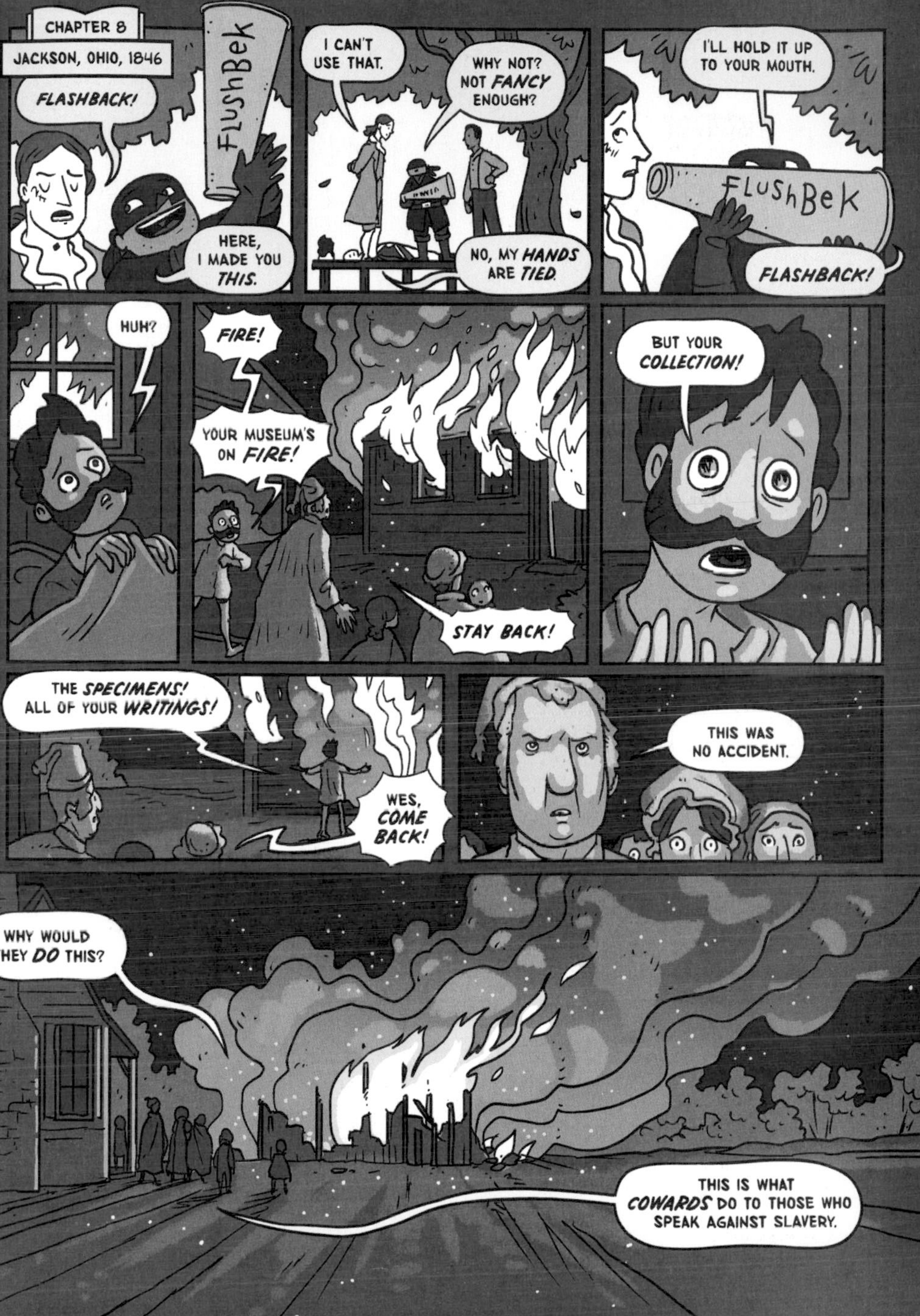
CHAPTER 8
JACKSON, OHIO, 1846
FLASHBACK!
FLUSHBEK
HERE, I MADE YOU THIS.
I CAN'T USE THAT.
WHY NOT? NOT FANCY ENOUGH?
NO, MY HANDS ARE TIED.
I'LL HOLD IT UP TO YOUR MOUTH.
FLUSHBEK
FLASHBACK!
HUH?
FIRE!
YOUR MUSEUM'S ON FIRE!
STAY BACK!
BUT YOUR COLLECTION!
THE SPECIMENS! ALL OF YOUR WRITINGS!
WES, COME BACK!
THIS WAS NO ACCIDENT.
WHY WOULD THEY DO THIS?
THIS IS WHAT COWARDS DO TO THOSE WHO SPEAK AGAINST SLAVERY.

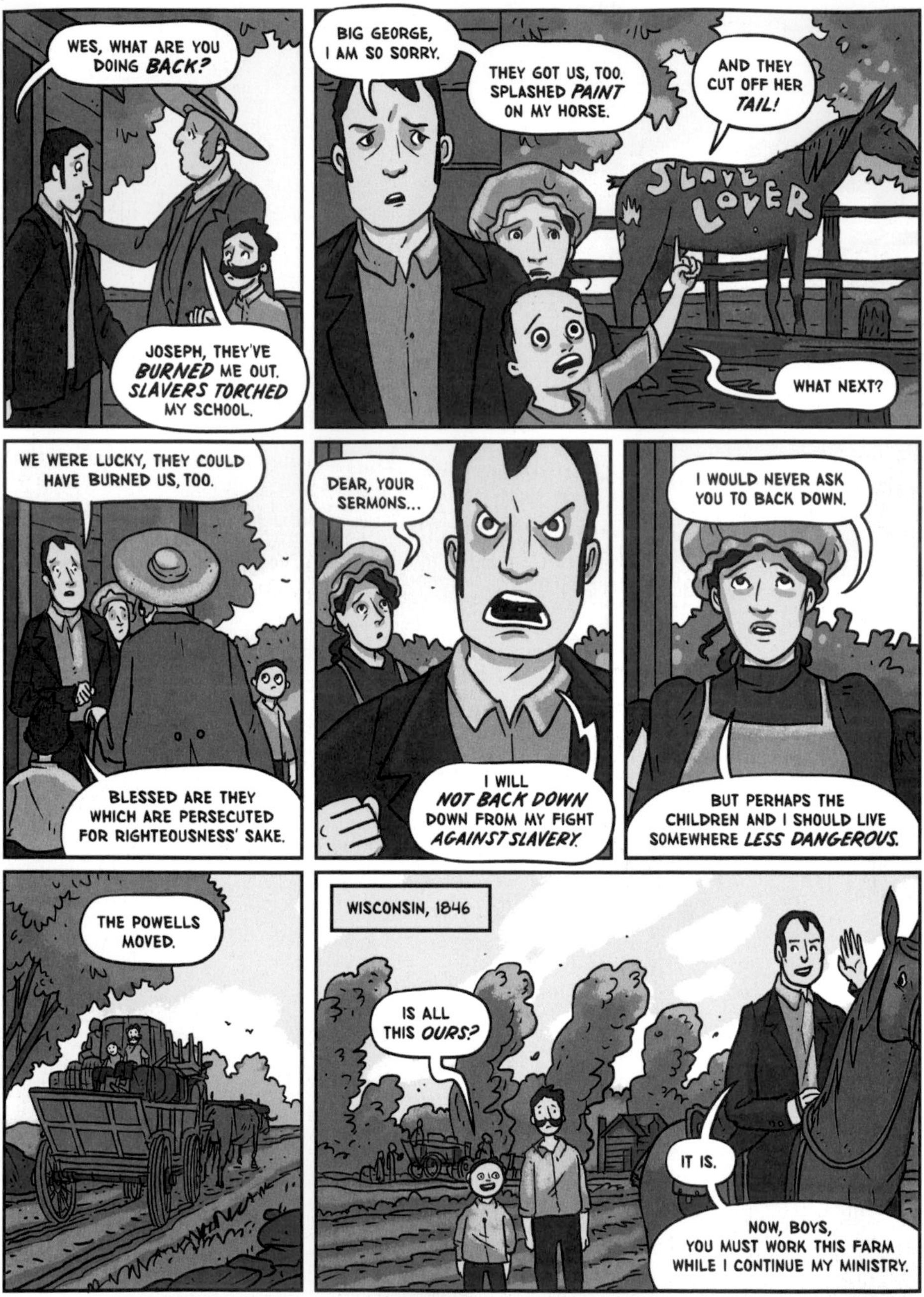
WES, WHAT ARE YOU DOING BACK?
JOSEPH, THEY'VE BURNED ME OUT. SLAVERS TORCHED MY SCHOOL.
BIG GEORGE, I AM SO SORRY.
THEY GOT US, TOO. SPLASHED PAINT ON MY HORSE.
AND THEY CUT OFF HER TAIL!
SLAVE LOVER
WHAT NEXT?
WE WERE LUCKY, THEY COULD HAVE BURNED US, TOO.
BLESSED ARE THEY WHICH ARE PERSECUTED FOR RIGHTEOUSNESS' SAKE.
DEAR, YOUR SERMONS...
I WILL NOT BACK DOWN DOWN FROM MY FIGHT AGAINST SLAVERY.
I WOULD NEVER ASK YOU TO BACK DOWN.
BUT PERHAPS THE CHILDREN AND I SHOULD LIVE SOMEWHERE LESS DANGEROUS.
THE POWELLS MOVED.
WISCONSIN, 1846
IS ALL THIS OURS?
IT IS.
NOW, BOYS, YOU MUST WORK THIS FARM WHILE I CONTINUE MY MINISTRY.

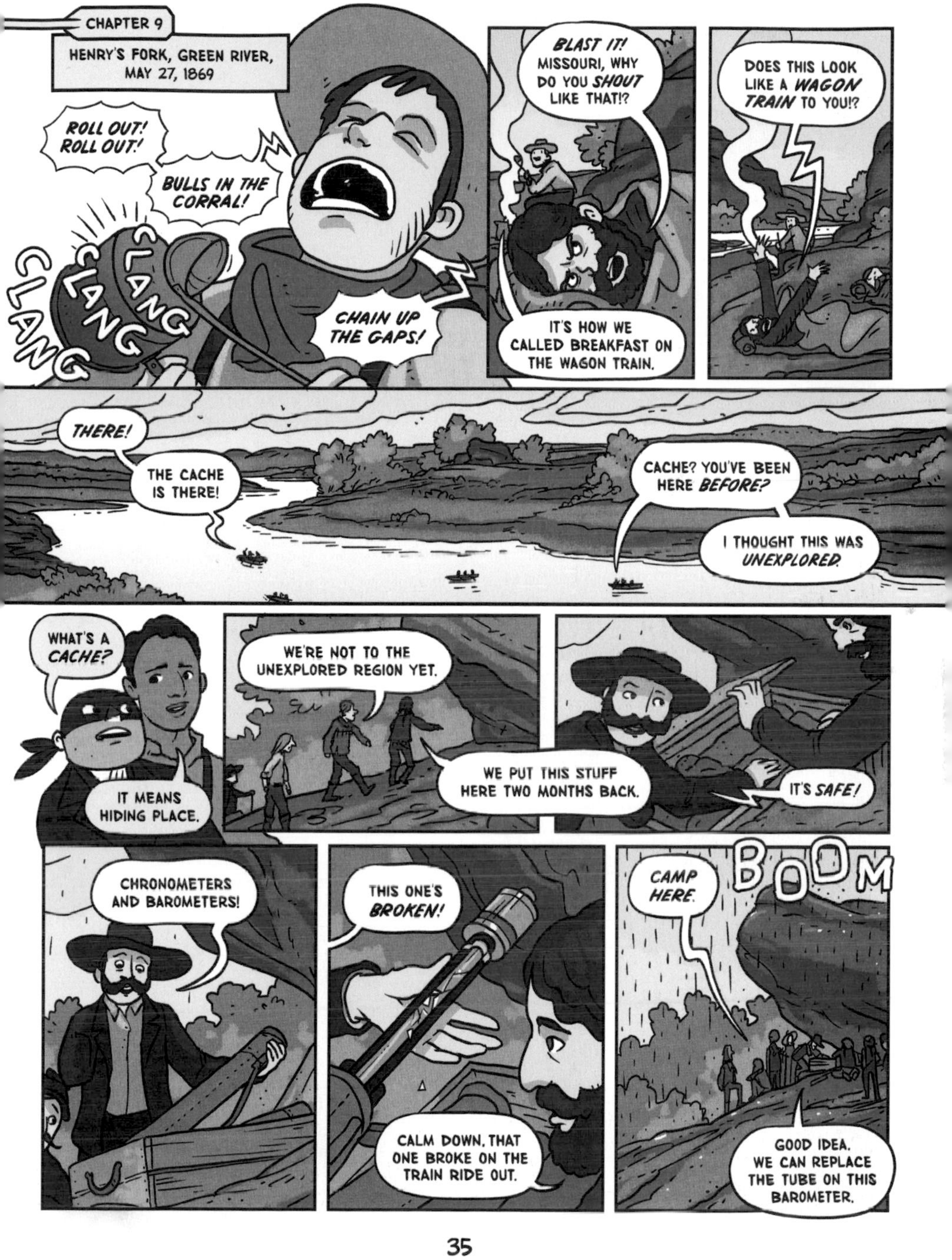
CHAPTER 9
HENRY'S FORK, GREEN RIVER, MAY 27, 1869
ROLL OUT! ROLL OUT!
BULLS IN THE CORRAL!
CLANG CLANG CLANG
CHAIN UP THE GAPS!
BLAST IT! MISSOURI, WHY DO YOU SHOUT LIKE THAT!?
IT'S HOW WE CALLED BREAKFAST ON THE WAGON TRAIN.
DOES THIS LOOK LIKE A WAGON TRAIN TO YOU!?
THERE!
THE CACHE IS THERE!
CACHE? YOU'VE BEEN HERE BEFORE?
I THOUGHT THIS WAS UNEXPLORED.
WHAT'S A CACHE?
IT MEANS HIDING PLACE.
WE'RE NOT TO THE UNEXPLORED REGION YET.
WE PUT THIS STUFF HERE TWO MONTHS BACK.
IT'S SAFE!
CHRONOMETERS AND BAROMETERS!
THIS ONE'S BROKEN!
CALM DOWN. THAT ONE BROKE ON THE TRAIN RIDE OUT.
BOOM
CAMP HERE.
GOOD IDEA. WE CAN REPLACE THE TUBE ON THIS BAROMETER.

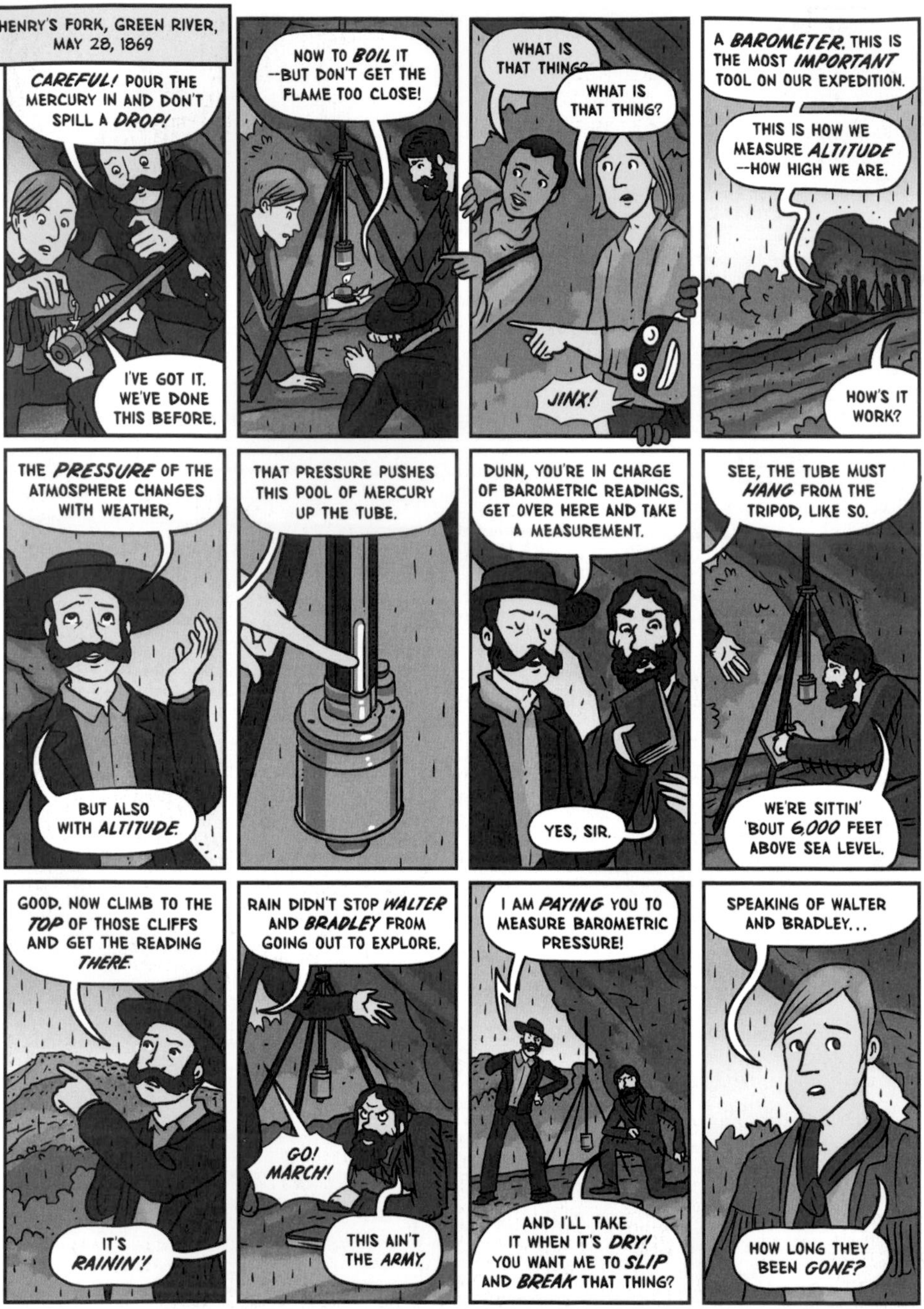
HENRY'S FORK, GREEN RIVER, MAY 28, 1869
CAREFUL! POUR THE MERCURY IN AND DON'T SPILL A DROP!
I'VE GOT IT. WE'VE DONE THIS BEFORE.
NOW TO BOIL IT --BUT DON'T GET THE FLAME TOO CLOSE!
WHAT IS THAT THING?
WHAT IS THAT THING?
JINX!
A BAROMETER. THIS IS THE MOST IMPORTANT TOOL ON OUR EXPEDITION.
THIS IS HOW WE MEASURE ALTITUDE --HOW HIGH WE ARE.
HOW'S IT WORK?
THE PRESSURE OF THE ATMOSPHERE CHANGES WITH WEATHER,
BUT ALSO WITH ALTITUDE.
THAT PRESSURE PUSHES THIS POOL OF MERCURY UP THE TUBE.
DUNN, YOU'RE IN CHARGE OF BAROMETRIC READINGS. GET OVER HERE AND TAKE A MEASUREMENT.
YES, SIR.
SEE, THE TUBE MUST HANG FROM THE TRIPOD, LIKE SO.
WE'RE SITTIN' 'BOUT 6,000 FEET ABOVE SEA LEVEL.
GOOD. NOW CLIMB TO THE TOP OF THOSE CLIFFS AND GET THE READING THERE.
IT'S RAININ'!
RAIN DIDN'T STOP WALTER AND BRADLEY FROM GOING OUT TO EXPLORE.
GO! MARCH!
THIS AIN'T THE ARMY.
I AM PAYING YOU TO MEASURE BAROMETRIC PRESSURE!
AND I'LL TAKE IT WHEN IT'S DRY! YOU WANT ME TO SLIP AND BREAK THAT THING?
SPEAKING OF WALTER AND BRADLEY...
HOW LONG THEY BEEN GONE?

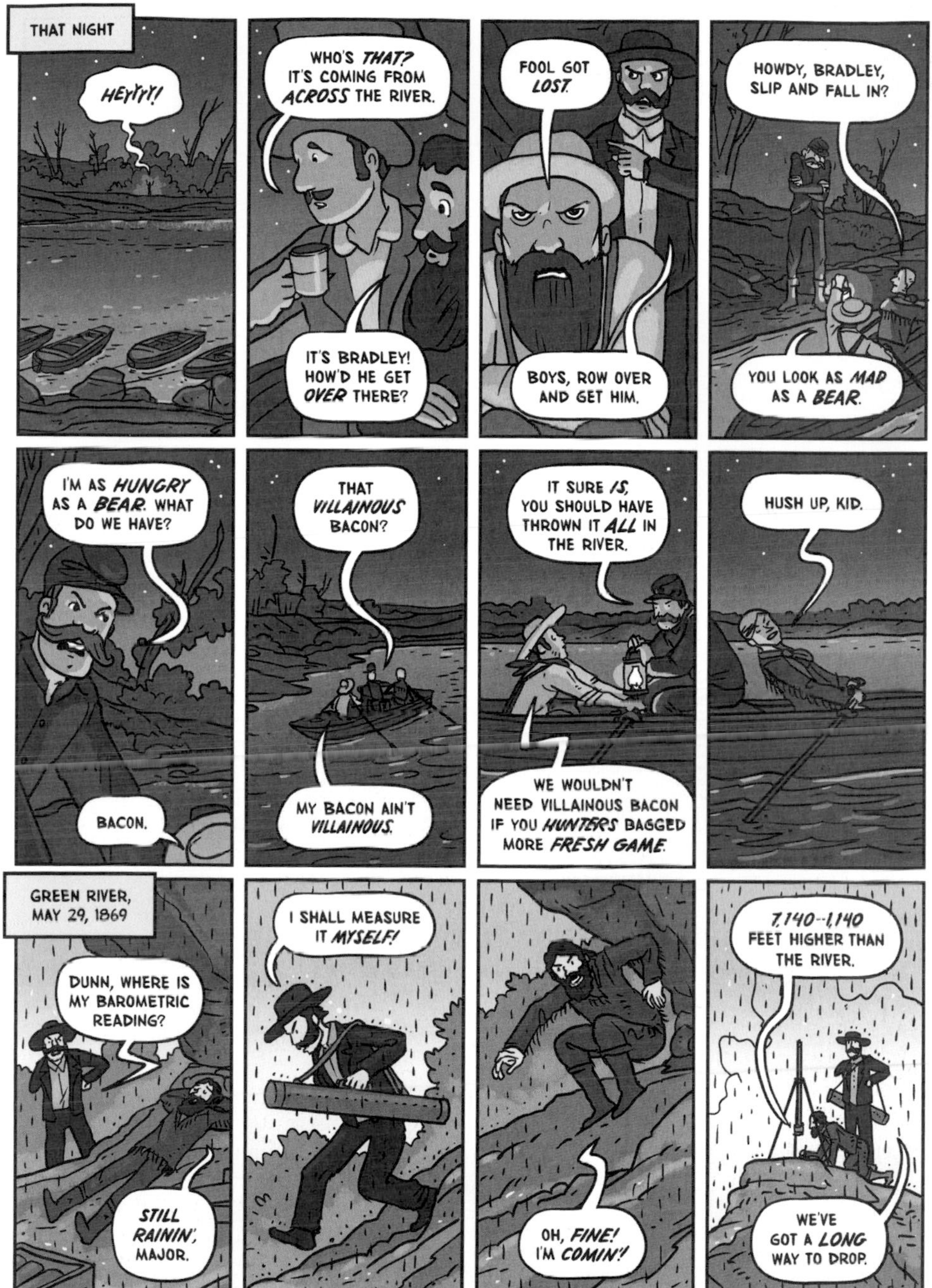
THAT NIGHT
HEYYYY!
WHO'S THAT? IT'S COMING FROM ACROSS THE RIVER.
IT'S BRADLEY! HOW'D HE GET OVER THERE?
FOOL GOT LOST.
BOYS, ROW OVER AND GET HIM.
HOWDY, BRADLEY, SLIP AND FALL IN?
YOU LOOK AS MAD AS A BEAR.
I'M AS HUNGRY AS A BEAR. WHAT DO WE HAVE?
BACON.
THAT VILLAINOUS BACON?
MY BACON AIN'T VILLAINOUS.
IT SURE IS, YOU SHOULD HAVE THROWN IT ALL IN THE RIVER.
WE WOULDN'T NEED VILLAINOUS BACON IF YOU HUNTERS BAGGED MORE FRESH GAME.
HUSH UP, KID.
GREEN RIVER, MAY 29, 1869
DUNN, WHERE IS MY BAROMETRIC READING?
STILL RAININ', MAJOR.
I SHALL MEASURE IT MYSELF!
OH, FINE! I'M COMIN'!
7,140--1,140 FEET HIGHER THAN THE RIVER.
WE'VE GOT A LONG WAY TO DROP.

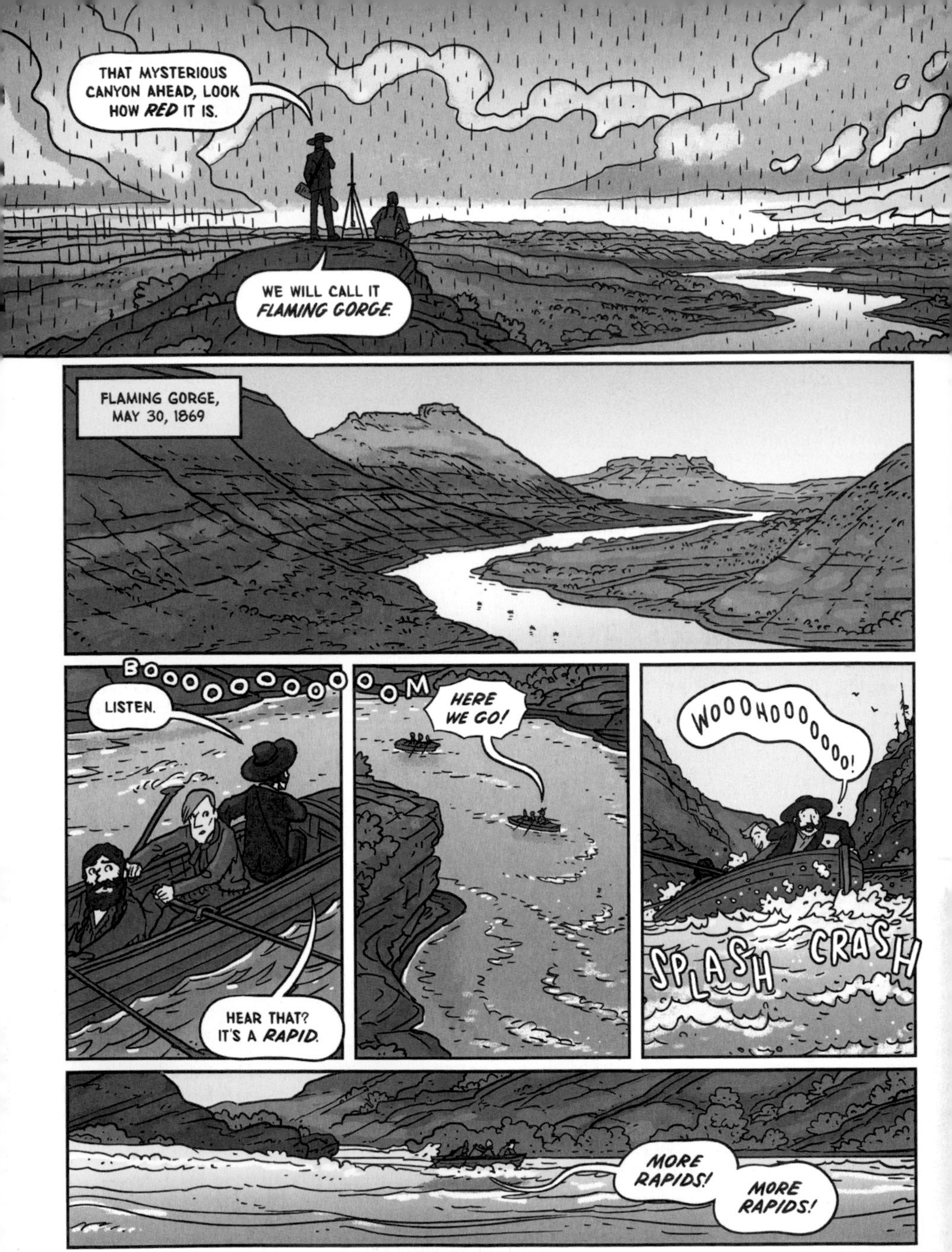
THAT MYSTERIOUS CANYON AHEAD, LOOK HOW *RED* IT IS.
WE WILL CALL IT *FLAMING GORGE.*
FLAMING GORGE, MAY 30, 1869
BOOOOOOOOOOOOOM
LISTEN.
HEAR THAT? IT'S A *RAPID.*
HERE WE GO!
WOOOHOOOOOOO!
SPLASH
CRASH
MORE RAPIDS!
MORE RAPIDS!

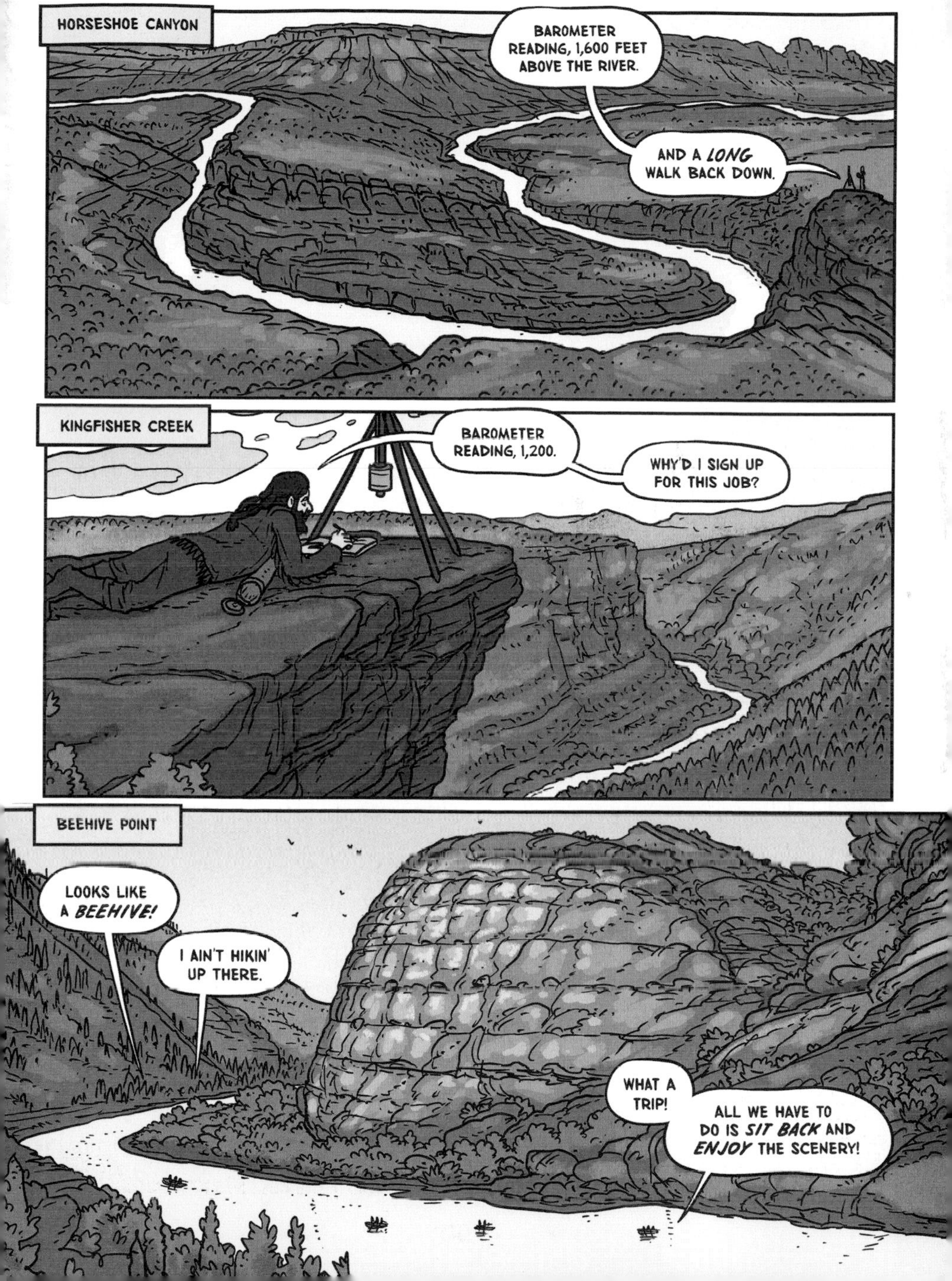
HORSESHOE CANYON
BAROMETER READING, 1,600 FEET ABOVE THE RIVER.
AND A LONG WALK BACK DOWN.
KINGFISHER CREEK
BAROMETER READING, 1,200.
WHY'D I SIGN UP FOR THIS JOB?
BEEHIVE POINT
LOOKS LIKE A BEEHIVE!
I AIN'T HIKIN' UP THERE.
WHAT A TRIP!
ALL WE HAVE TO DO IS SIT BACK AND ENJOY THE SCENERY!

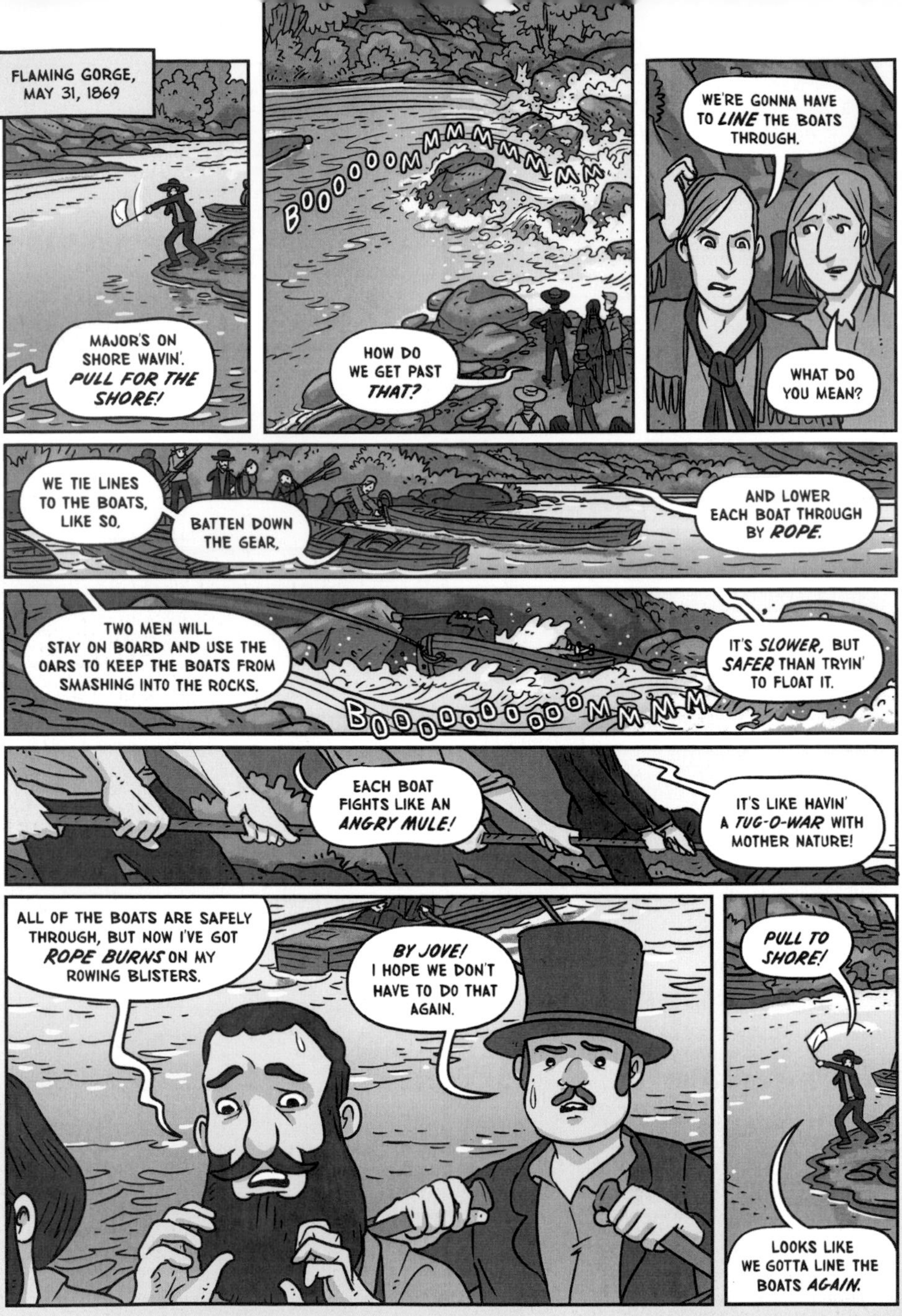
FLAMING GORGE, MAY 31, 1869
MAJOR'S ON SHORE WAVIN'. PULL FOR THE SHORE!
BOOOOOOMMMMMMMMMM
HOW DO WE GET PAST THAT?
WE'RE GONNA HAVE TO LINE THE BOATS THROUGH.
WHAT DO YOU MEAN?
WE TIE LINES TO THE BOATS, LIKE SO,
BATTEN DOWN THE GEAR,
AND LOWER EACH BOAT THROUGH BY ROPE.
TWO MEN WILL STAY ON BOARD AND USE THE OARS TO KEEP THE BOATS FROM SMASHING INTO THE ROCKS.
IT'S SLOWER, BUT SAFER THAN TRYIN' TO FLOAT IT.
BOOOOOOOOOOMMMM
EACH BOAT FIGHTS LIKE AN ANGRY MULE!
IT'S LIKE HAVIN' A TUG-O-WAR WITH MOTHER NATURE!
ALL OF THE BOATS ARE SAFELY THROUGH, BUT NOW I'VE GOT ROPE BURNS ON MY ROWING BLISTERS.
BY JOVE! I HOPE WE DON'T HAVE TO DO THAT AGAIN.
PULL TO SHORE!
LOOKS LIKE WE GOTTA LINE THE BOATS AGAIN.

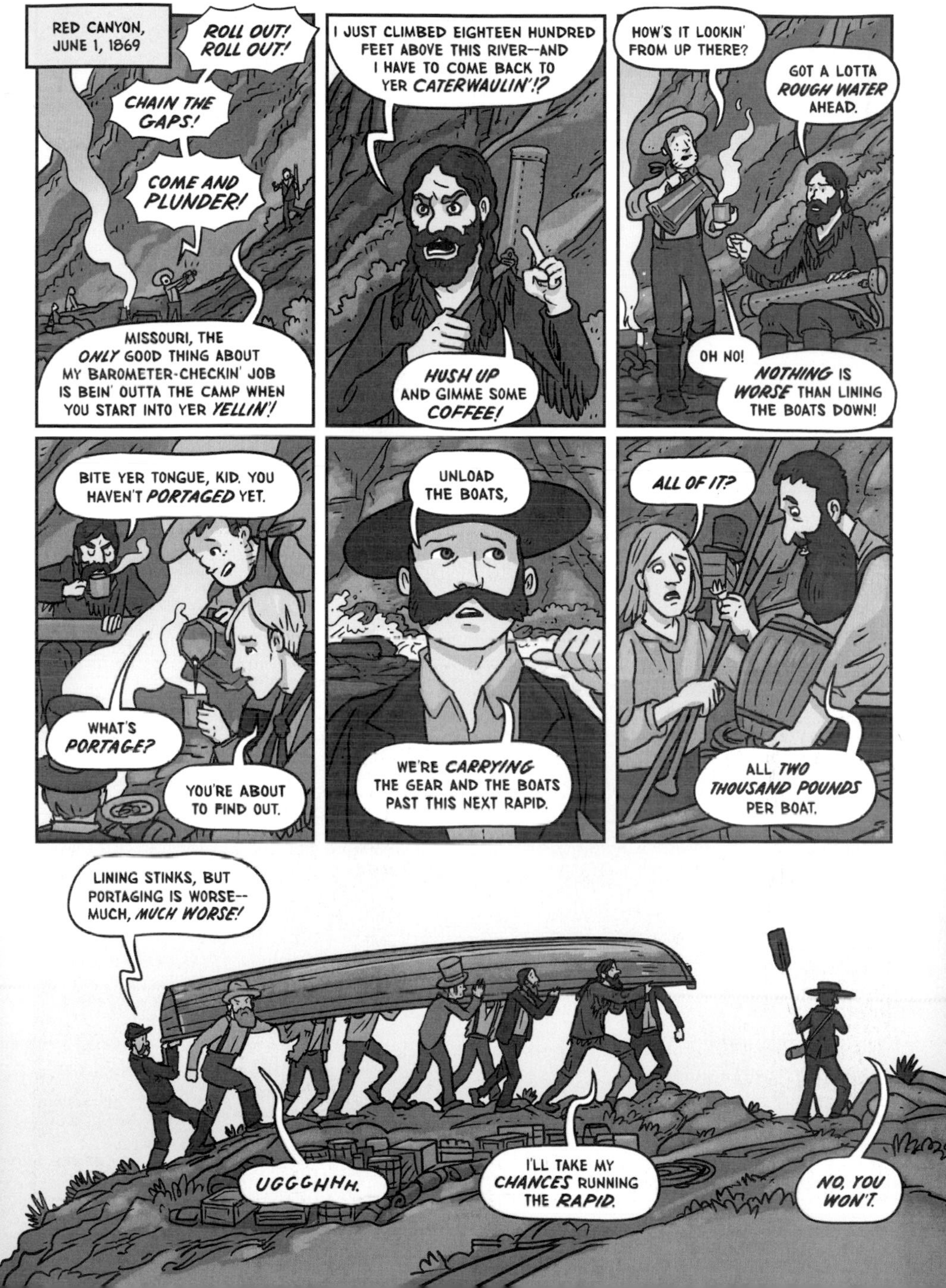
RED CANYON, JUNE 1, 1869
ROLL OUT! ROLL OUT!
CHAIN THE GAPS!
COME AND PLUNDER!
MISSOURI, THE ONLY GOOD THING ABOUT MY BAROMETER-CHECKIN' JOB IS BEIN' OUTTA THE CAMP WHEN YOU START INTO YER YELLIN'!
I JUST CLIMBED EIGHTEEN HUNDRED FEET ABOVE THIS RIVER--AND I HAVE TO COME BACK TO YER CATERWAULIN'!?
HUSH UP AND GIMME SOME COFFEE!
HOW'S IT LOOKIN' FROM UP THERE?
GOT A LOTTA ROUGH WATER AHEAD.
OH NO!
NOTHING IS WORSE THAN LINING THE BOATS DOWN!
BITE YER TONGUE, KID. YOU HAVEN'T PORTAGED YET.
WHAT'S PORTAGE?
YOU'RE ABOUT TO FIND OUT.
UNLOAD THE BOATS,
WE'RE CARRYING THE GEAR AND THE BOATS PAST THIS NEXT RAPID.
ALL OF IT?
ALL TWO THOUSAND POUNDS PER BOAT.
LINING STINKS, BUT PORTAGING IS WORSE-- MUCH, MUCH WORSE!
UGGGHHH.
I'LL TAKE MY CHANCES RUNNING THE RAPID.
NO, YOU WON'T.

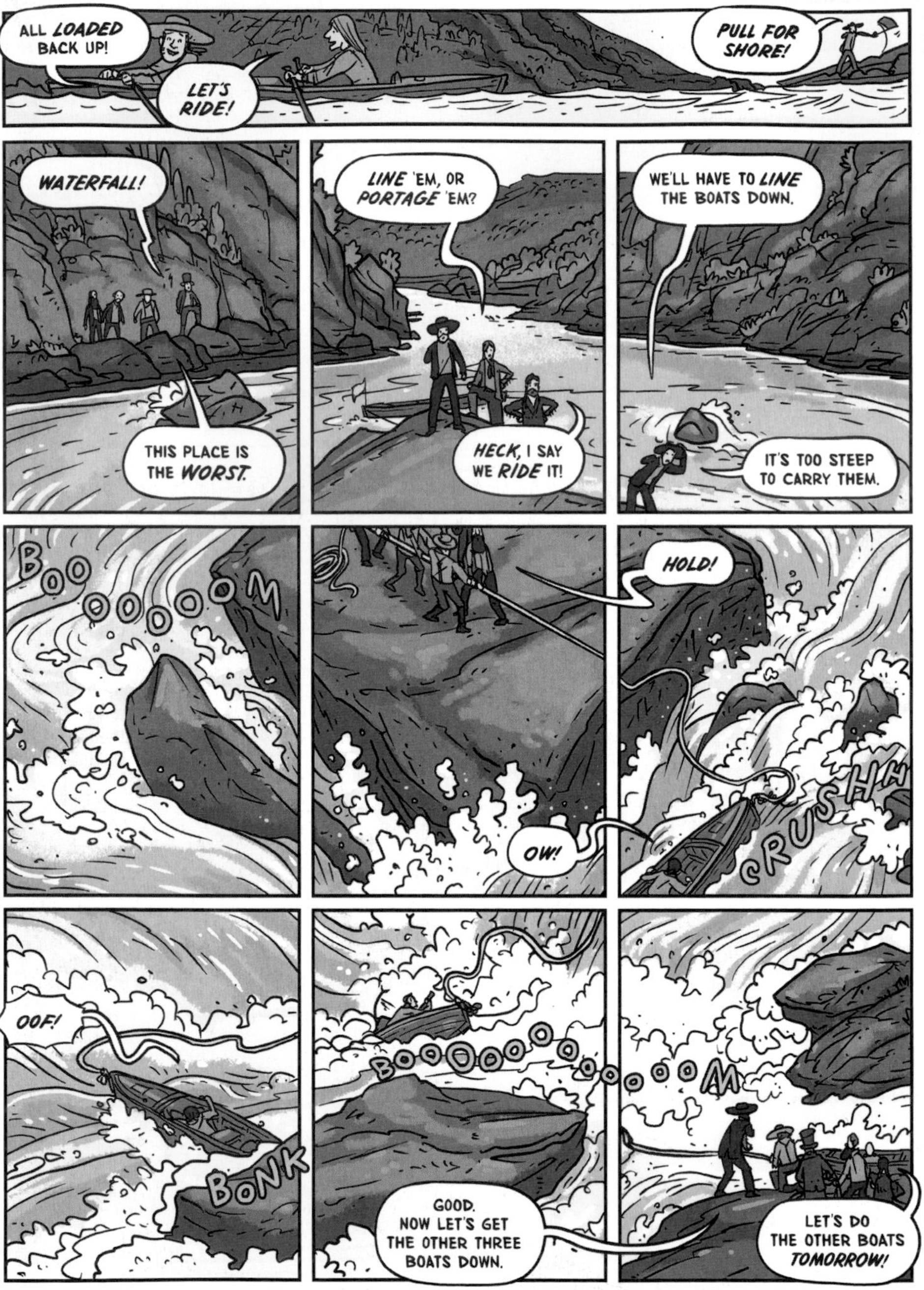
ALL LOADED BACK UP!
LET'S RIDE!
PULL FOR SHORE!
WATERFALL!
THIS PLACE IS THE WORST.
LINE 'EM, OR PORTAGE 'EM?
HECK, I SAY WE RIDE IT!
WE'LL HAVE TO LINE THE BOATS DOWN.
IT'S TOO STEEP TO CARRY THEM.
BOOOOOOOM
HOLD!
OW!
CRUSHH
OOF!
BONK
BOOOOOOOOOOOOM
GOOD. NOW LET'S GET THE OTHER THREE BOATS DOWN.
LET'S DO THE OTHER BOATS TOMORROW!

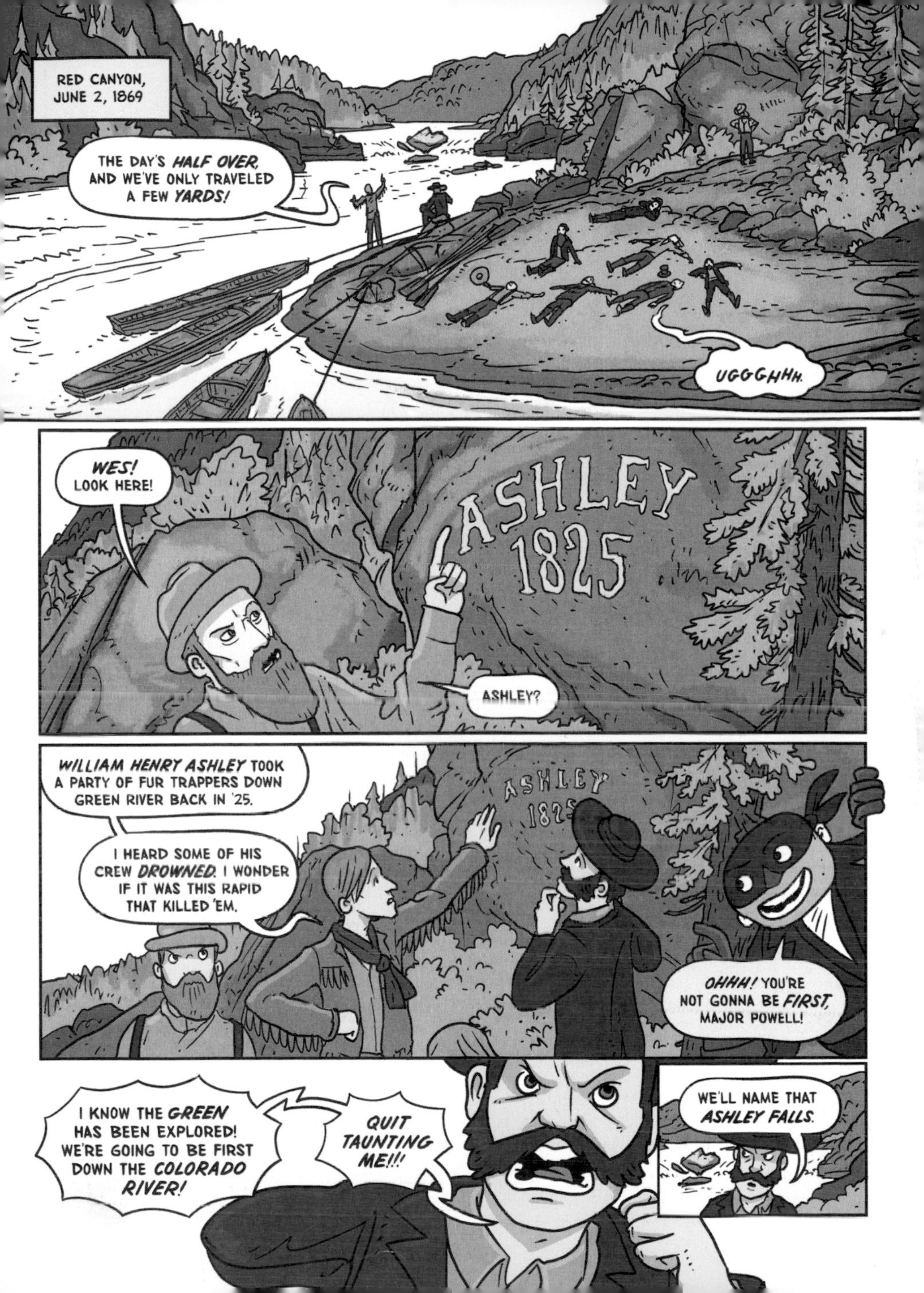
RED CANYON, JUNE 2, 1869
THE DAY'S HALF OVER, AND WE'VE ONLY TRAVELED A FEW YARDS!
UGGGHHH.
WES! LOOK HERE!
ASHLEY 1825
ASHLEY?
WILLIAM HENRY ASHLEY TOOK A PARTY OF FUR TRAPPERS DOWN GREEN RIVER BACK IN '25.
I HEARD SOME OF HIS CREW DROWNED. I WONDER IF IT WAS THIS RAPID THAT KILLED 'EM.
OHHH! YOU'RE NOT GONNA BE FIRST, MAJOR POWELL!
I KNOW THE GREEN HAS BEEN EXPLORED! WE'RE GOING TO BE FIRST DOWN THE COLORADO RIVER!
QUIT TAUNTING ME!!!
WE'LL NAME THAT ASHLEY FALLS.

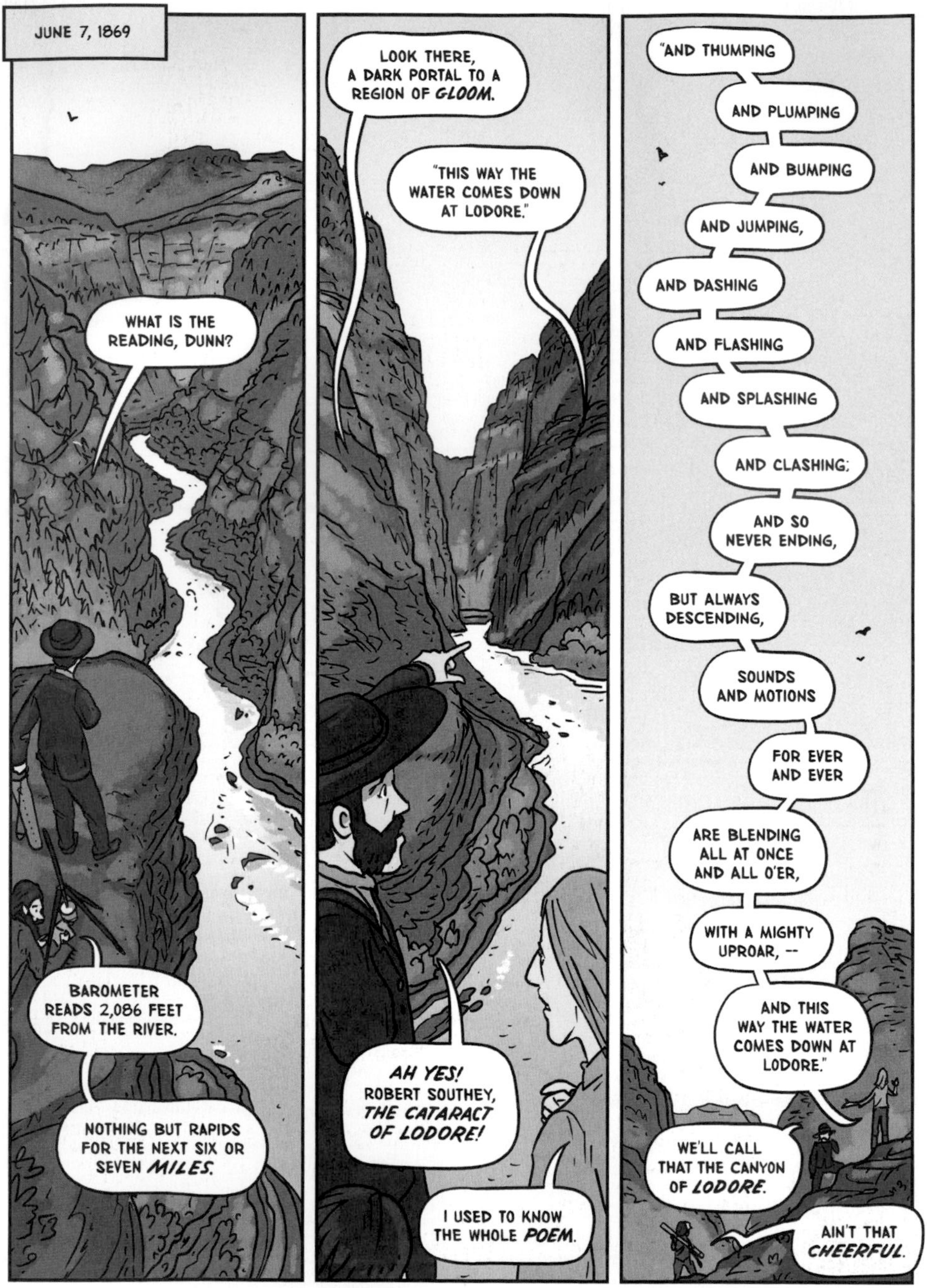
JUNE 7, 1869
WHAT IS THE READING, DUNN?
BAROMETER READS 2,086 FEET FROM THE RIVER.
NOTHING BUT RAPIDS FOR THE NEXT SIX OR SEVEN *MILES.*
LOOK THERE, A DARK PORTAL TO A REGION OF *GLOOM.*
"THIS WAY THE WATER COMES DOWN AT LODORE."
AH YES! ROBERT SOUTHEY, *THE CATARACT OF LODORE!*
I USED TO KNOW THE WHOLE *POEM.*
"AND THUMPING
AND PLUMPING
AND BUMPING
AND JUMPING,
AND DASHING
AND FLASHING
AND SPLASHING
AND CLASHING;
AND SO NEVER ENDING,
BUT ALWAYS DESCENDING,
SOUNDS AND MOTIONS
FOR EVER AND EVER
ARE BLENDING ALL AT ONCE AND ALL O'ER,
WITH A MIGHTY UPROAR, --
AND THIS WAY THE WATER COMES DOWN AT LODORE."
WE'LL CALL THAT THE CANYON OF *LODORE.*
AIN'T THAT *CHEERFUL.*

CHAPTER 10

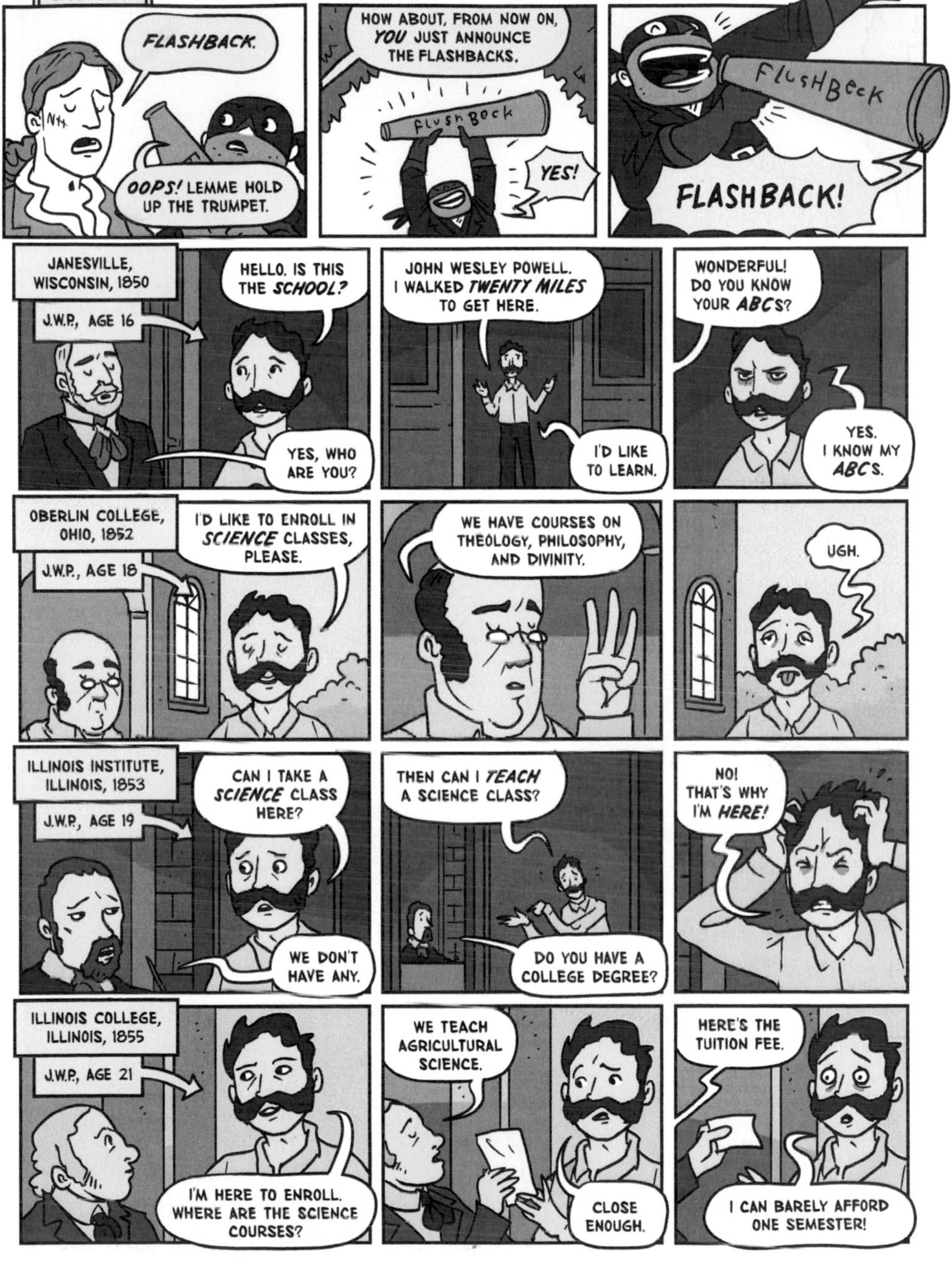

FLASHBACK.
OOPS! LEMME HOLD UP THE TRUMPET.
HOW ABOUT, FROM NOW ON, YOU JUST ANNOUNCE THE FLASHBACKS.
FLUSHBECK
YES!
FLUSHBECK
FLASHBACK!
JANESVILLE, WISCONSIN, 1850
J.W.P., AGE 16
HELLO. IS THIS THE SCHOOL?
YES, WHO ARE YOU?
JOHN WESLEY POWELL. I WALKED TWENTY MILES TO GET HERE.
I'D LIKE TO LEARN.
WONDERFUL! DO YOU KNOW YOUR ABCS?
YES. I KNOW MY ABCS.
OBERLIN COLLEGE, OHIO, 1852
J.W.P., AGE 18
I'D LIKE TO ENROLL IN SCIENCE CLASSES, PLEASE.
WE HAVE COURSES ON THEOLOGY, PHILOSOPHY, AND DIVINITY.
UGH.
ILLINOIS INSTITUTE, ILLINOIS, 1853
J.W.P., AGE 19
CAN I TAKE A SCIENCE CLASS HERE?
WE DON'T HAVE ANY.
THEN CAN I TEACH A SCIENCE CLASS?
DO YOU HAVE A COLLEGE DEGREE?
NO! THAT'S WHY I'M HERE!
ILLINOIS COLLEGE, ILLINOIS, 1855
J.W.P., AGE 21
I'M HERE TO ENROLL. WHERE ARE THE SCIENCE COURSES?
WE TEACH AGRICULTURAL SCIENCE.
CLOSE ENOUGH.
HERE'S THE TUITION FEE.
I CAN BARELY AFFORD ONE SEMESTER!

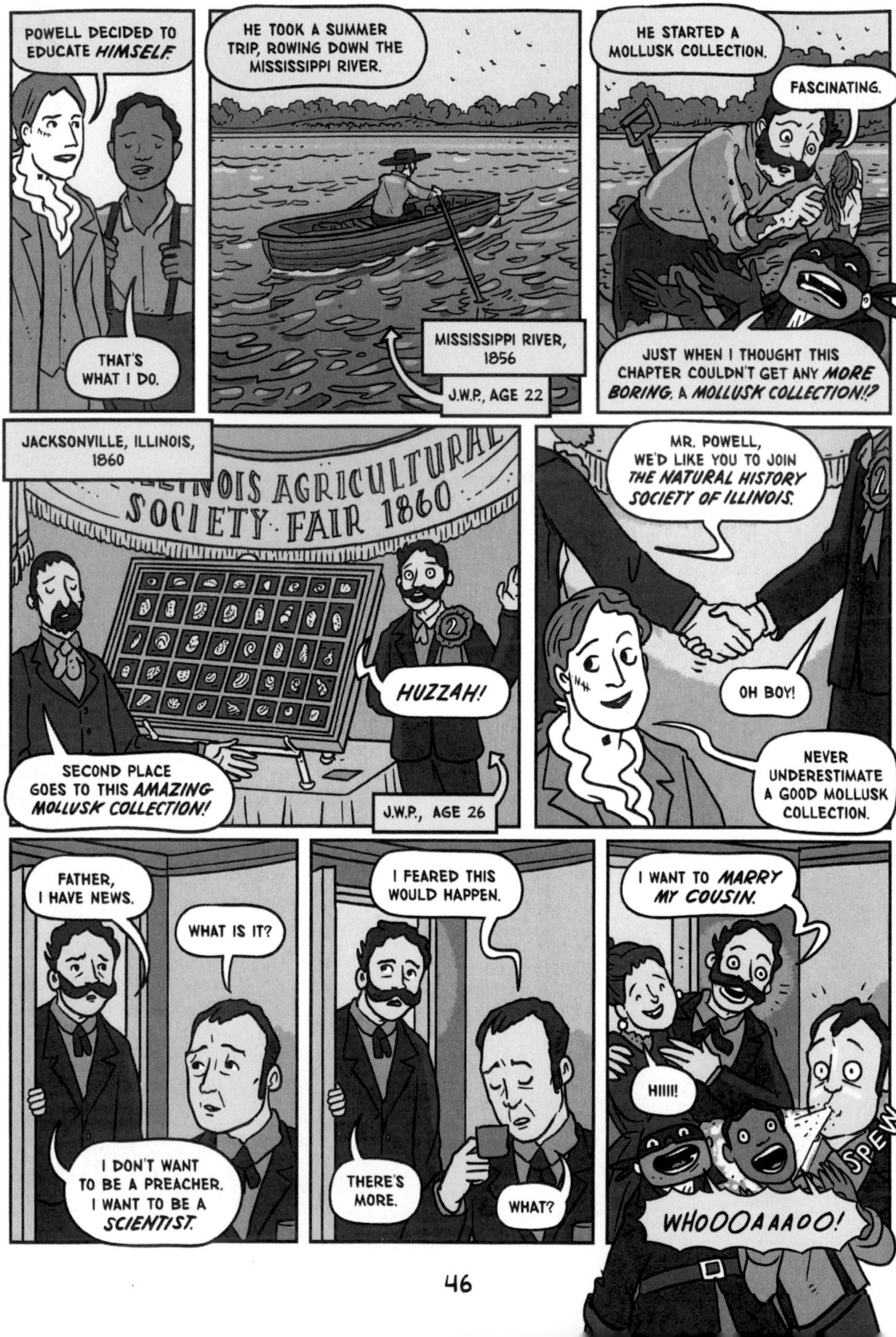
POWELL DECIDED TO EDUCATE HIMSELF.
THAT'S WHAT I DO.
HE TOOK A SUMMER TRIP, ROWING DOWN THE MISSISSIPPI RIVER.
MISSISSIPPI RIVER, 1856
J.W.P., AGE 22
HE STARTED A MOLLUSK COLLECTION.
FASCINATING.
JUST WHEN I THOUGHT THIS CHAPTER COULDN'T GET ANY MORE BORING, A MOLLUSK COLLECTION!?
JACKSONVILLE, ILLINOIS, 1860
ILLINOIS AGRICULTURAL SOCIETY FAIR 1860
SECOND PLACE GOES TO THIS AMAZING MOLLUSK COLLECTION!
HUZZAH!
J.W.P., AGE 26
MR. POWELL, WE'D LIKE YOU TO JOIN THE NATURAL HISTORY SOCIETY OF ILLINOIS.
OH BOY!
NEVER UNDERESTIMATE A GOOD MOLLUSK COLLECTION.
FATHER, I HAVE NEWS.
WHAT IS IT?
I DON'T WANT TO BE A PREACHER. I WANT TO BE A SCIENTIST.
I FEARED THIS WOULD HAPPEN.
THERE'S MORE.
WHAT?
I WANT TO MARRY MY COUSIN.
HIIII!
SPEW
WHOOOAAAOO!

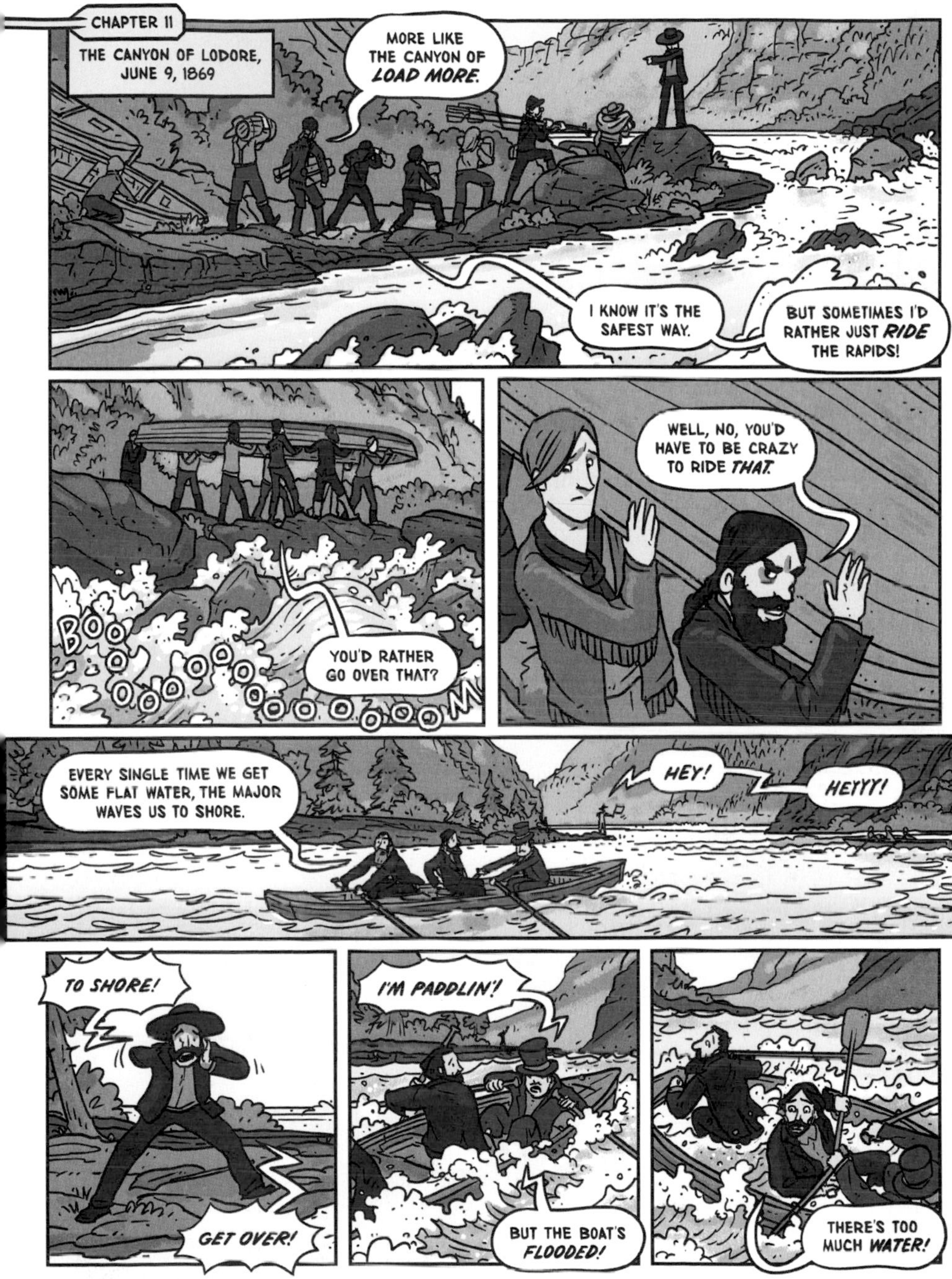
CHAPTER 11
THE CANYON OF LODORE, JUNE 9, 1869
MORE LIKE THE CANYON OF LOAD MORE.
I KNOW IT'S THE SAFEST WAY.
BUT SOMETIMES I'D RATHER JUST RIDE THE RAPIDS!
BOOOOOOOOOOOOOOOOOOOM
YOU'D RATHER GO OVER THAT?
WELL, NO, YOU'D HAVE TO BE CRAZY TO RIDE THAT.
EVERY SINGLE TIME WE GET SOME FLAT WATER, THE MAJOR WAVES US TO SHORE.
HEY!
HEYYY!
TO SHORE!
GET OVER!
I'M PADDLIN'!
BUT THE BOAT'S FLOODED!
THERE'S TOO MUCH WATER!

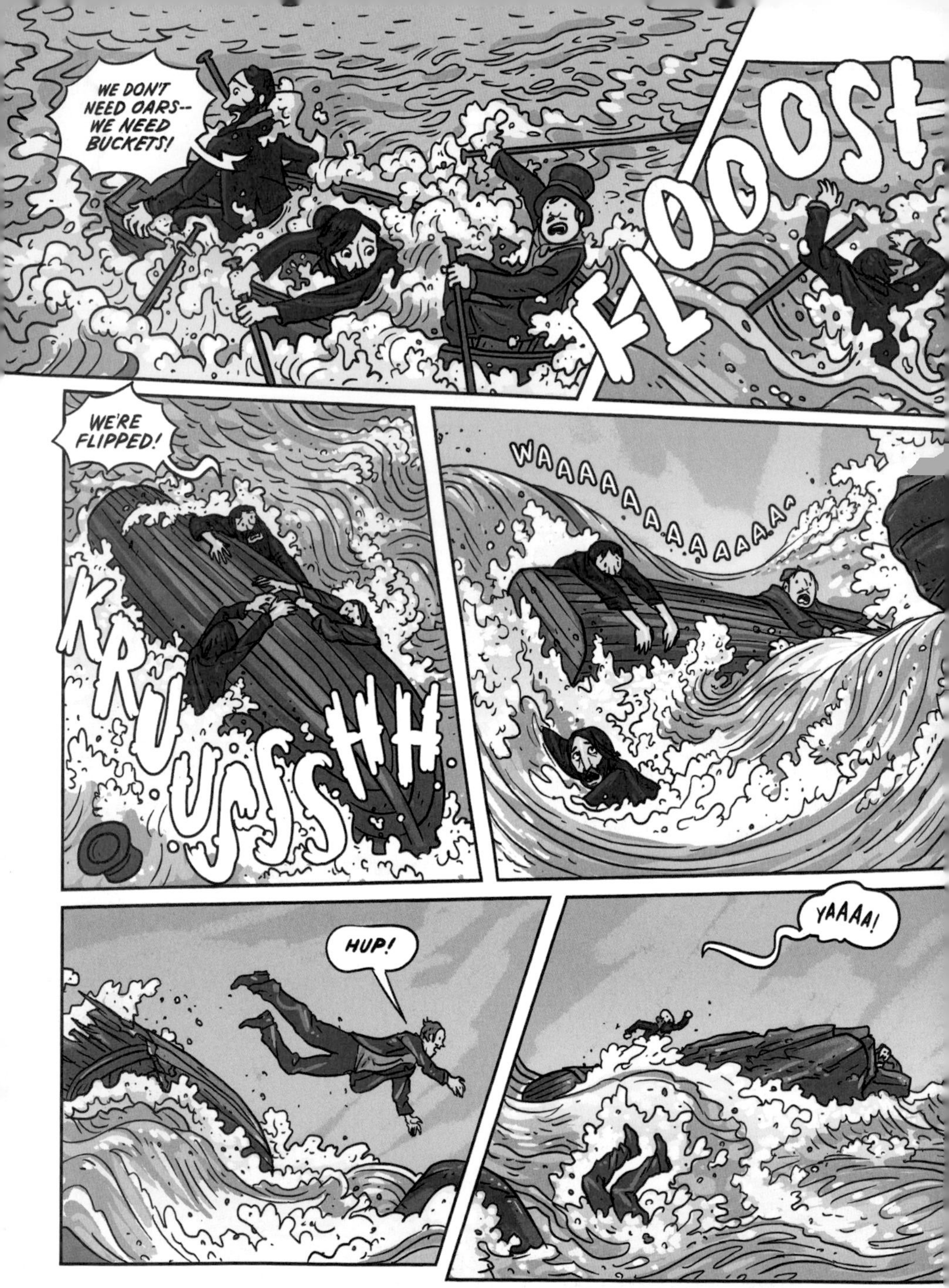
WE DON'T NEED OARS-- WE NEED BUCKETS!
FLOOOSH
WE'RE FLIPPED!
KRUUSSHH
WAAAAAAAAAAAAAAA
HUP!
YAAAA!

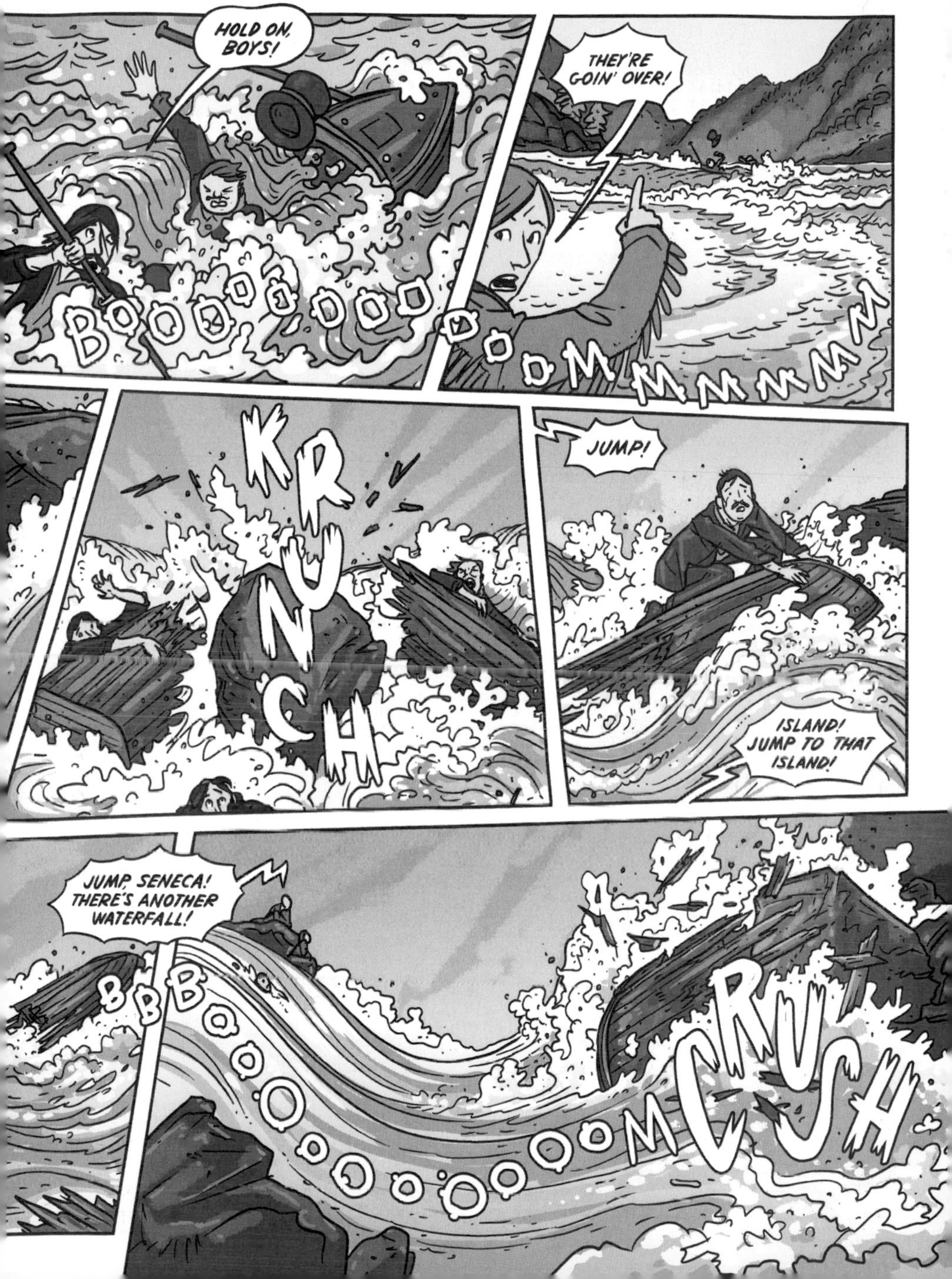
HOLD ON, BOYS!
THEY'RE GOIN' OVER!
BOOOOOOOOOOOOOMMMMMMMMM
KRUNCH
JUMP!
ISLAND! JUMP TO THAT ISLAND!
JUMP, SENECA! THERE'S ANOTHER WATERFALL!
BBBOOOOOOOOOOOOOOM
CRUSH

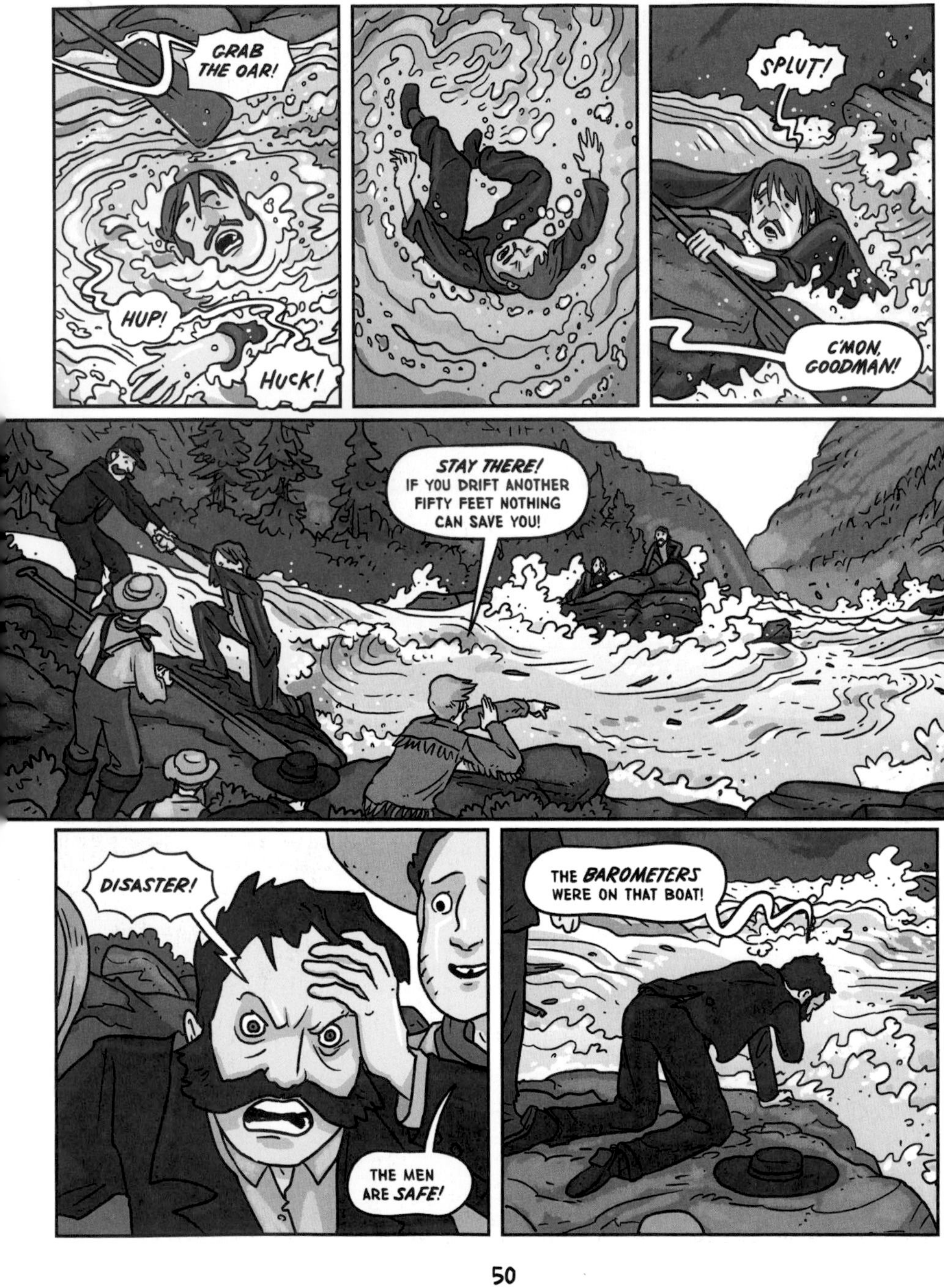
GRAB THE OAR!
HUP!
HUCK!
SPLUT!
C'MON, GOODMAN!
STAY THERE! IF YOU DRIFT ANOTHER FIFTY FEET NOTHING CAN SAVE YOU!
DISASTER!
THE MEN ARE SAFE!
THE BAROMETERS WERE ON THAT BOAT!

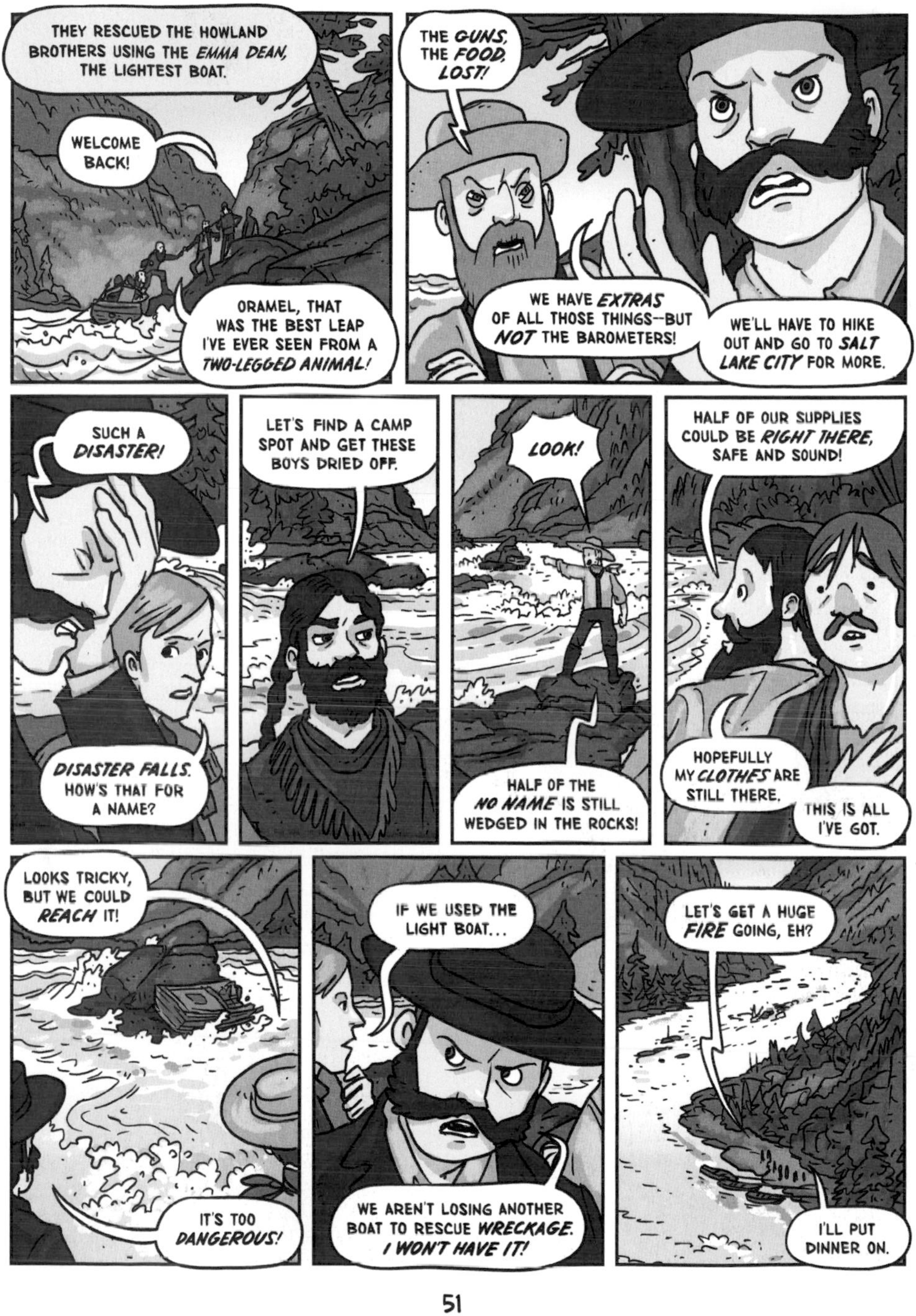
THEY RESCUED THE HOWLAND BROTHERS USING THE EMMA DEAN, THE LIGHTEST BOAT.
WELCOME BACK!
ORAMEL, THAT WAS THE BEST LEAP I'VE EVER SEEN FROM A TWO-LEGGED ANIMAL!
THE GUNS, THE FOOD, LOST!
WE HAVE EXTRAS OF ALL THOSE THINGS--BUT NOT THE BAROMETERS!
WE'LL HAVE TO HIKE OUT AND GO TO SALT LAKE CITY FOR MORE.
SUCH A DISASTER!
DISASTER FALLS. HOW'S THAT FOR A NAME?
LET'S FIND A CAMP SPOT AND GET THESE BOYS DRIED OFF.
LOOK!
HALF OF THE NO NAME IS STILL WEDGED IN THE ROCKS!
HALF OF OUR SUPPLIES COULD BE RIGHT THERE, SAFE AND SOUND!
HOPEFULLY MY CLOTHES ARE STILL THERE.
THIS IS ALL I'VE GOT.
LOOKS TRICKY, BUT WE COULD REACH IT!
IT'S TOO DANGEROUS!
IF WE USED THE LIGHT BOAT...
WE AREN'T LOSING ANOTHER BOAT TO RESCUE WRECKAGE. I WON'T HAVE IT!
LET'S GET A HUGE FIRE GOING, EH?
I'LL PUT DINNER ON.

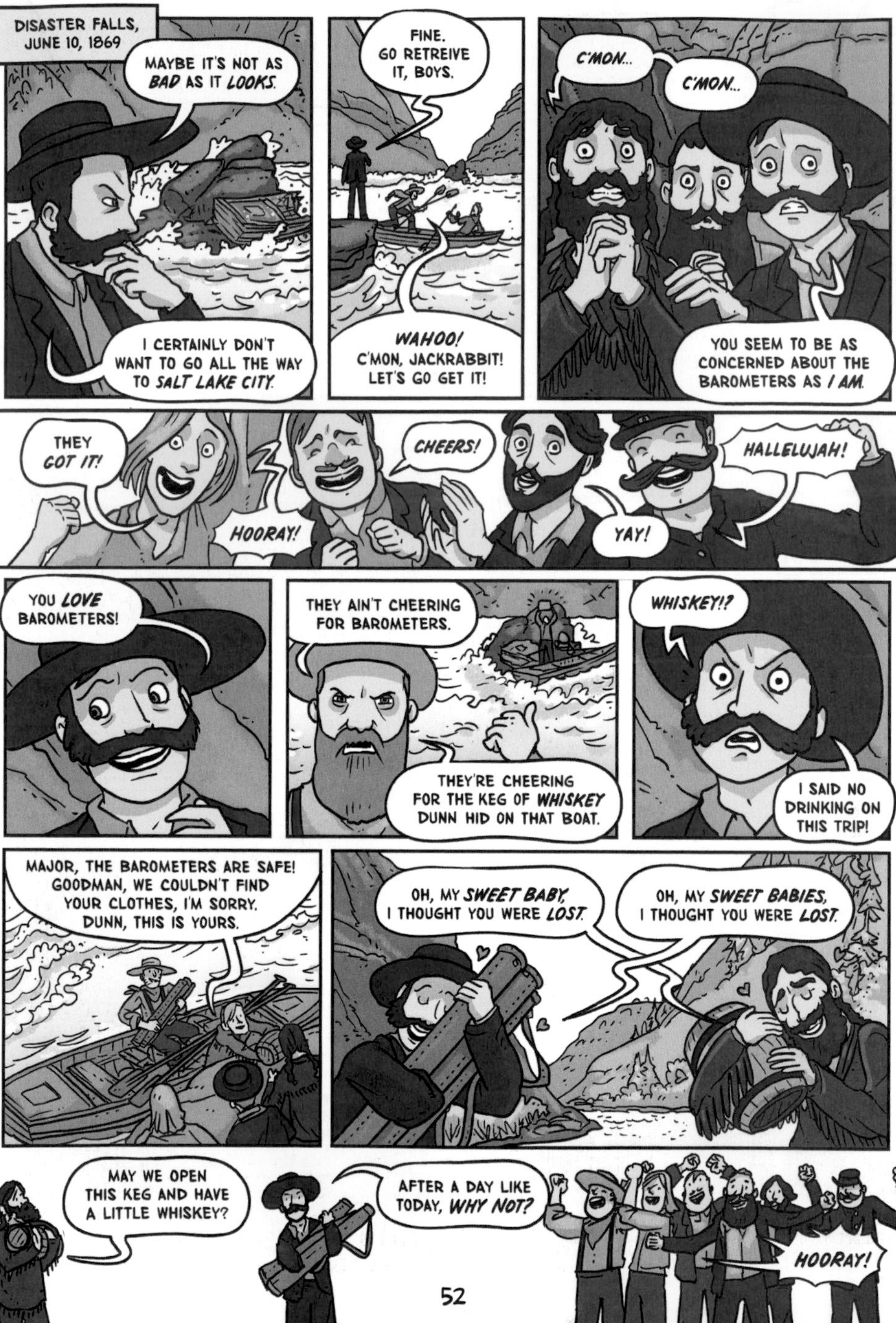
DISASTER FALLS, JUNE 10, 1869
MAYBE IT'S NOT AS BAD AS IT LOOKS.
I CERTAINLY DON'T WANT TO GO ALL THE WAY TO SALT LAKE CITY.
FINE. GO RETREIVE IT, BOYS.
WAHOO! C'MON, JACKRABBIT! LET'S GO GET IT!
C'MON...
C'MON...
YOU SEEM TO BE AS CONCERNED ABOUT THE BAROMETERS AS I AM.
THEY GOT IT!
HOORAY!
CHEERS!
YAY!
HALLELUJAH!
YOU LOVE BAROMETERS!
THEY AIN'T CHEERING FOR BAROMETERS.
THEY'RE CHEERING FOR THE KEG OF WHISKEY DUNN HID ON THAT BOAT.
WHISKEY!?
I SAID NO DRINKING ON THIS TRIP!
MAJOR, THE BAROMETERS ARE SAFE! GOODMAN, WE COULDN'T FIND YOUR CLOTHES, I'M SORRY. DUNN, THIS IS YOURS.
OH, MY SWEET BABY, I THOUGHT YOU WERE LOST.
OH, MY SWEET BABIES, I THOUGHT YOU WERE LOST.
MAY WE OPEN THIS KEG AND HAVE A LITTLE WHISKEY?
AFTER A DAY LIKE TODAY, WHY NOT?
HOORAY!

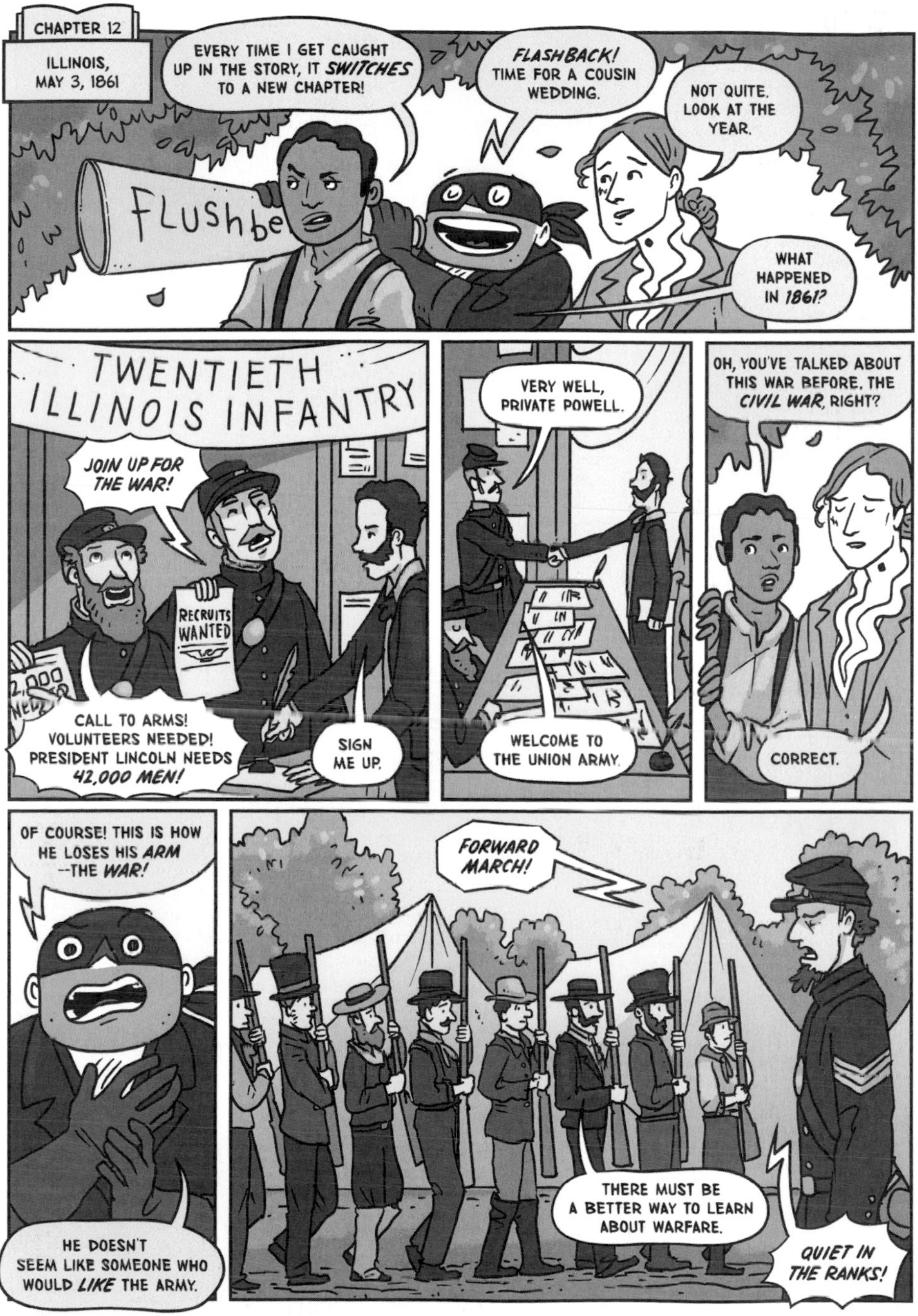
CHAPTER 12
ILLINOIS, MAY 3, 1861
EVERY TIME I GET CAUGHT UP IN THE STORY, IT *SWITCHES* TO A NEW CHAPTER!
FLUSHbe
FLASHBACK! TIME FOR A COUSIN WEDDING.
NOT QUITE. LOOK AT THE YEAR.
WHAT HAPPENED IN *1861?*
TWENTIETH ILLINOIS INFANTRY
JOIN UP FOR THE WAR!
RECRUITS WANTED
CALL TO ARMS! VOLUNTEERS NEEDED! PRESIDENT LINCOLN NEEDS *42,000 MEN!*
SIGN ME UP.
VERY WELL, PRIVATE POWELL.
WELCOME TO THE UNION ARMY.
OH, YOU'VE TALKED ABOUT THIS WAR BEFORE. THE *CIVIL WAR*, RIGHT?
CORRECT.
OF COURSE! THIS IS HOW HE LOSES HIS *ARM* --THE *WAR!*
HE DOESN'T SEEM LIKE SOMEONE WHO WOULD *LIKE* THE ARMY.
FORWARD MARCH!
THERE MUST BE A BETTER WAY TO LEARN ABOUT WARFARE.
QUIET IN THE RANKS!

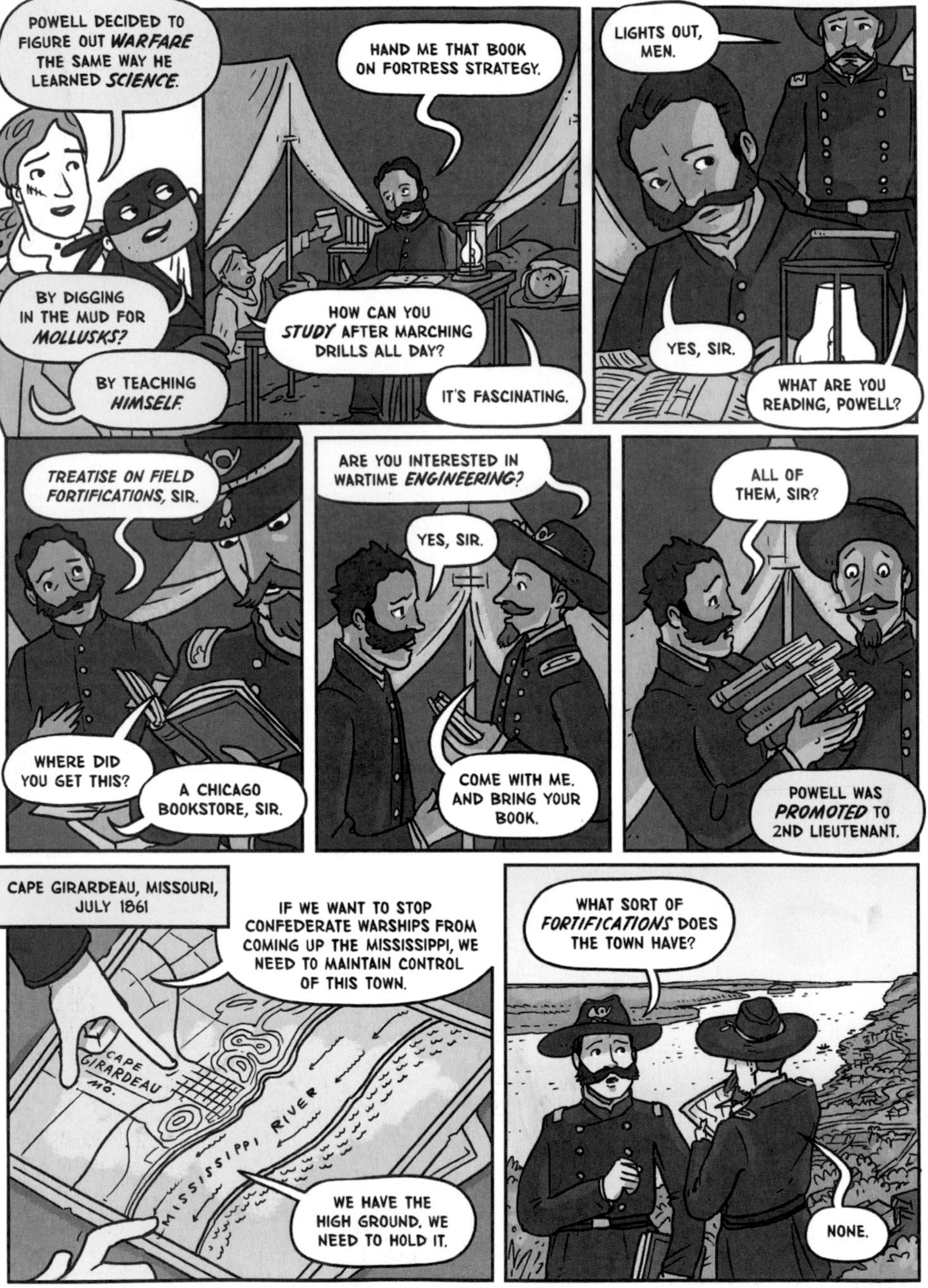
POWELL DECIDED TO FIGURE OUT WARFARE THE SAME WAY HE LEARNED SCIENCE.
BY DIGGING IN THE MUD FOR MOLLUSKS?
BY TEACHING HIMSELF.
HAND ME THAT BOOK ON FORTRESS STRATEGY.
HOW CAN YOU STUDY AFTER MARCHING DRILLS ALL DAY?
IT'S FASCINATING.
LIGHTS OUT, MEN.
YES, SIR.
WHAT ARE YOU READING, POWELL?
TREATISE ON FIELD FORTIFICATIONS, SIR.
WHERE DID YOU GET THIS?
A CHICAGO BOOKSTORE, SIR.
ARE YOU INTERESTED IN WARTIME ENGINEERING?
YES, SIR.
COME WITH ME. AND BRING YOUR BOOK.
ALL OF THEM, SIR?
POWELL WAS PROMOTED TO 2ND LIEUTENANT.
CAPE GIRARDEAU, MISSOURI, JULY 1861
IF WE WANT TO STOP CONFEDERATE WARSHIPS FROM COMING UP THE MISSISSIPPI, WE NEED TO MAINTAIN CONTROL OF THIS TOWN.
CAPE GIRARDEAU MO.
MISSISSIPPI RIVER
MISSISSIPPI
WE HAVE THE HIGH GROUND. WE NEED TO HOLD IT.
WHAT SORT OF FORTIFICATIONS DOES THE TOWN HAVE?
NONE.

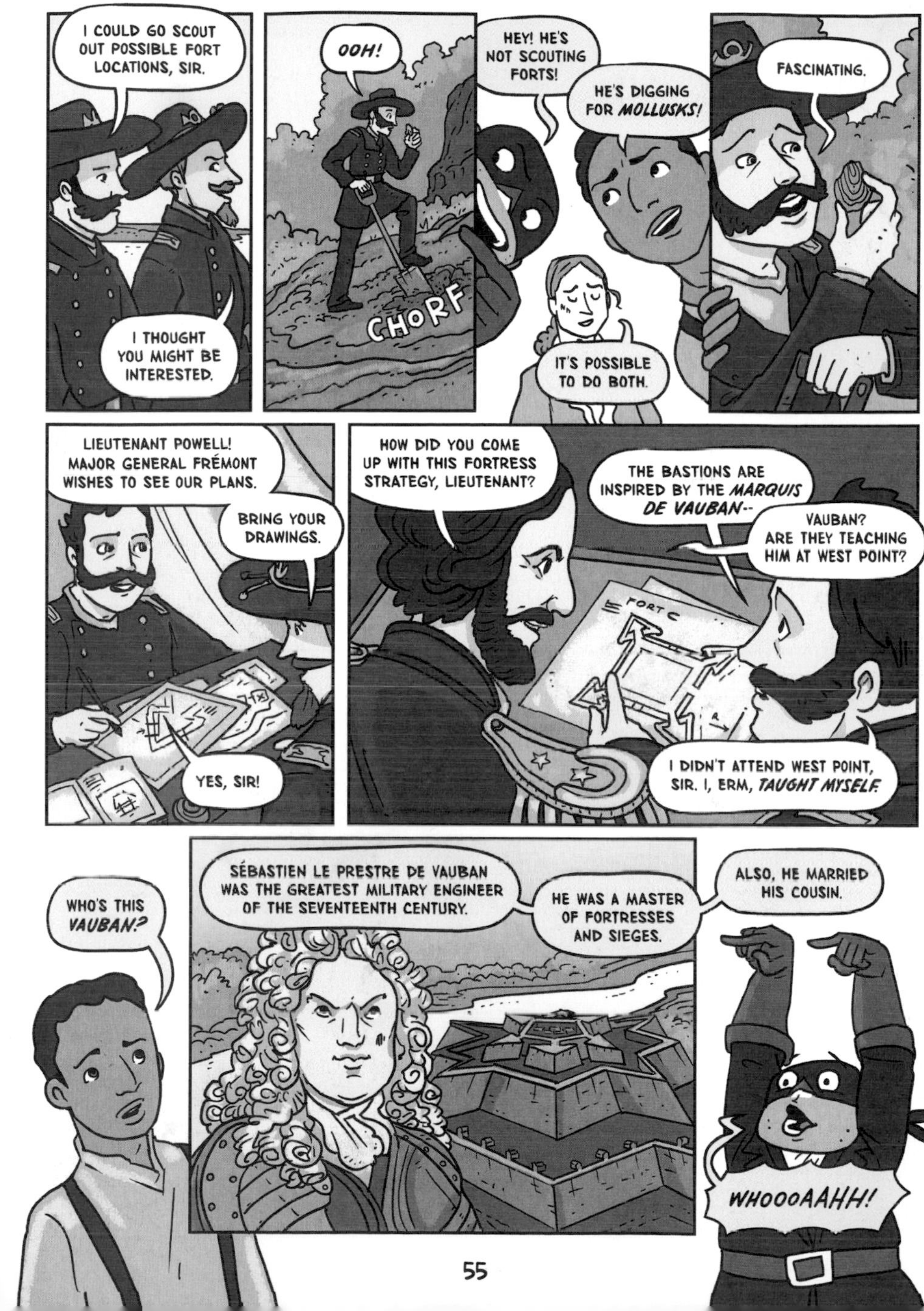
I COULD GO SCOUT OUT POSSIBLE FORT LOCATIONS, SIR.
I THOUGHT YOU MIGHT BE INTERESTED.
OOH!
CHORF
HEY! HE'S NOT SCOUTING FORTS!
HE'S DIGGING FOR MOLLUSKS!
IT'S POSSIBLE TO DO BOTH.
FASCINATING.
LIEUTENANT POWELL! MAJOR GENERAL FRÉMONT WISHES TO SEE OUR PLANS.
BRING YOUR DRAWINGS.
YES, SIR!
HOW DID YOU COME UP WITH THIS FORTRESS STRATEGY, LIEUTENANT?
THE BASTIONS ARE INSPIRED BY THE MARQUIS DE VAUBAN--
VAUBAN? ARE THEY TEACHING HIM AT WEST POINT?
FORT C
I DIDN'T ATTEND WEST POINT, SIR. I, ERM, TAUGHT MYSELF.
WHO'S THIS VAUBAN?
SÉBASTIEN LE PRESTRE DE VAUBAN WAS THE GREATEST MILITARY ENGINEER OF THE SEVENTEENTH CENTURY.
HE WAS A MASTER OF FORTRESSES AND SIEGES.
ALSO, HE MARRIED HIS COUSIN.
WHOOOAAHH!

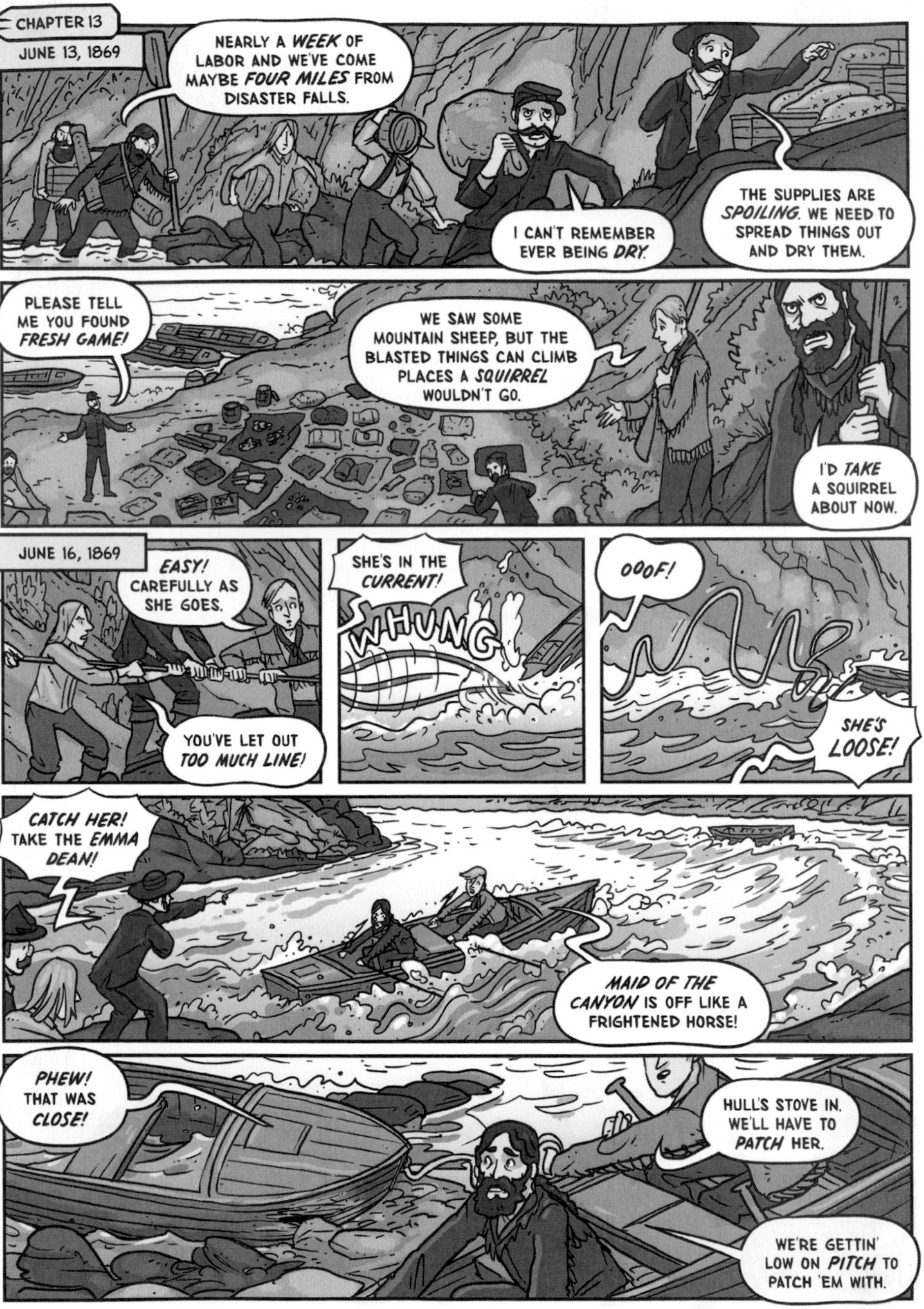
CHAPTER 13
JUNE 13, 1869
NEARLY A WEEK OF LABOR AND WE'VE COME MAYBE FOUR MILES FROM DISASTER FALLS.
I CAN'T REMEMBER EVER BEING DRY.
THE SUPPLIES ARE SPOILING. WE NEED TO SPREAD THINGS OUT AND DRY THEM.
PLEASE TELL ME YOU FOUND FRESH GAME!
WE SAW SOME MOUNTAIN SHEEP, BUT THE BLASTED THINGS CAN CLIMB PLACES A SQUIRREL WOULDN'T GO.
I'D TAKE A SQUIRREL ABOUT NOW.
JUNE 16, 1869
EASY! CAREFULLY AS SHE GOES.
YOU'VE LET OUT TOO MUCH LINE!
SHE'S IN THE CURRENT!
WHUNG
OOOF!
SHE'S LOOSE!
CATCH HER! TAKE THE EMMA DEAN!
MAID OF THE CANYON IS OFF LIKE A FRIGHTENED HORSE!
PHEW! THAT WAS CLOSE!
HULL'S STOVE IN. WE'LL HAVE TO PATCH HER.
WE'RE GETTIN' LOW ON PITCH TO PATCH 'EM WITH.

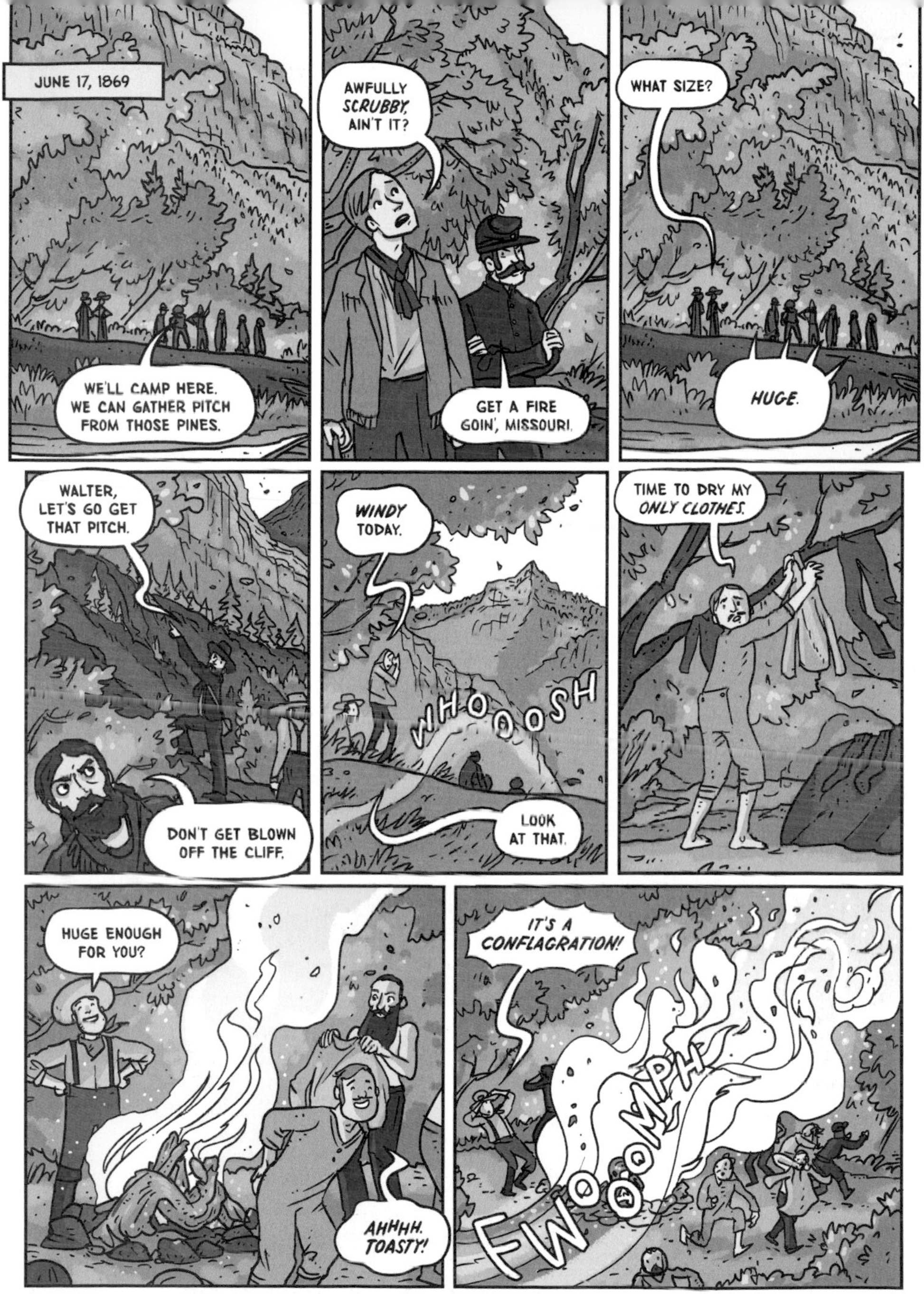
JUNE 17, 1869
WE'LL CAMP HERE. WE CAN GATHER PITCH FROM THOSE PINES.
AWFULLY SCRUBBY, AIN'T IT?
GET A FIRE GOIN', MISSOURI.
WHAT SIZE?
HUGE.
WALTER, LET'S GO GET THAT PITCH.
DON'T GET BLOWN OFF THE CLIFF.
WINDY TODAY.
WHOOOSH
LOOK AT THAT.
TIME TO DRY MY ONLY CLOTHES.
HUGE ENOUGH FOR YOU?
AHHHH. TOASTY!
IT'S A CONFLAGRATION!
FWOOOMPH

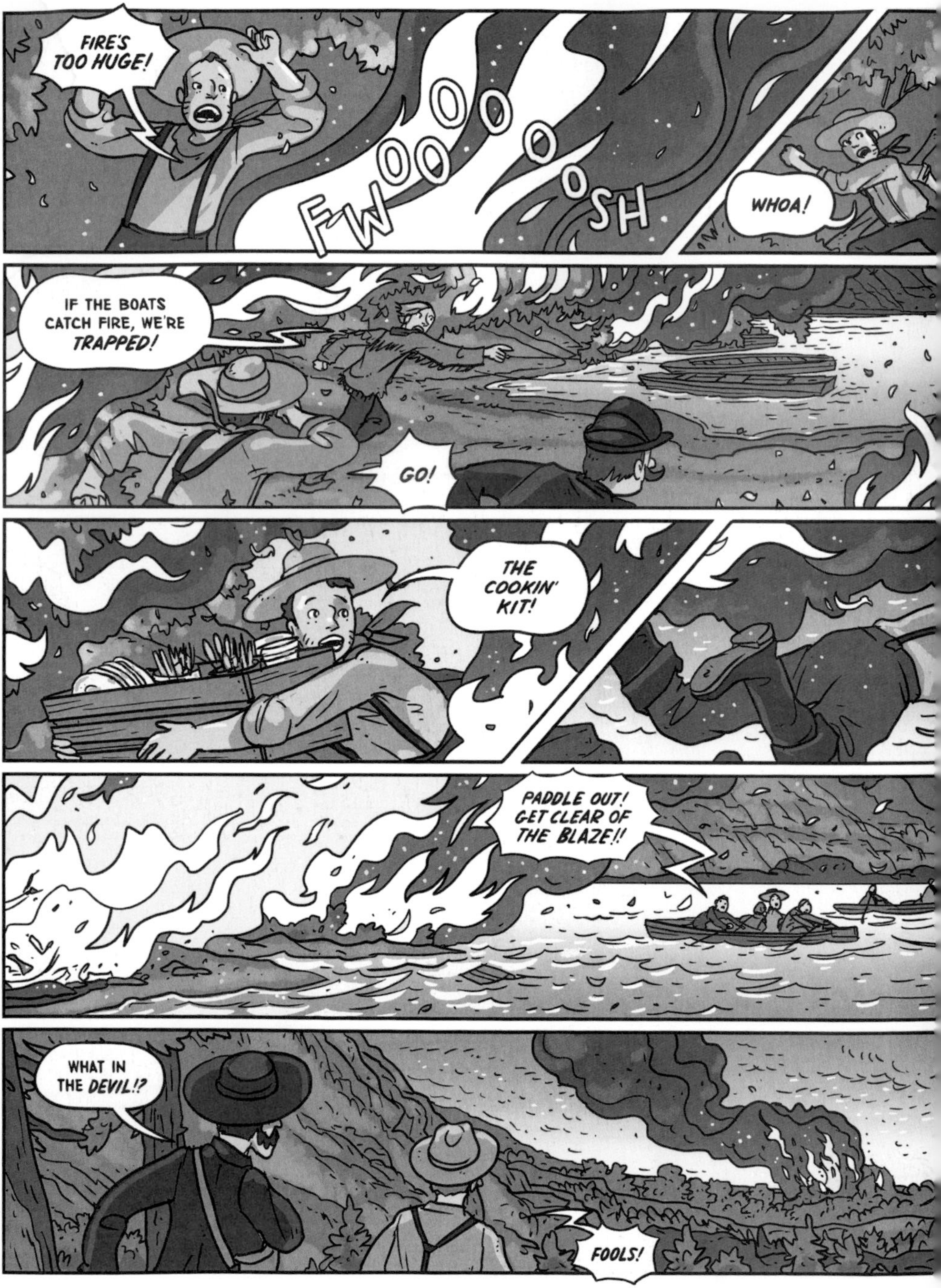
FIRE'S TOO HUGE!
FWOOOOOOOSH
WHOA!
IF THE BOATS CATCH FIRE, WE'RE TRAPPED!
GO!
THE COOKIN' KIT!
PADDLE OUT! GET CLEAR OF THE BLAZE!!
WHAT IN THE DEVIL!?
FOOLS!

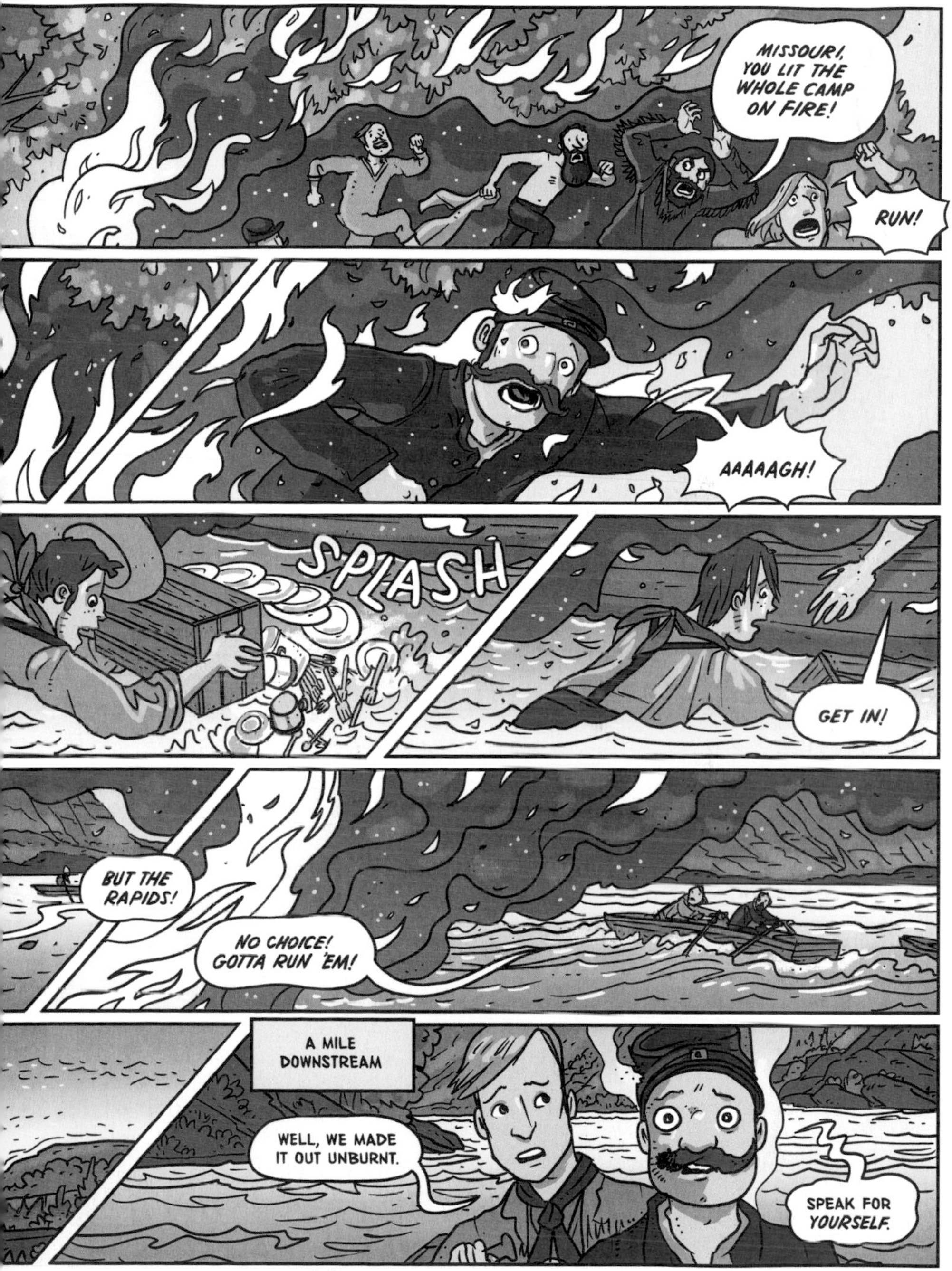
MISSOURI, YOU LIT THE WHOLE CAMP ON FIRE!
RUN!
AAAAAGH!
SPLASH
GET IN!
BUT THE RAPIDS!
NO CHOICE! GOTTA RUN 'EM!
A MILE DOWNSTREAM
WELL, WE MADE IT OUT UNBURNT.
SPEAK FOR YOURSELF.

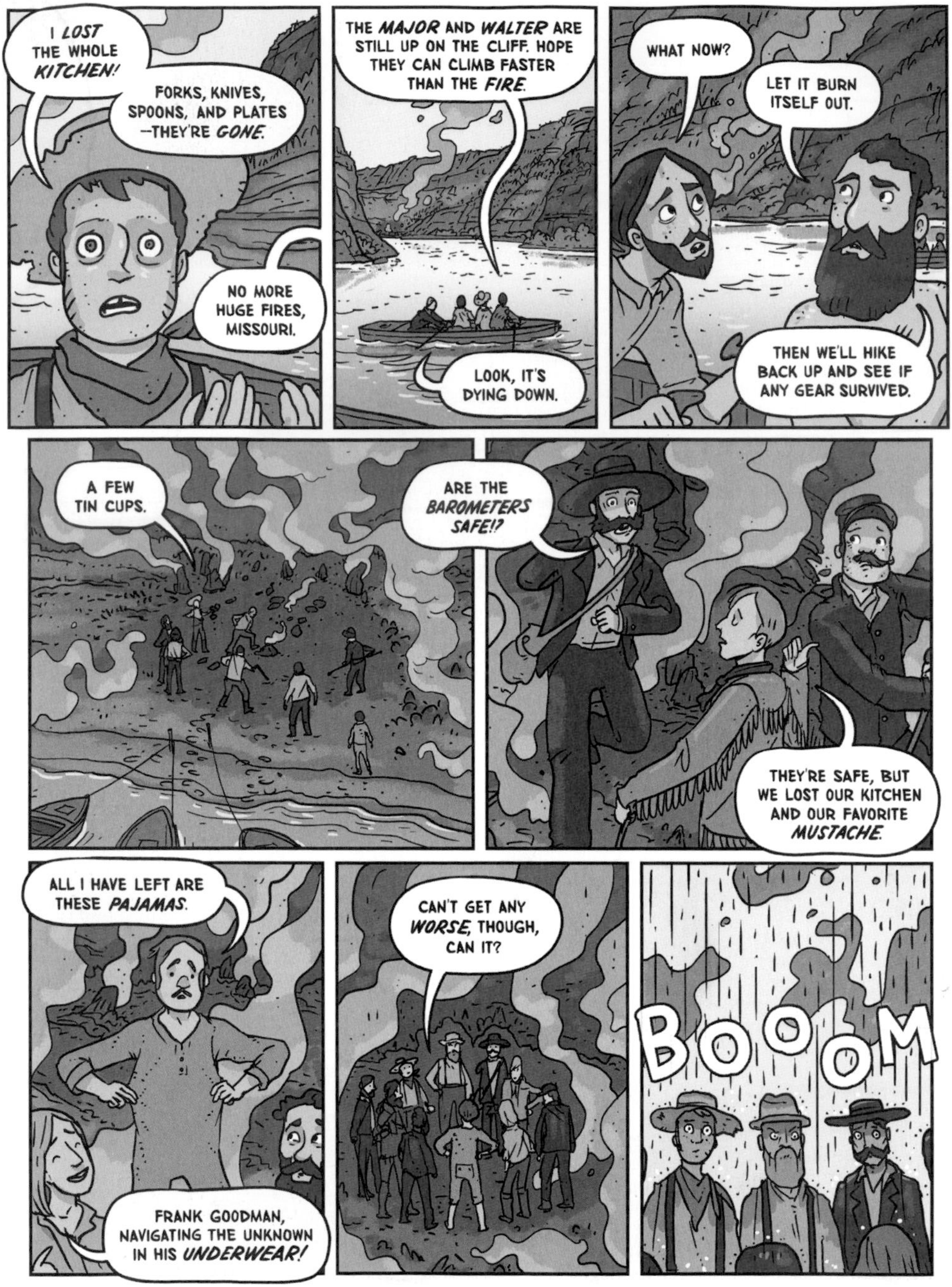
I LOST THE WHOLE KITCHEN!
FORKS, KNIVES, SPOONS, AND PLATES —THEY'RE GONE.
NO MORE HUGE FIRES, MISSOURI.
THE MAJOR AND WALTER ARE STILL UP ON THE CLIFF. HOPE THEY CAN CLIMB FASTER THAN THE FIRE.
LOOK, IT'S DYING DOWN.
WHAT NOW?
LET IT BURN ITSELF OUT.
THEN WE'LL HIKE BACK UP AND SEE IF ANY GEAR SURVIVED.
A FEW TIN CUPS.
ARE THE BAROMETERS SAFE!?
THEY'RE SAFE, BUT WE LOST OUR KITCHEN AND OUR FAVORITE MUSTACHE.
ALL I HAVE LEFT ARE THESE PAJAMAS.
FRANK GOODMAN, NAVIGATING THE UNKNOWN IN HIS UNDERWEAR!
CAN'T GET ANY WORSE, THOUGH, CAN IT?
BOOOM

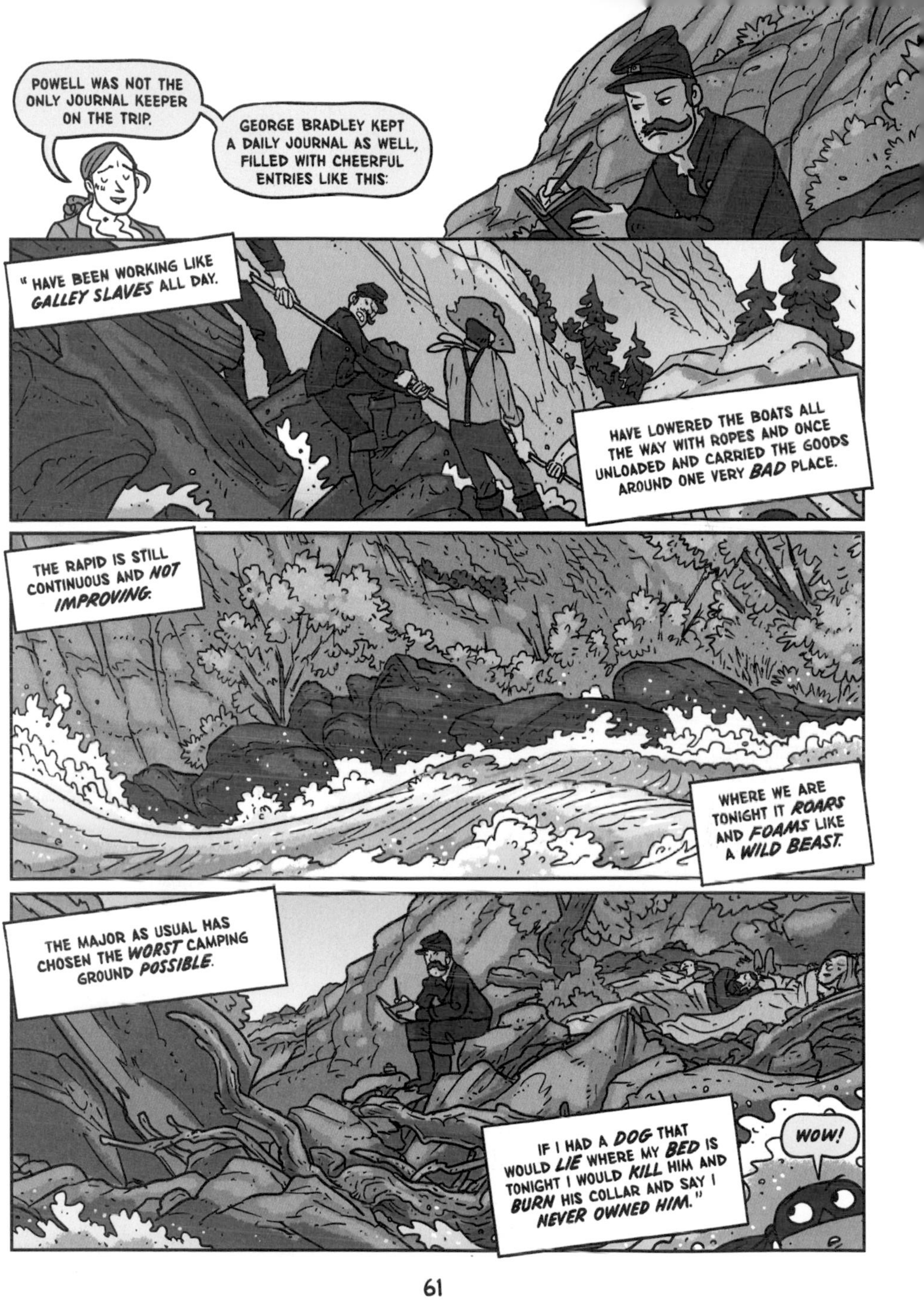
POWELL WAS NOT THE ONLY JOURNAL KEEPER ON THE TRIP.
GEORGE BRADLEY KEPT A DAILY JOURNAL AS WELL, FILLED WITH CHEERFUL ENTRIES LIKE THIS:
"HAVE BEEN WORKING LIKE GALLEY SLAVES ALL DAY.
HAVE LOWERED THE BOATS ALL THE WAY WITH ROPES AND ONCE UNLOADED AND CARRIED THE GOODS AROUND ONE VERY BAD PLACE.
THE RAPID IS STILL CONTINUOUS AND NOT IMPROVING.
WHERE WE ARE TONIGHT IT ROARS AND FOAMS LIKE A WILD BEAST.
THE MAJOR AS USUAL HAS CHOSEN THE WORST CAMPING GROUND POSSIBLE.
IF I HAD A DOG THAT WOULD LIE WHERE MY BED IS TONIGHT I WOULD KILL HIM AND BURN HIS COLLAR AND SAY I NEVER OWNED HIM."
WOW!

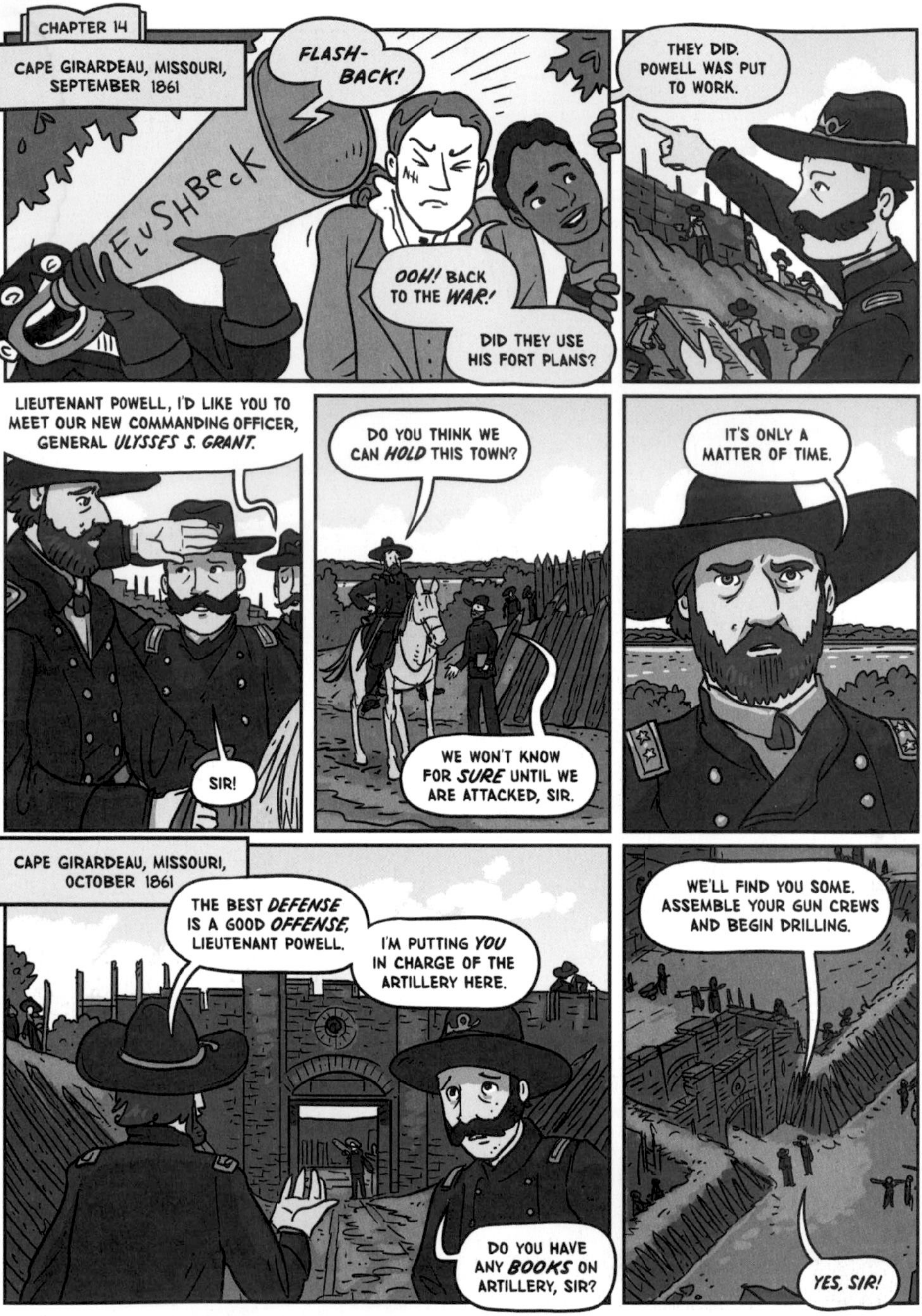
CHAPTER 14
CAPE GIRARDEAU, MISSOURI, SEPTEMBER 1861
FLASH-BACK!
FLUSHBECK
OOH! BACK TO THE WAR!
DID THEY USE HIS FORT PLANS?
THEY DID. POWELL WAS PUT TO WORK.
LIEUTENANT POWELL, I'D LIKE YOU TO MEET OUR NEW COMMANDING OFFICER, GENERAL ULYSSES S. GRANT.
SIR!
DO YOU THINK WE CAN HOLD THIS TOWN?
WE WON'T KNOW FOR SURE UNTIL WE ARE ATTACKED, SIR.
IT'S ONLY A MATTER OF TIME.
CAPE GIRARDEAU, MISSOURI, OCTOBER 1861
THE BEST DEFENSE IS A GOOD OFFENSE, LIEUTENANT POWELL.
I'M PUTTING YOU IN CHARGE OF THE ARTILLERY HERE.
DO YOU HAVE ANY BOOKS ON ARTILLERY, SIR?
WE'LL FIND YOU SOME. ASSEMBLE YOUR GUN CREWS AND BEGIN DRILLING.
YES, SIR!

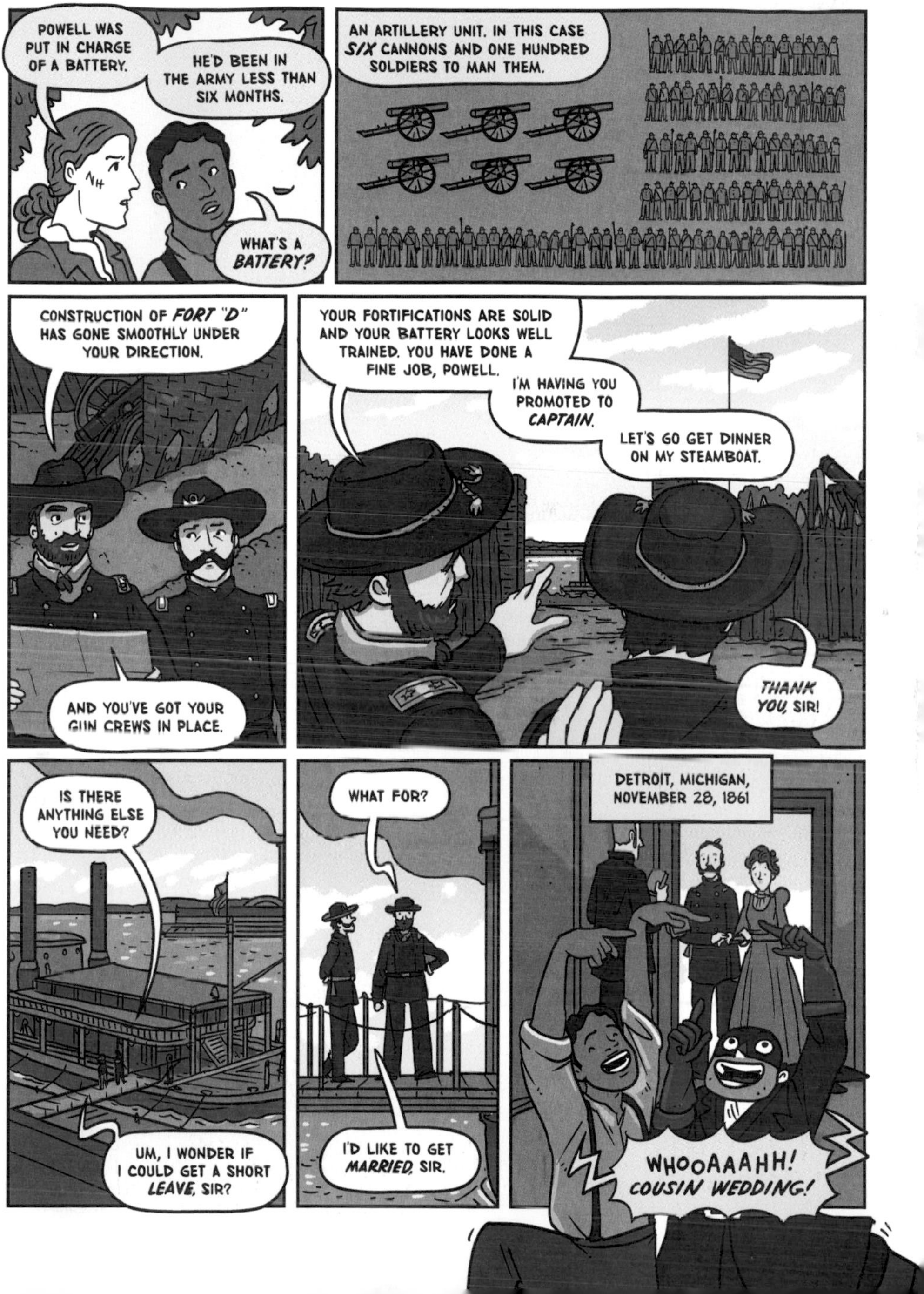
POWELL WAS PUT IN CHARGE OF A BATTERY.
HE'D BEEN IN THE ARMY LESS THAN SIX MONTHS.
WHAT'S A BATTERY?
AN ARTILLERY UNIT. IN THIS CASE SIX CANNONS AND ONE HUNDRED SOLDIERS TO MAN THEM.
CONSTRUCTION OF FORT "D" HAS GONE SMOOTHLY UNDER YOUR DIRECTION.
AND YOU'VE GOT YOUR GUN CREWS IN PLACE.
YOUR FORTIFICATIONS ARE SOLID AND YOUR BATTERY LOOKS WELL TRAINED. YOU HAVE DONE A FINE JOB, POWELL.
I'M HAVING YOU PROMOTED TO CAPTAIN.
LET'S GO GET DINNER ON MY STEAMBOAT.
THANK YOU, SIR!
IS THERE ANYTHING ELSE YOU NEED?
UM, I WONDER IF I COULD GET A SHORT LEAVE, SIR?
WHAT FOR?
I'D LIKE TO GET MARRIED, SIR.
DETROIT, MICHIGAN, NOVEMBER 28, 1861
WHOOAAAHH! COUSIN WEDDING!

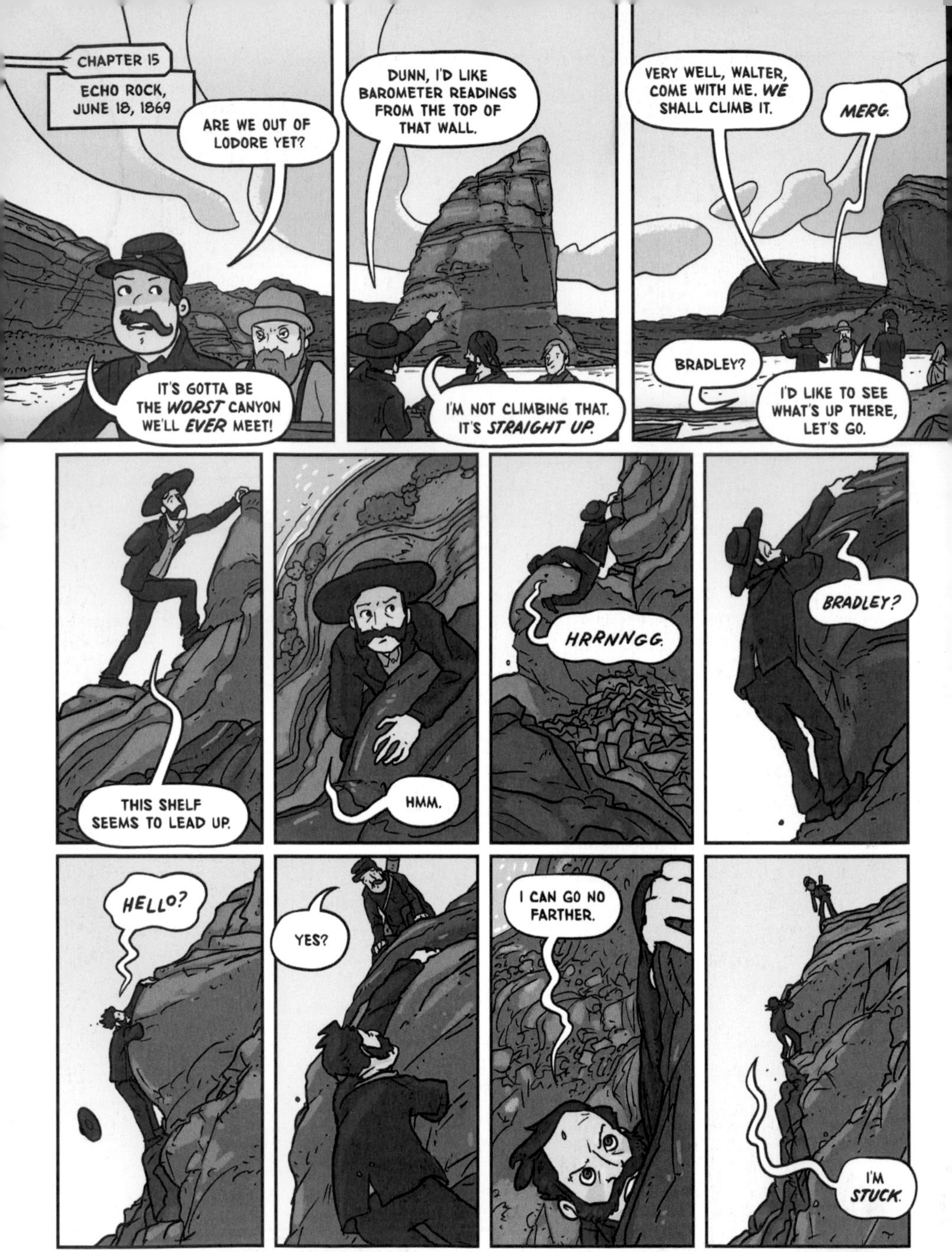

CHAPTER 15
ECHO ROCK, JUNE 18, 1869
ARE WE OUT OF LODORE YET?
IT'S GOTTA BE THE WORST CANYON WE'LL EVER MEET!
DUNN, I'D LIKE BAROMETER READINGS FROM THE TOP OF THAT WALL.
I'M NOT CLIMBING THAT. IT'S STRAIGHT UP.
VERY WELL, WALTER, COME WITH ME. WE SHALL CLIMB IT.
MERG.
BRADLEY?
I'D LIKE TO SEE WHAT'S UP THERE, LET'S GO.
THIS SHELF SEEMS TO LEAD UP.
HMM.
HRRNNGG.
BRADLEY?
HELLO?
YES?
I CAN GO NO FARTHER.
I'M STUCK.

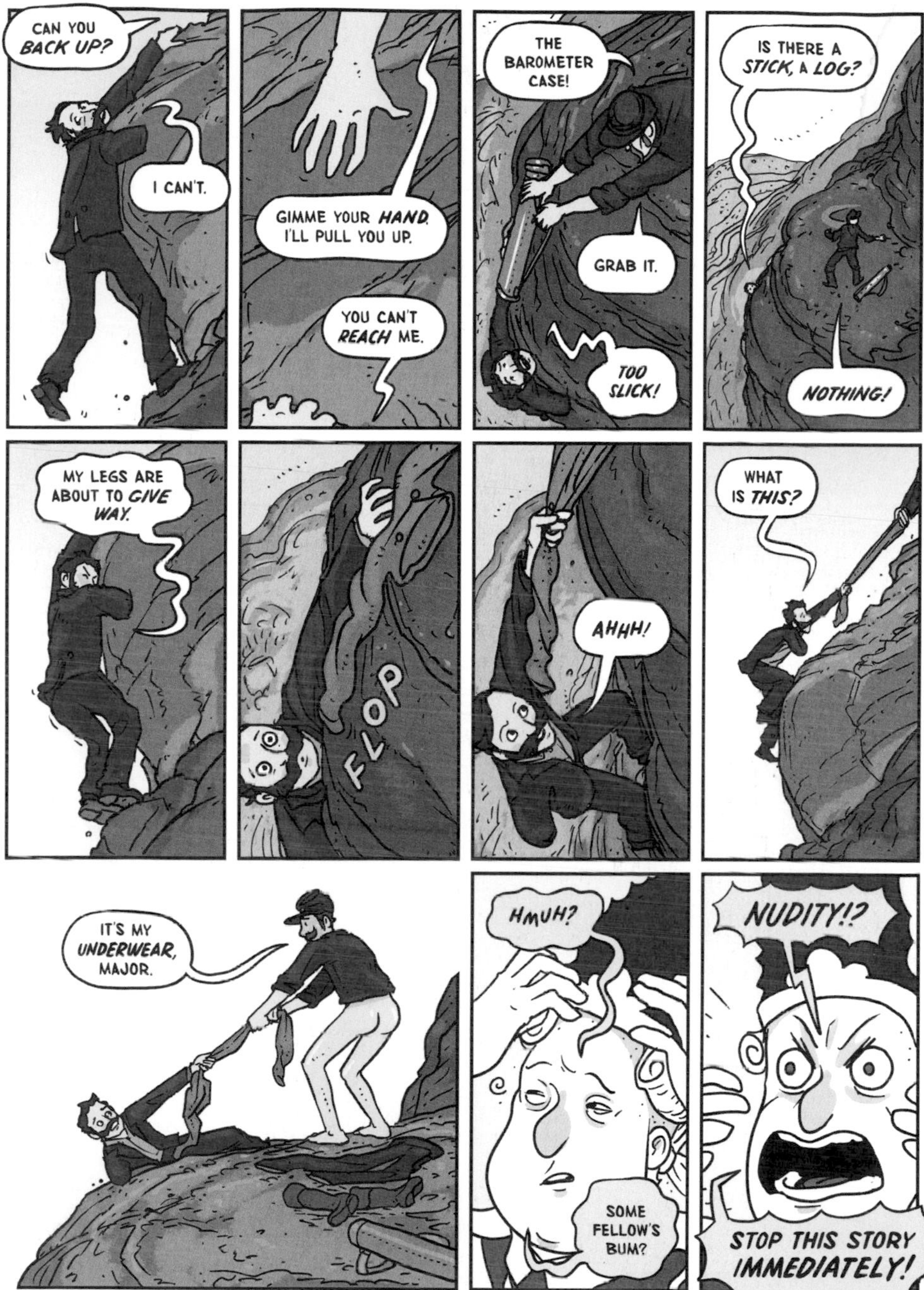
CAN YOU BACK UP?
I CAN'T.
GIMME YOUR HAND. I'LL PULL YOU UP.
YOU CAN'T REACH ME.
THE BAROMETER CASE!
GRAB IT.
TOO SLICK!
IS THERE A STICK, A LOG?
NOTHING!
MY LEGS ARE ABOUT TO GIVE WAY.
FLOP
AHHH!
WHAT IS THIS?
IT'S MY UNDERWEAR, MAJOR.
HMUH?
SOME FELLOW'S BUM?
NUDITY!?
STOP THIS STORY IMMEDIATELY!

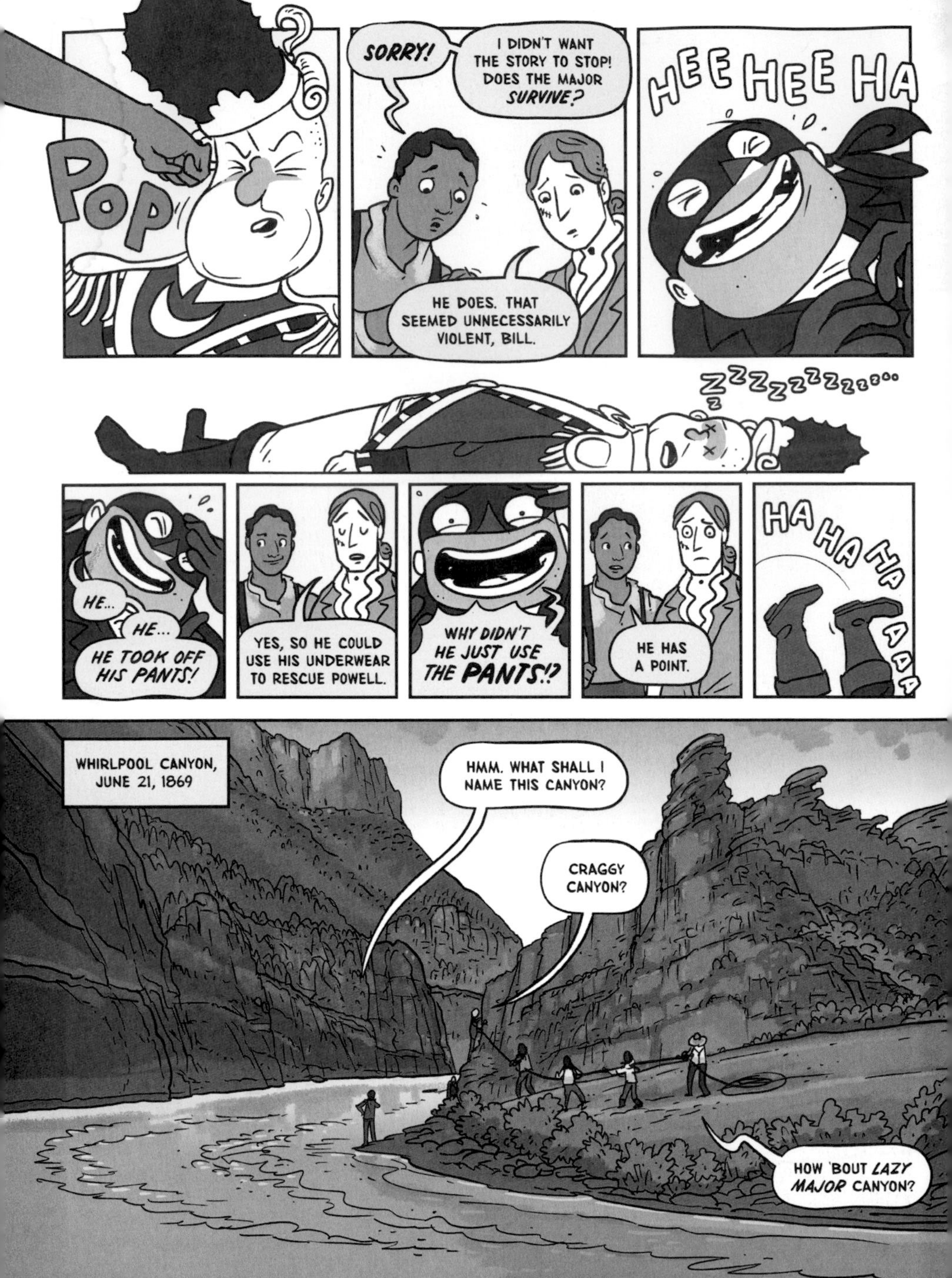
POP
SORRY!
I DIDN'T WANT THE STORY TO STOP! DOES THE MAJOR SURVIVE?
HE DOES. THAT SEEMED UNNECESSARILY VIOLENT, BILL.
HEE HEE HA
ZZZZZZZZzzz...
HE... HE... HE TOOK OFF HIS PANTS!
YES, SO HE COULD USE HIS UNDERWEAR TO RESCUE POWELL.
WHY DIDN'T HE JUST USE THE PANTS!?
HE HAS A POINT.
HA HA HA HAAA
WHIRLPOOL CANYON, JUNE 21, 1869
HMM. WHAT SHALL I NAME THIS CANYON?
CRAGGY CANYON?
HOW 'BOUT LAZY MAJOR CANYON?

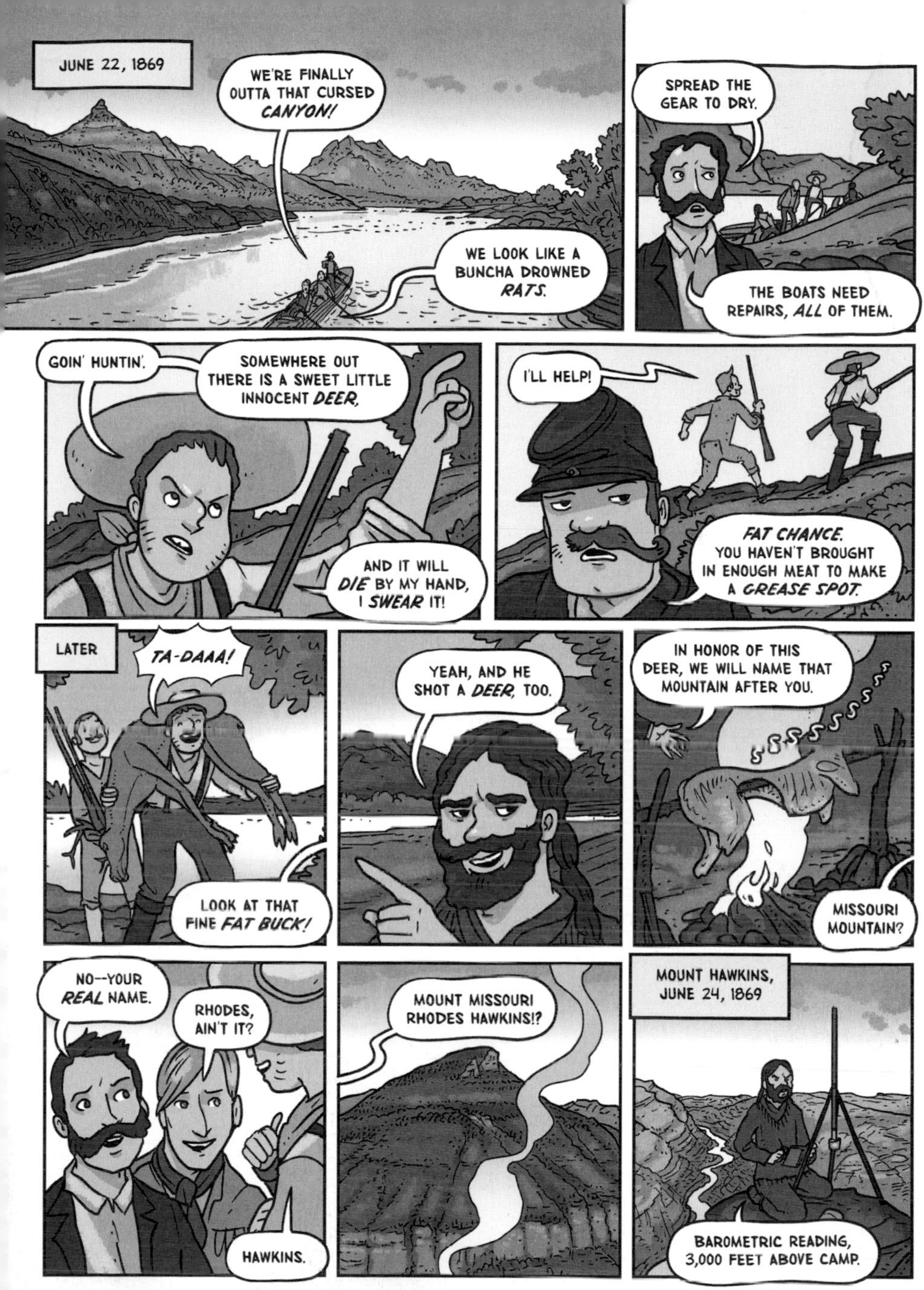
JUNE 22, 1869
WE'RE FINALLY OUTTA THAT CURSED CANYON!
WE LOOK LIKE A BUNCHA DROWNED RATS.
SPREAD THE GEAR TO DRY.
THE BOATS NEED REPAIRS, ALL OF THEM.
GOIN' HUNTIN'.
SOMEWHERE OUT THERE IS A SWEET LITTLE INNOCENT DEER,
AND IT WILL DIE BY MY HAND, I SWEAR IT!
I'LL HELP!
FAT CHANCE. YOU HAVEN'T BROUGHT IN ENOUGH MEAT TO MAKE A GREASE SPOT.
LATER
TA-DAAA!
LOOK AT THAT FINE FAT BUCK!
YEAH, AND HE SHOT A DEER, TOO.
IN HONOR OF THIS DEER, WE WILL NAME THAT MOUNTAIN AFTER YOU.
MISSOURI MOUNTAIN?
NO--YOUR REAL NAME.
RHODES, AIN'T IT?
HAWKINS.
MOUNT MISSOURI RHODES HAWKINS!?
MOUNT HAWKINS, JUNE 24, 1869
BAROMETRIC READING, 3,000 FEET ABOVE CAMP.

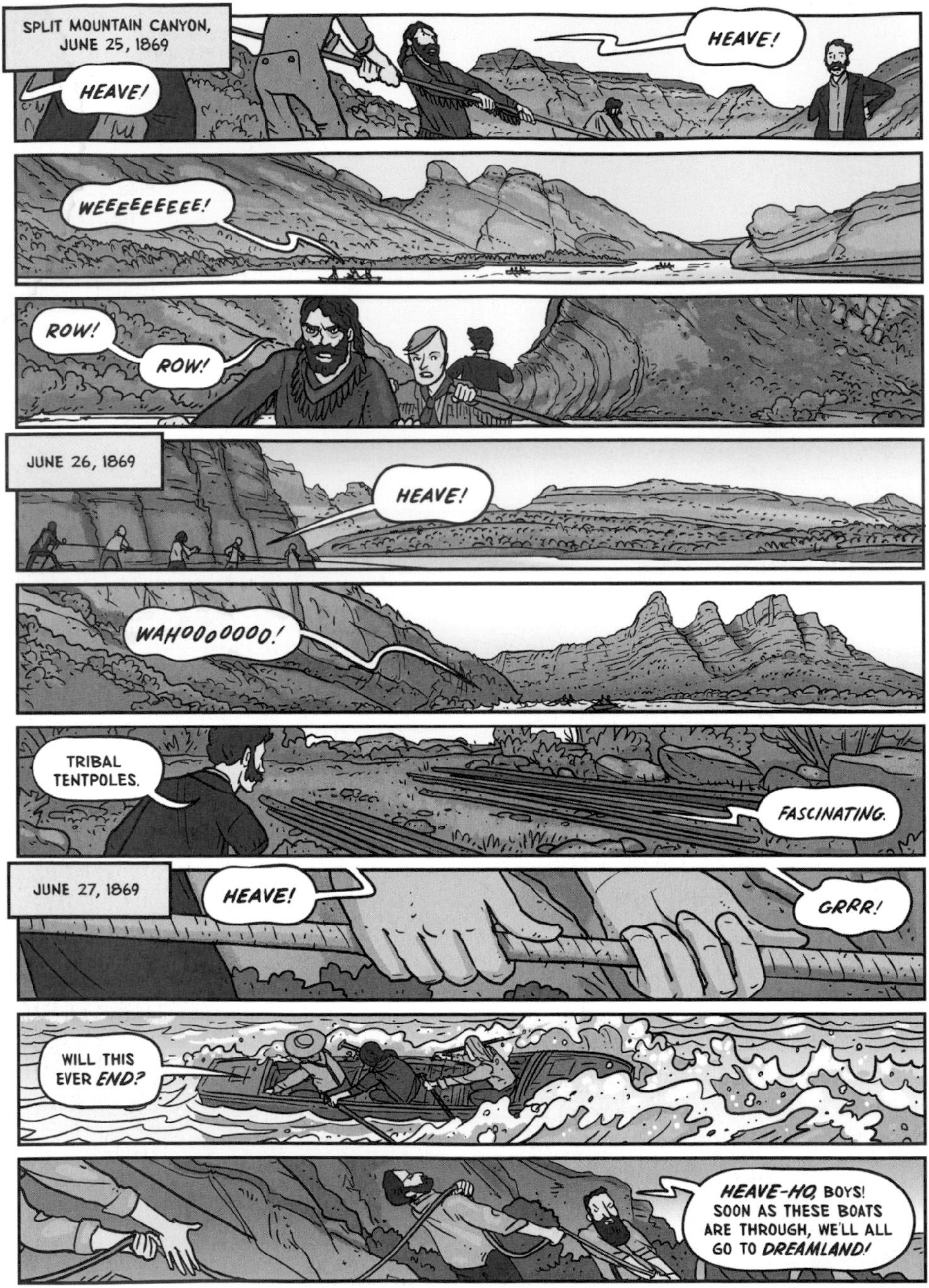
SPLIT MOUNTAIN CANYON, JUNE 25, 1869
HEAVE!
HEAVE!
WEEEEEEEEE!
ROW!
ROW!
JUNE 26, 1869
HEAVE!
WAHOOOOOOO!
TRIBAL TENTPOLES.
FASCINATING.
JUNE 27, 1869
HEAVE!
GRRR!
WILL THIS EVER END?
HEAVE-HO, BOYS! SOON AS THESE BOATS ARE THROUGH, WE'LL ALL GO TO DREAMLAND!

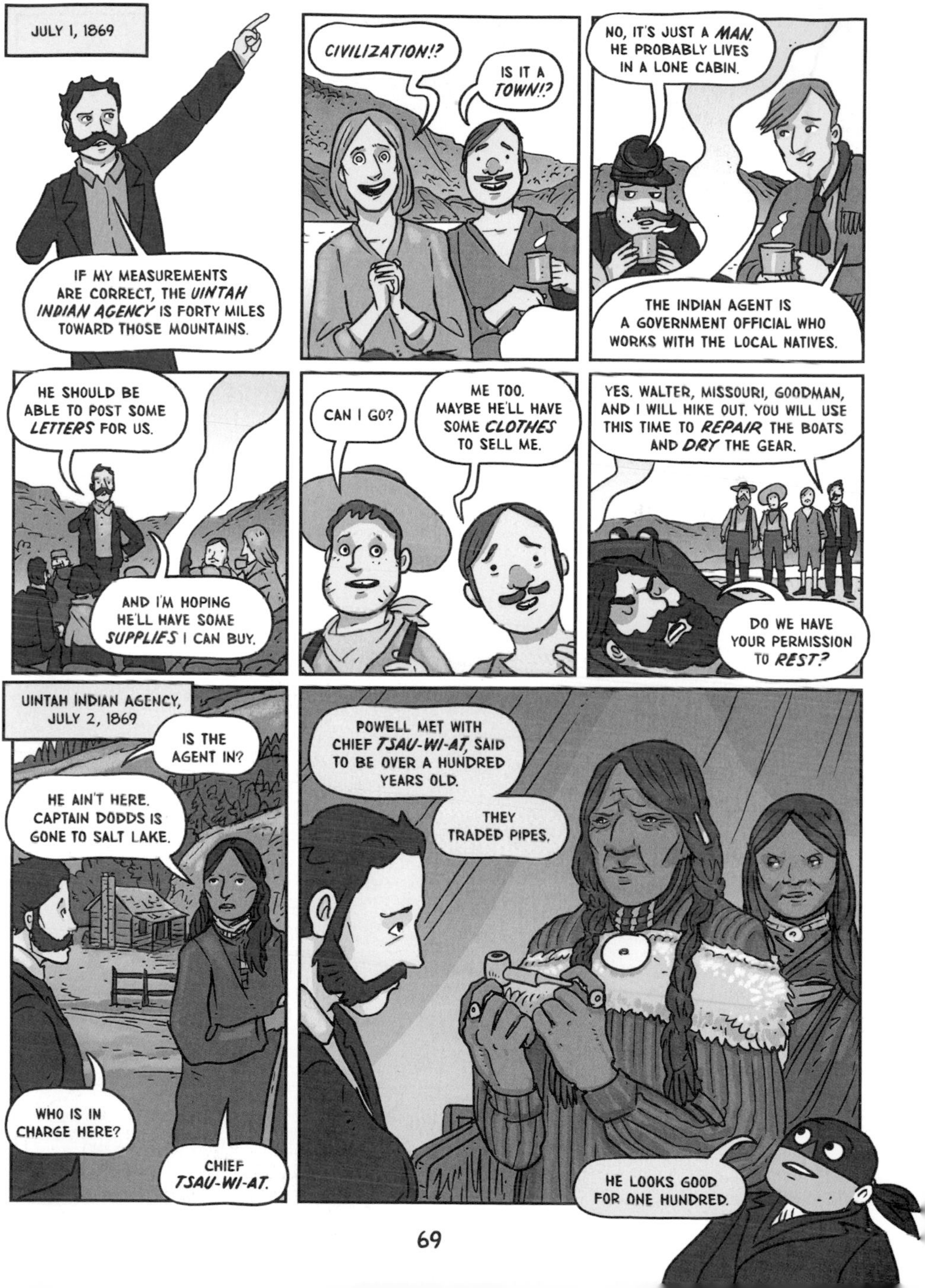
JULY 1, 1869
IF MY MEASUREMENTS ARE CORRECT, THE UINTAH INDIAN AGENCY IS FORTY MILES TOWARD THOSE MOUNTAINS.
CIVILIZATION!?
IS IT A TOWN!?
NO, IT'S JUST A MAN. HE PROBABLY LIVES IN A LONE CABIN.
THE INDIAN AGENT IS A GOVERNMENT OFFICIAL WHO WORKS WITH THE LOCAL NATIVES.
HE SHOULD BE ABLE TO POST SOME LETTERS FOR US.
AND I'M HOPING HE'LL HAVE SOME SUPPLIES I CAN BUY.
CAN I GO?
ME TOO. MAYBE HE'LL HAVE SOME CLOTHES TO SELL ME.
YES. WALTER, MISSOURI, GOODMAN, AND I WILL HIKE OUT. YOU WILL USE THIS TIME TO REPAIR THE BOATS AND DRY THE GEAR.
DO WE HAVE YOUR PERMISSION TO REST?
UINTAH INDIAN AGENCY, JULY 2, 1869
IS THE AGENT IN?
HE AIN'T HERE. CAPTAIN DODDS IS GONE TO SALT LAKE.
WHO IS IN CHARGE HERE?
CHIEF TSAU-WI-AT.
POWELL MET WITH CHIEF TSAU-WI-AT, SAID TO BE OVER A HUNDRED YEARS OLD.
THEY TRADED PIPES.
HE LOOKS GOOD FOR ONE HUNDRED.

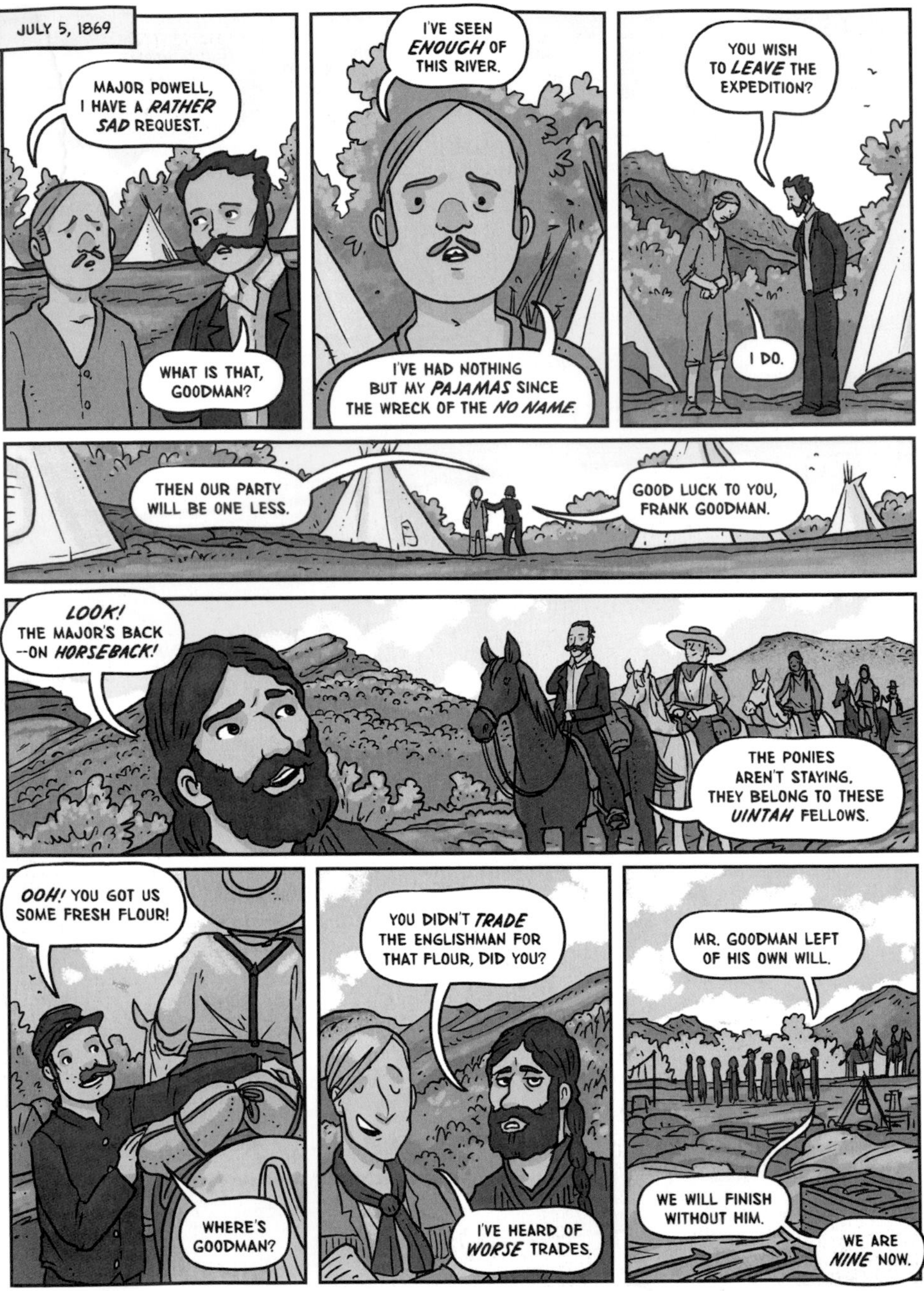
JULY 5, 1869
MAJOR POWELL, I HAVE A RATHER SAD REQUEST.
WHAT IS THAT, GOODMAN?
I'VE SEEN ENOUGH OF THIS RIVER.
I'VE HAD NOTHING BUT MY PAJAMAS SINCE THE WRECK OF THE NO NAME.
YOU WISH TO LEAVE THE EXPEDITION?
I DO.
THEN OUR PARTY WILL BE ONE LESS.
GOOD LUCK TO YOU, FRANK GOODMAN.
LOOK! THE MAJOR'S BACK --ON HORSEBACK!
THE PONIES AREN'T STAYING. THEY BELONG TO THESE UINTAH FELLOWS.
OOH! YOU GOT US SOME FRESH FLOUR!
WHERE'S GOODMAN?
YOU DIDN'T TRADE THE ENGLISHMAN FOR THAT FLOUR, DID YOU?
I'VE HEARD OF WORSE TRADES.
MR. GOODMAN LEFT OF HIS OWN WILL.
WE WILL FINISH WITHOUT HIM.
WE ARE NINE NOW.

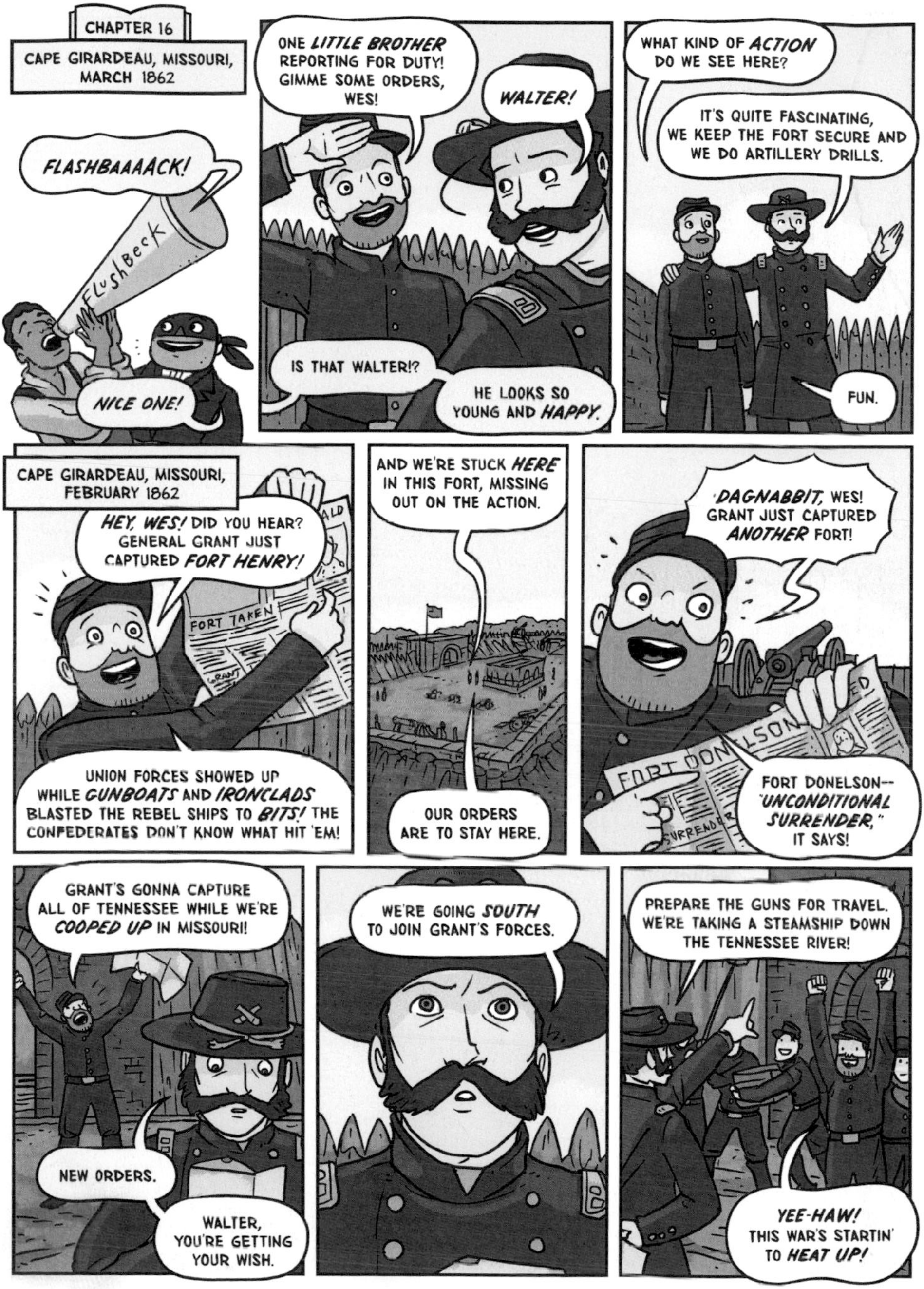

CHAPTER 16
CAPE GIRARDEAU, MISSOURI, MARCH 1862
FLASHBAAAACK!
FLUSHBECK
NICE ONE!
ONE LITTLE BROTHER REPORTING FOR DUTY! GIMME SOME ORDERS, WES!
WALTER!
IS THAT WALTER!?
HE LOOKS SO YOUNG AND HAPPY.
WHAT KIND OF ACTION DO WE SEE HERE?
IT'S QUITE FASCINATING, WE KEEP THE FORT SECURE AND WE DO ARTILLERY DRILLS.
FUN.
CAPE GIRARDEAU, MISSOURI, FEBRUARY 1862
HEY, WES! DID YOU HEAR? GENERAL GRANT JUST CAPTURED FORT HENRY!
FORT TAKEN
UNION FORCES SHOWED UP WHILE GUNBOATS AND IRONCLADS BLASTED THE REBEL SHIPS TO BITS! THE CONFEDERATES DON'T KNOW WHAT HIT 'EM!
AND WE'RE STUCK HERE IN THIS FORT, MISSING OUT ON THE ACTION.
OUR ORDERS ARE TO STAY HERE.
DAGNABBIT, WES! GRANT JUST CAPTURED ANOTHER FORT!
FORT DONELSON
SURRENDER
FORT DONELSON-- "UNCONDITIONAL SURRENDER," IT SAYS!
GRANT'S GONNA CAPTURE ALL OF TENNESSEE WHILE WE'RE COOPED UP IN MISSOURI!
NEW ORDERS.
WALTER, YOU'RE GETTING YOUR WISH.
WE'RE GOING SOUTH TO JOIN GRANT'S FORCES.
PREPARE THE GUNS FOR TRAVEL. WE'RE TAKING A STEAMSHIP DOWN THE TENNESSEE RIVER!
YEE-HAW! THIS WAR'S STARTIN' TO HEAT UP!

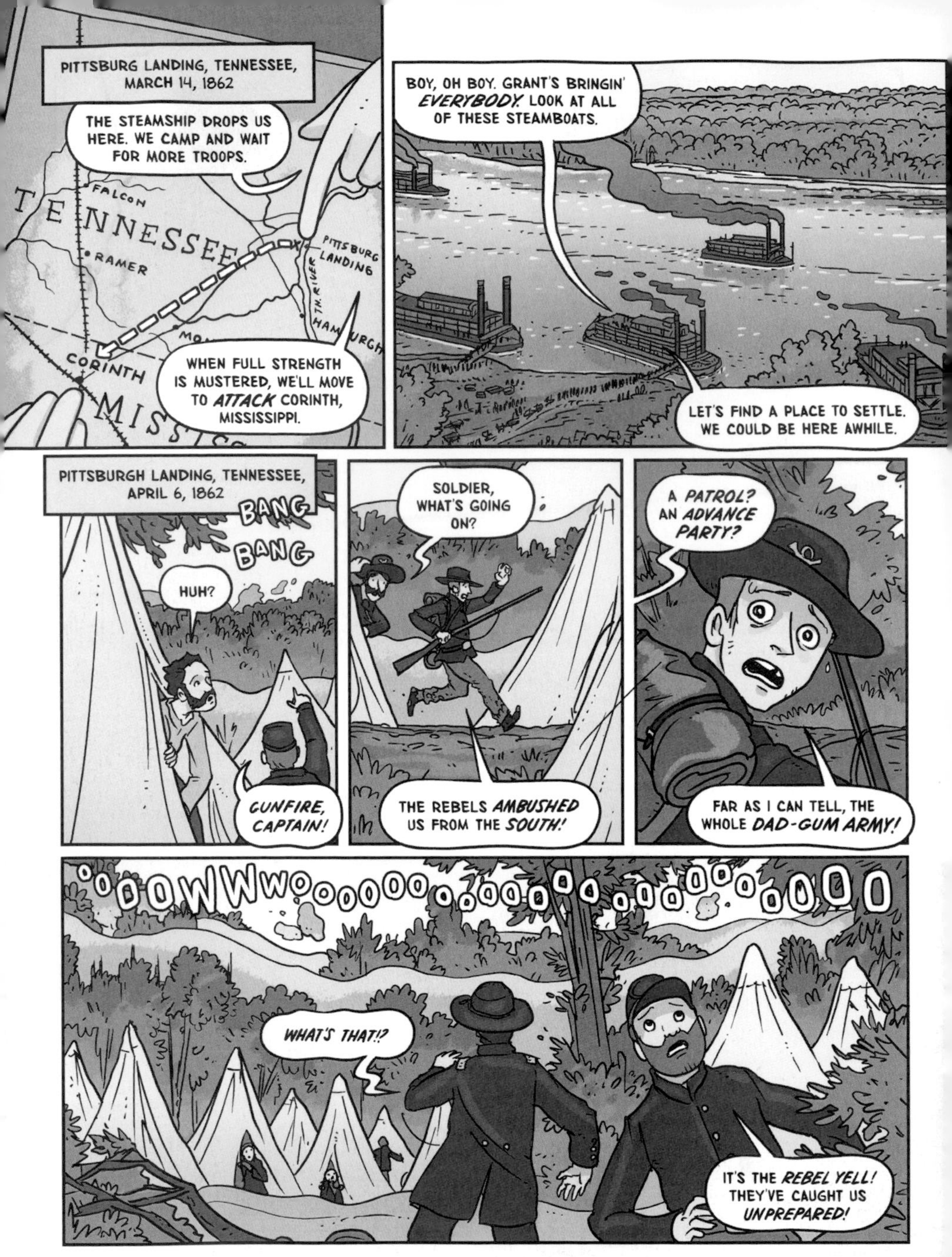
PITTSBURG LANDING, TENNESSEE, MARCH 14, 1862
THE STEAMSHIP DROPS US HERE. WE CAMP AND WAIT FOR MORE TROOPS.
FALCON
TENNESSEE
RAMER
PITTSBURG LANDING
TN. RIVER
HAMBURGH
CORINTH
MISSIS
WHEN FULL STRENGTH IS MUSTERED, WE'LL MOVE TO ATTACK CORINTH, MISSISSIPPI.
BOY, OH BOY. GRANT'S BRINGIN' EVERYBODY. LOOK AT ALL OF THESE STEAMBOATS.
LET'S FIND A PLACE TO SETTLE. WE COULD BE HERE AWHILE.
PITTSBURGH LANDING, TENNESSEE, APRIL 6, 1862
BANG
BANG
HUH?
GUNFIRE, CAPTAIN!
SOLDIER, WHAT'S GOING ON?
THE REBELS AMBUSHED US FROM THE SOUTH!
A PATROL? AN ADVANCE PARTY?
FAR AS I CAN TELL, THE WHOLE DAD-GUM ARMY!
OOOWWWOOOOOOOOOOOOOOOOOOOOOOOOOOO
WHAT'S THAT!?
IT'S THE REBEL YELL! THEY'VE CAUGHT US UNPREPARED!

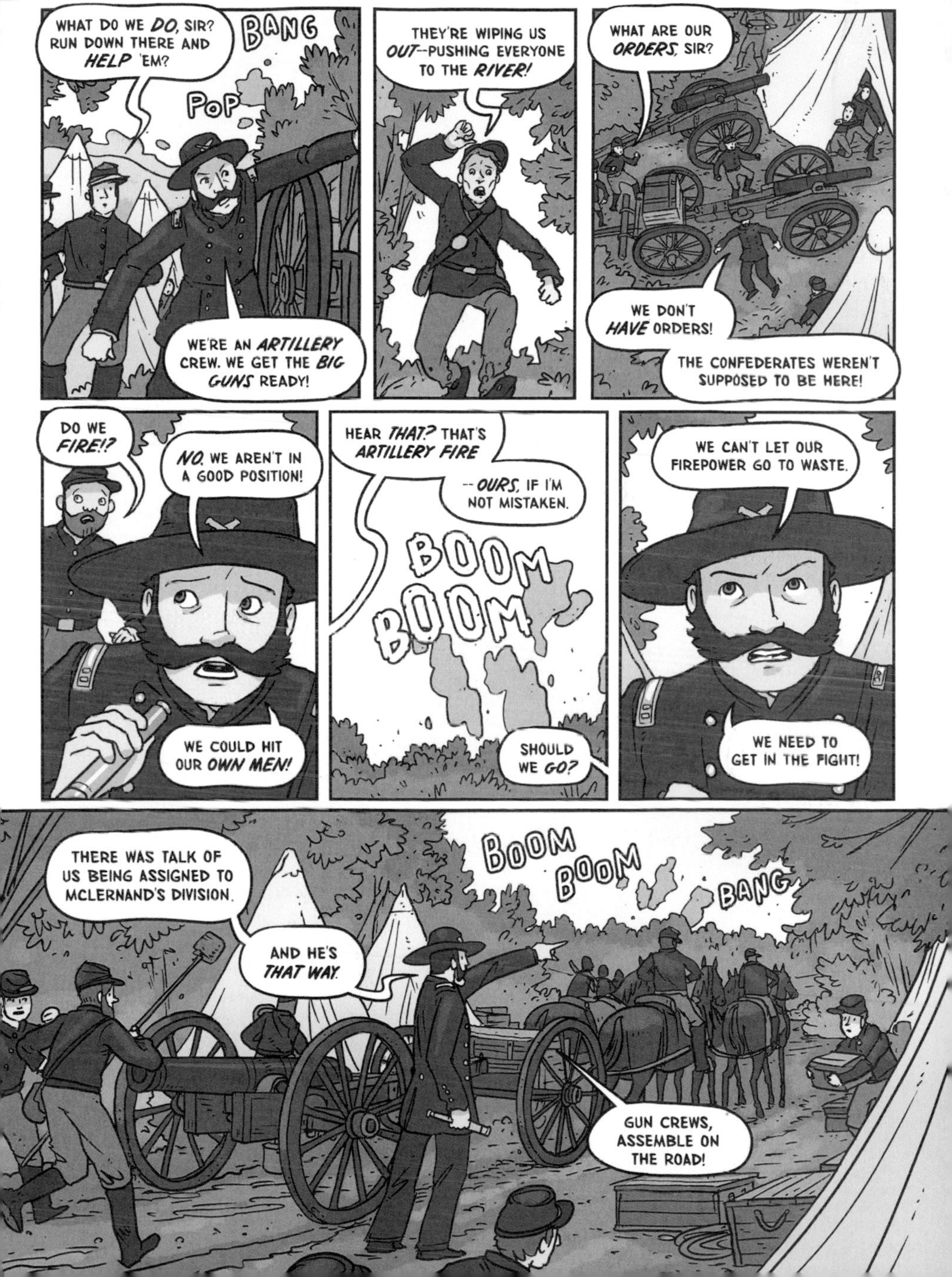
WHAT DO WE *DO*, SIR? RUN DOWN THERE AND *HELP* 'EM?
BANG
POP
WE'RE AN *ARTILLERY* CREW. WE GET THE *BIG GUNS* READY!
THEY'RE WIPING US *OUT*--PUSHING EVERYONE TO THE *RIVER!*
WHAT ARE OUR *ORDERS*, SIR?
WE DON'T *HAVE* ORDERS!
THE CONFEDERATES WEREN'T SUPPOSED TO BE HERE!
DO WE *FIRE!?*
NO. WE AREN'T IN A GOOD POSITION!
WE COULD HIT OUR *OWN MEN!*
HEAR *THAT?* THAT'S *ARTILLERY FIRE*
--*OURS*, IF I'M NOT MISTAKEN.
BOOM
BOOM
SHOULD WE *GO?*
WE CAN'T LET OUR FIREPOWER GO TO WASTE.
WE NEED TO GET IN THE FIGHT!
THERE WAS TALK OF US BEING ASSIGNED TO MCLERNAND'S DIVISION.
AND HE'S *THAT WAY.*
BOOM
BOOM
BANG
GUN CREWS, ASSEMBLE ON THE ROAD!

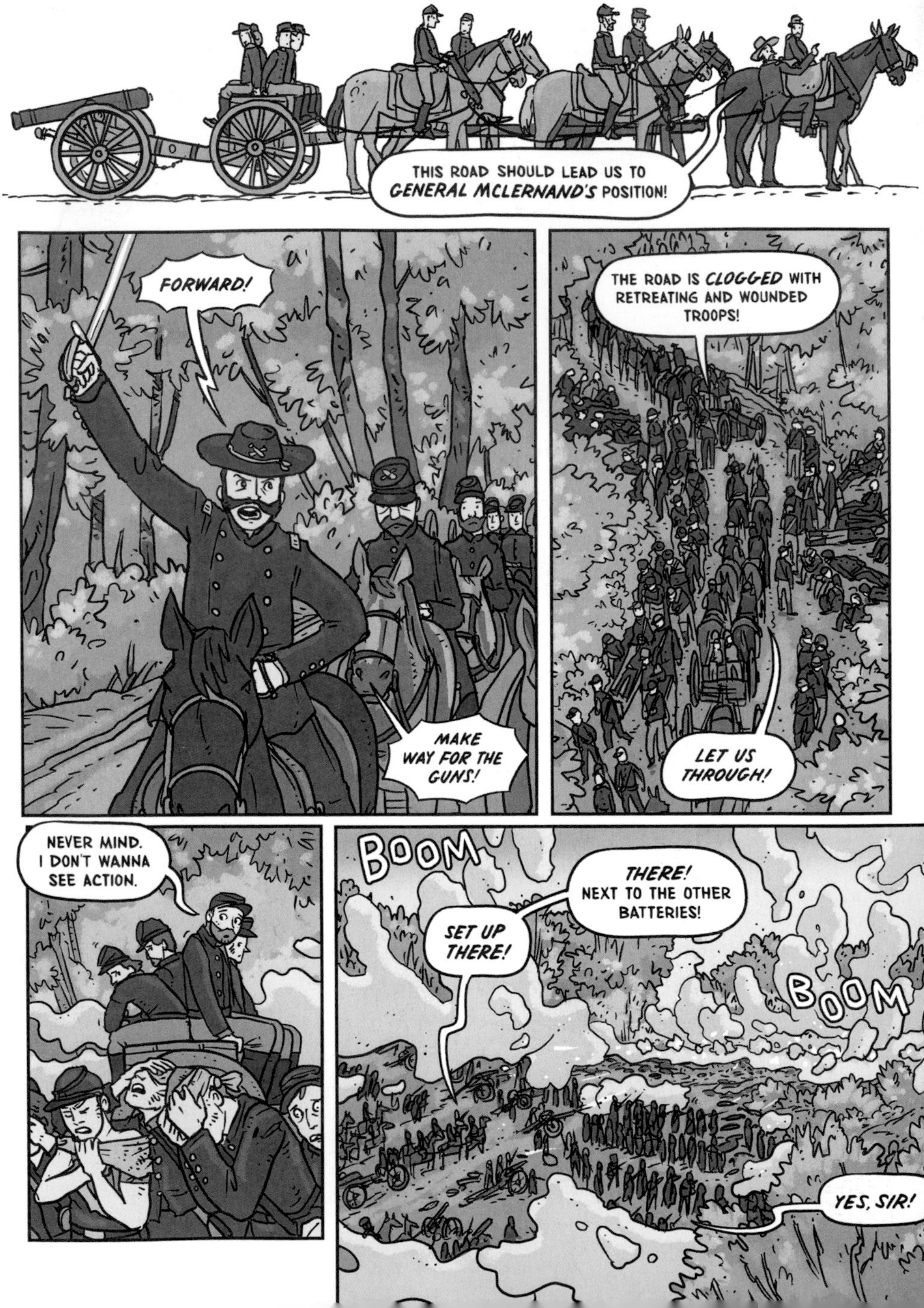
THIS ROAD SHOULD LEAD US TO GENERAL MCLERNAND'S POSITION!
FORWARD!
MAKE WAY FOR THE GUNS!
THE ROAD IS CLOGGED WITH RETREATING AND WOUNDED TROOPS!
LET US THROUGH!
NEVER MIND. I DON'T WANNA SEE ACTION.
BOOM
SET UP THERE!
THERE! NEXT TO THE OTHER BATTERIES!
BOOM
YES, SIR!

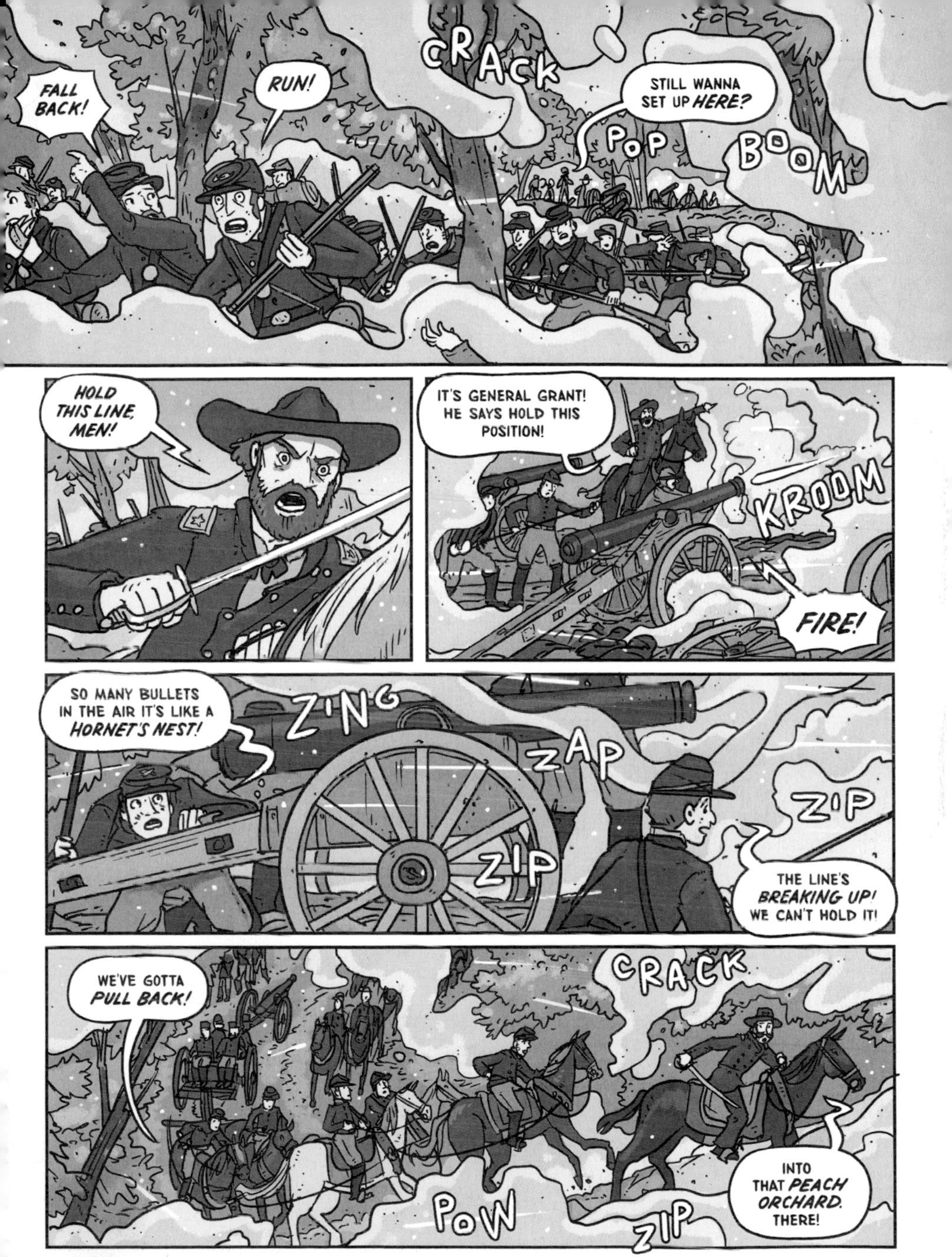
FALL BACK!
RUN!
CRACK
STILL WANNA SET UP HERE?
POP
BOOM
HOLD THIS LINE, MEN!
IT'S GENERAL GRANT! HE SAYS HOLD THIS POSITION!
KROOM
FIRE!
SO MANY BULLETS IN THE AIR IT'S LIKE A HORNET'S NEST!
ZING
ZAP
ZIP
ZIP
THE LINE'S BREAKING UP! WE CAN'T HOLD IT!
WE'VE GOTTA PULL BACK!
CRACK
POW
ZIP
INTO THAT PEACH ORCHARD. THERE!

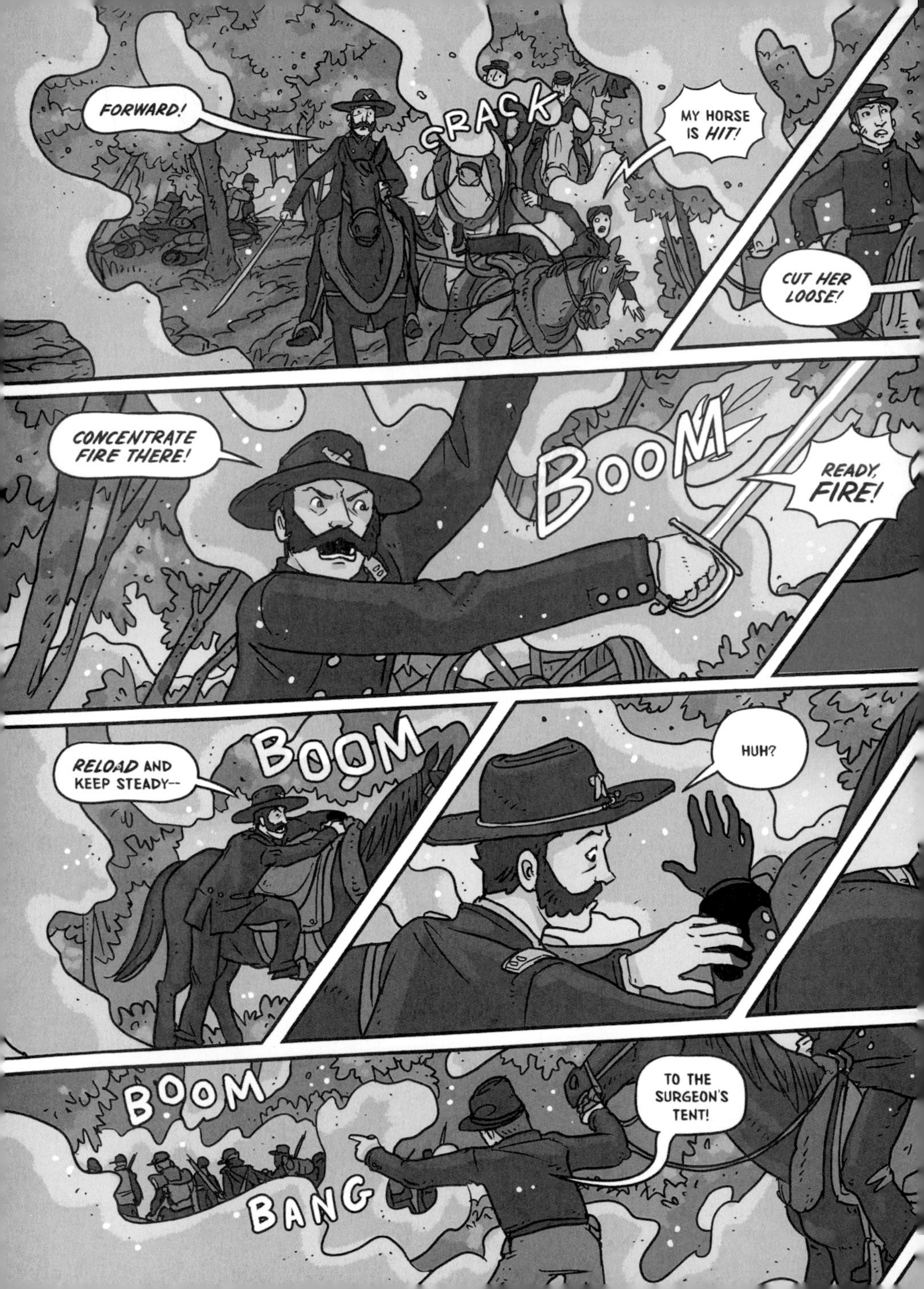
FORWARD!
CRACK
MY HORSE IS HIT!
CUT HER LOOSE!
CONCENTRATE FIRE THERE!
BOOM
READY, FIRE!
RELOAD AND KEEP STEADY--
BOOM
HUH?
BOOM
TO THE SURGEON'S TENT!
BANG

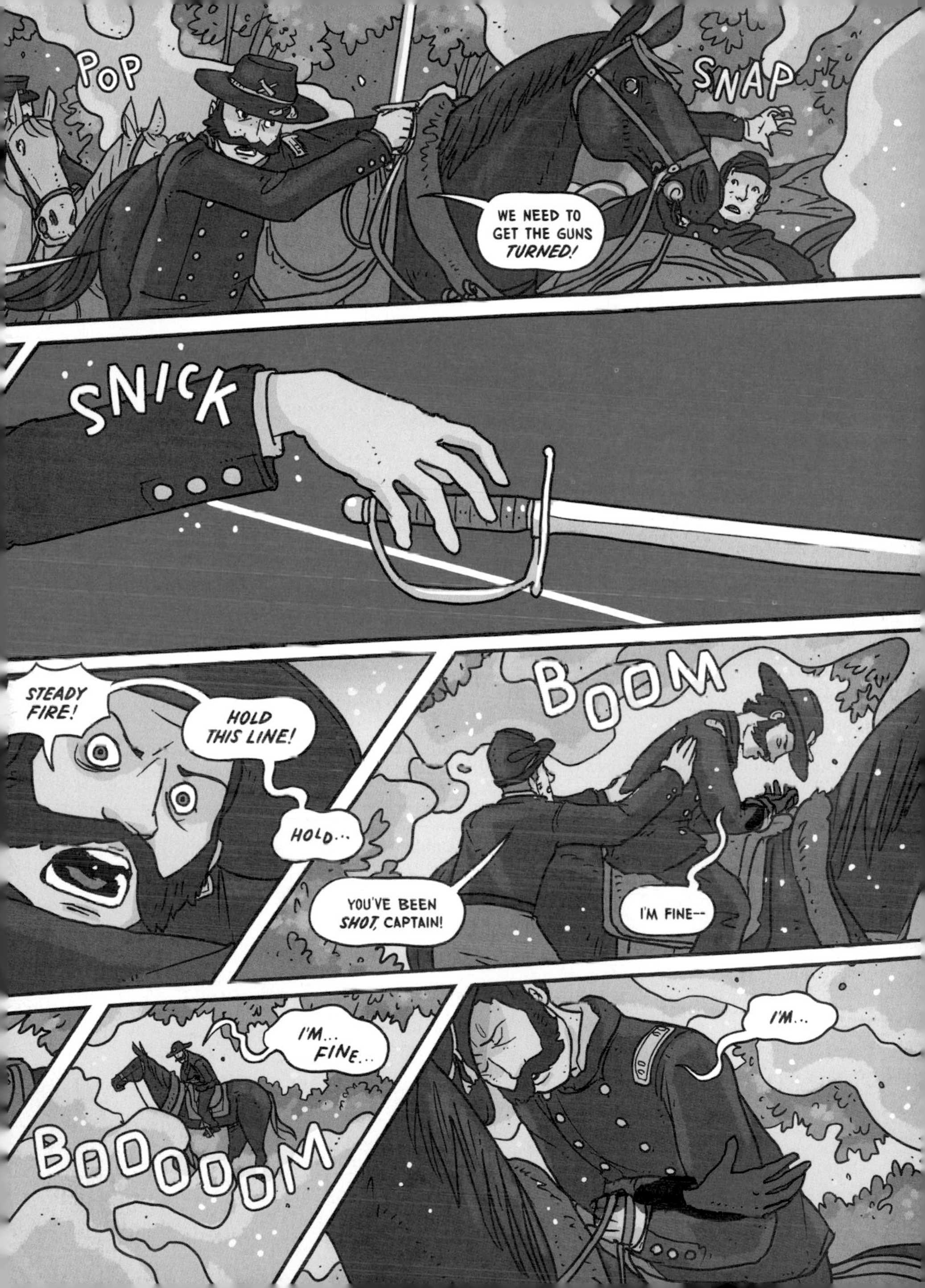
POP
SNAP
WE NEED TO GET THE GUNS TURNED!
SNICK
STEADY FIRE!
HOLD THIS LINE!
HOLD...
BOOM
YOU'VE BEEN SHOT, CAPTAIN!
I'M FINE--
I'M... FINE...
BOOOOOM
I'M...

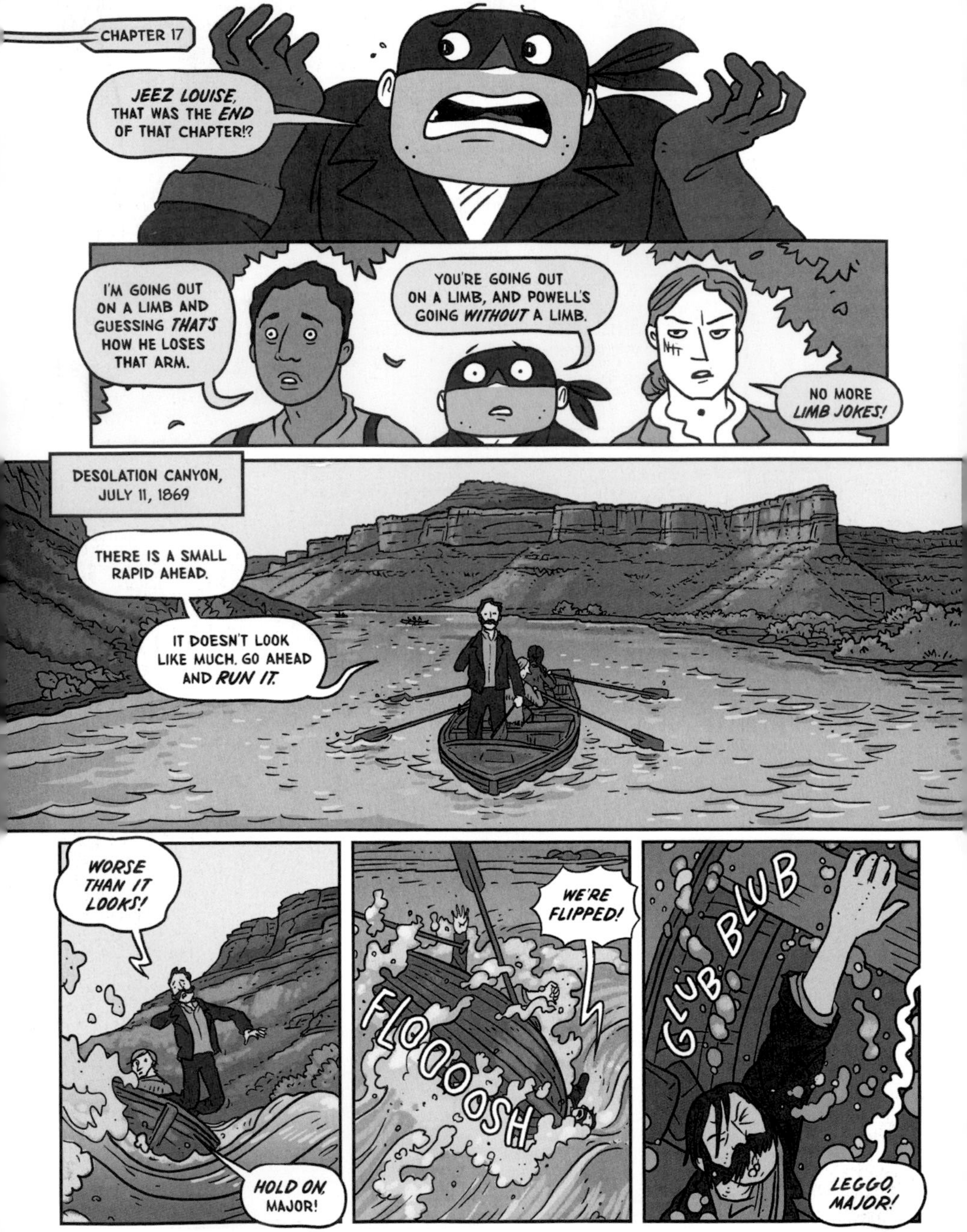
CHAPTER 17
JEEZ LOUISE, THAT WAS THE END OF THAT CHAPTER!?
I'M GOING OUT ON A LIMB AND GUESSING THAT'S HOW HE LOSES THAT ARM.
YOU'RE GOING OUT ON A LIMB, AND POWELL'S GOING WITHOUT A LIMB.
NO MORE LIMB JOKES!
DESOLATION CANYON, JULY 11, 1869
THERE IS A SMALL RAPID AHEAD.
IT DOESN'T LOOK LIKE MUCH. GO AHEAD AND RUN IT.
WORSE THAN IT LOOKS!
HOLD ON, MAJOR!
WE'RE FLIPPED!
FLOOOOSH
GLUB BLUB
LEGGO, MAJOR!

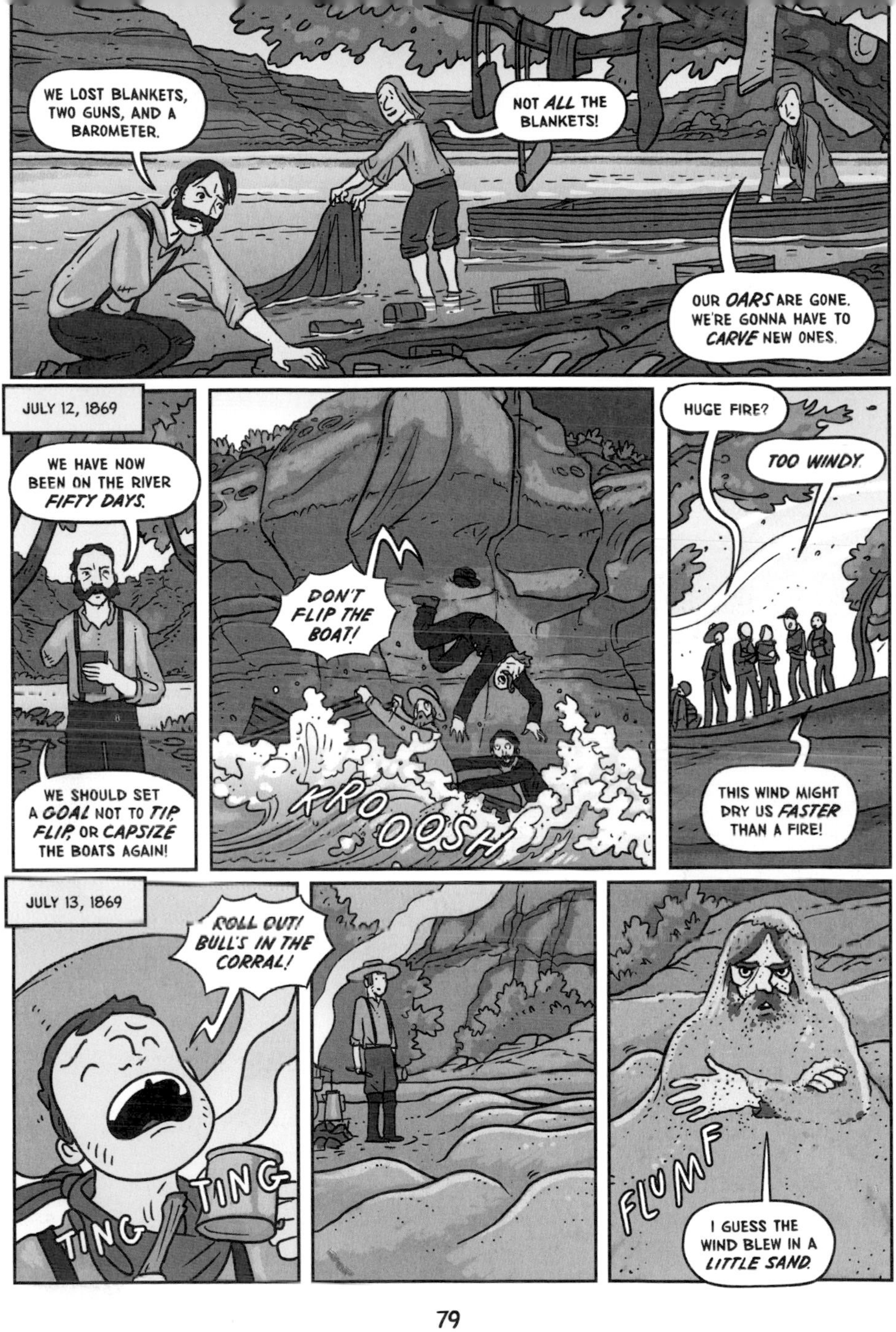
WE LOST BLANKETS, TWO GUNS, AND A BAROMETER.
NOT ALL THE BLANKETS!
OUR OARS ARE GONE. WE'RE GONNA HAVE TO CARVE NEW ONES.
JULY 12, 1869
WE HAVE NOW BEEN ON THE RIVER FIFTY DAYS.
WE SHOULD SET A GOAL NOT TO TIP, FLIP, OR CAPSIZE THE BOATS AGAIN!
DON'T FLIP THE BOAT!
KROOOSH
HUGE FIRE?
TOO WINDY.
THIS WIND MIGHT DRY US FASTER THAN A FIRE!
JULY 13, 1869
ROLL OUT! BULL'S IN THE CORRAL!
TING TING
FLUMF
I GUESS THE WIND BLEW IN A LITTLE SAND.

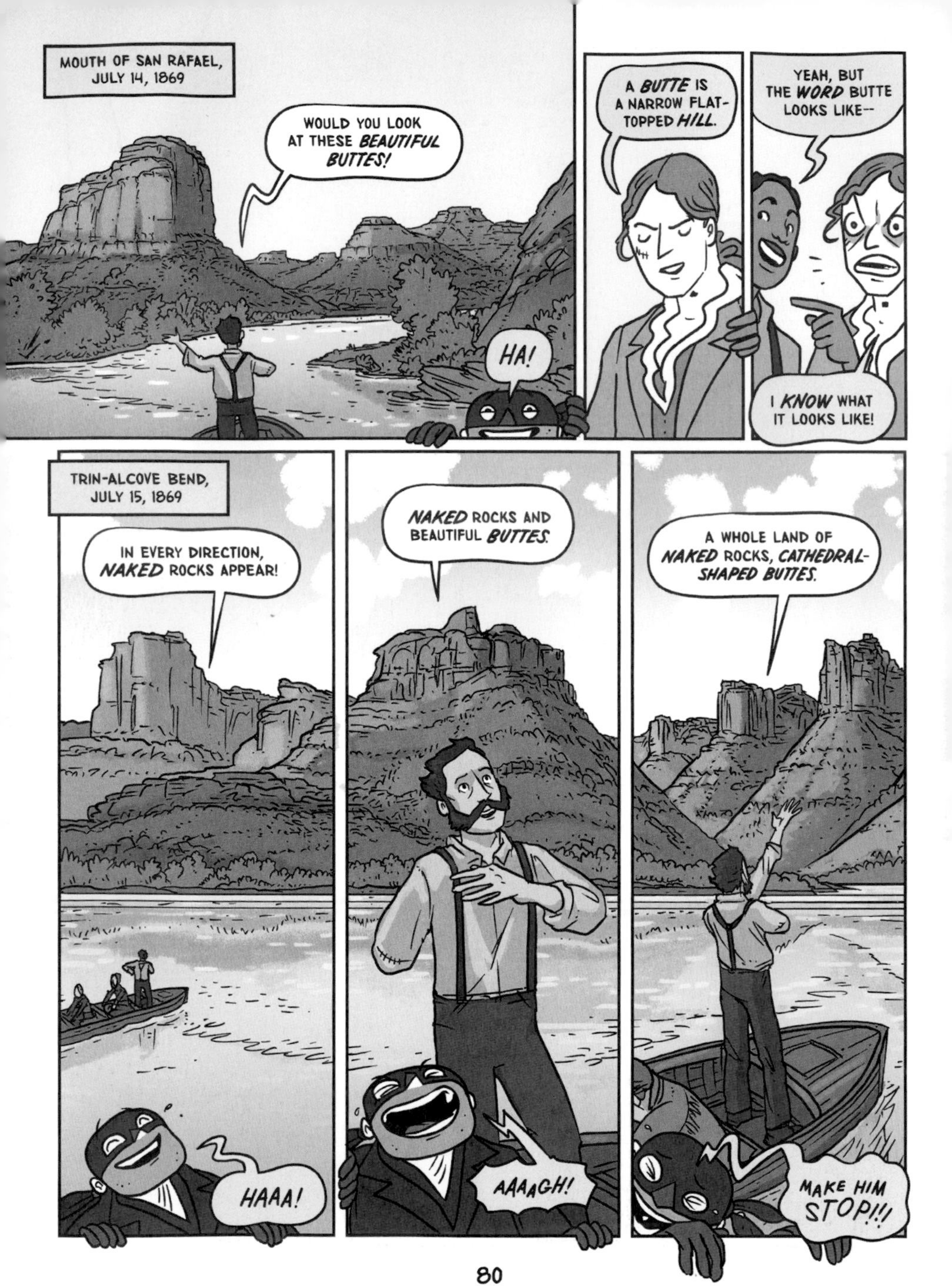
MOUTH OF SAN RAFAEL, JULY 14, 1869
WOULD YOU LOOK AT THESE BEAUTIFUL BUTTES!
HA!
A BUTTE IS A NARROW FLAT-TOPPED HILL.
YEAH, BUT THE WORD BUTTE LOOKS LIKE--
I KNOW WHAT IT LOOKS LIKE!
TRIN-ALCOVE BEND, JULY 15, 1869
IN EVERY DIRECTION, NAKED ROCKS APPEAR!
HAAA!
NAKED ROCKS AND BEAUTIFUL BUTTES.
AAAAGH!
A WHOLE LAND OF NAKED ROCKS, CATHEDRAL-SHAPED BUTTES.
MAKE HIM STOP!!!

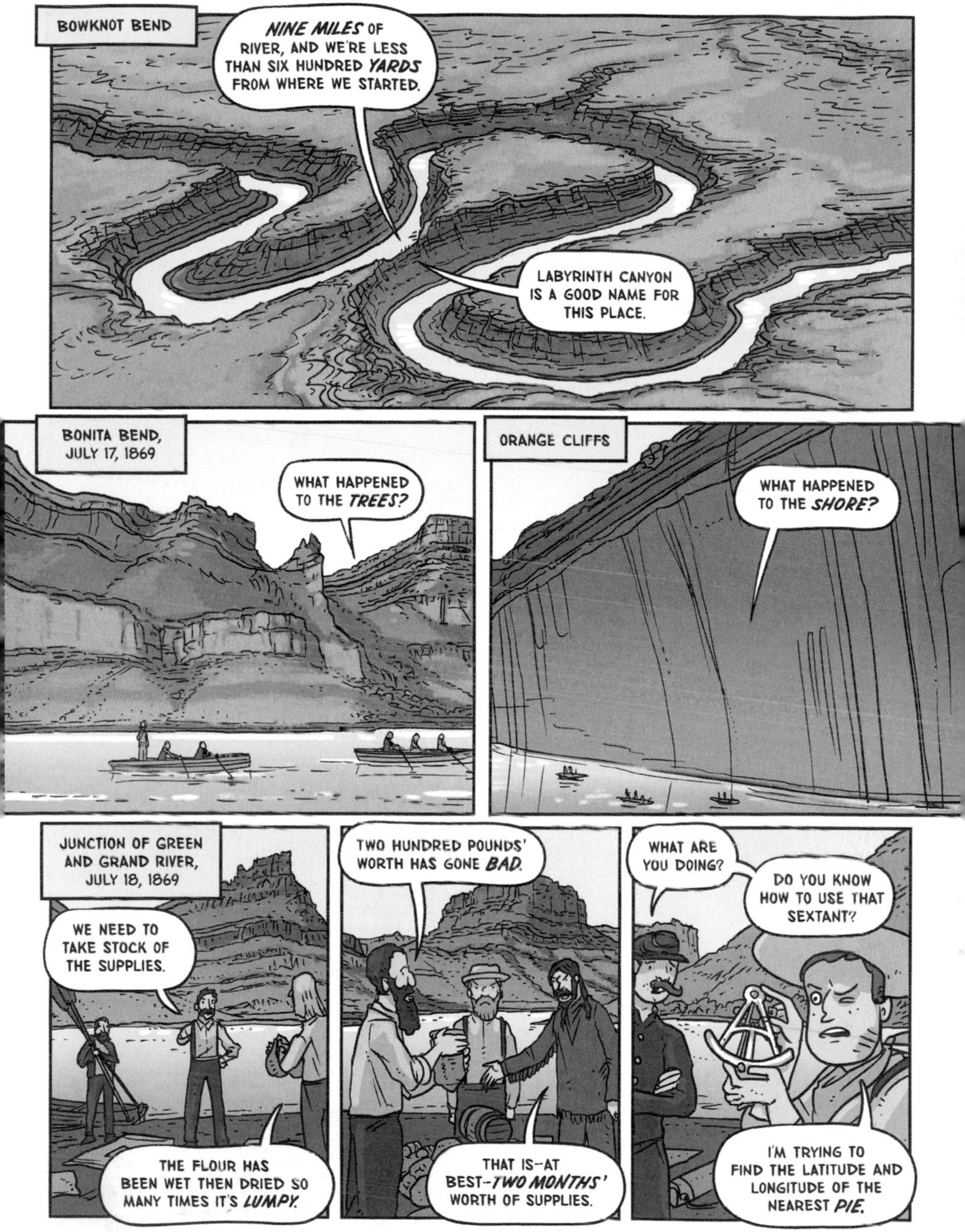
BOWKNOT BEND
NINE MILES OF RIVER, AND WE'RE LESS THAN SIX HUNDRED YARDS FROM WHERE WE STARTED.
LABYRINTH CANYON IS A GOOD NAME FOR THIS PLACE.
BONITA BEND, JULY 17, 1869
WHAT HAPPENED TO THE TREES?
ORANGE CLIFFS
WHAT HAPPENED TO THE SHORE?
JUNCTION OF GREEN AND GRAND RIVER, JULY 18, 1869
WE NEED TO TAKE STOCK OF THE SUPPLIES.
THE FLOUR HAS BEEN WET THEN DRIED SO MANY TIMES IT'S LUMPY.
TWO HUNDRED POUNDS' WORTH HAS GONE BAD.
THAT IS--AT BEST--TWO MONTHS' WORTH OF SUPPLIES.
WHAT ARE YOU DOING?
DO YOU KNOW HOW TO USE THAT SEXTANT?
I'M TRYING TO FIND THE LATITUDE AND LONGITUDE OF THE NEAREST PIE.

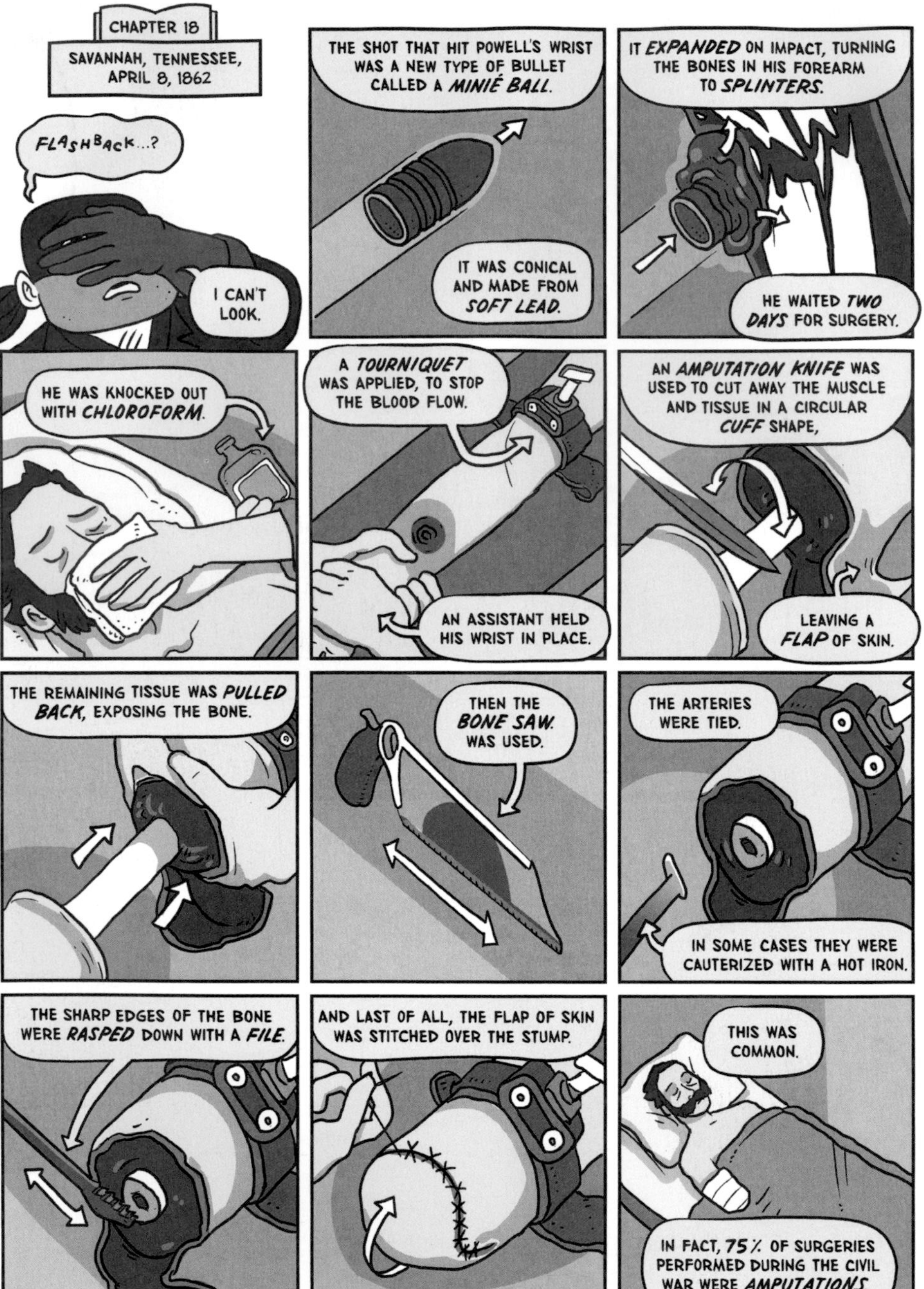
CHAPTER 18
SAVANNAH, TENNESSEE, APRIL 8, 1862
FLASHBACK...?
I CAN'T LOOK.
THE SHOT THAT HIT POWELL'S WRIST WAS A NEW TYPE OF BULLET CALLED A MINIÉ BALL.
IT WAS CONICAL AND MADE FROM SOFT LEAD.
IT EXPANDED ON IMPACT, TURNING THE BONES IN HIS FOREARM TO SPLINTERS.
HE WAITED TWO DAYS FOR SURGERY.
HE WAS KNOCKED OUT WITH CHLOROFORM.
A TOURNIQUET WAS APPLIED, TO STOP THE BLOOD FLOW.
AN ASSISTANT HELD HIS WRIST IN PLACE.
AN AMPUTATION KNIFE WAS USED TO CUT AWAY THE MUSCLE AND TISSUE IN A CIRCULAR CUFF SHAPE,
LEAVING A FLAP OF SKIN.
THE REMAINING TISSUE WAS PULLED BACK, EXPOSING THE BONE.
THEN THE BONE SAW WAS USED.
THE ARTERIES WERE TIED.
IN SOME CASES THEY WERE CAUTERIZED WITH A HOT IRON.
THE SHARP EDGES OF THE BONE WERE RASPED DOWN WITH A FILE.
AND LAST OF ALL, THE FLAP OF SKIN WAS STITCHED OVER THE STUMP.
THIS WAS COMMON.
IN FACT, 75% OF SURGERIES PERFORMED DURING THE CIVIL WAR WERE AMPUTATIONS.

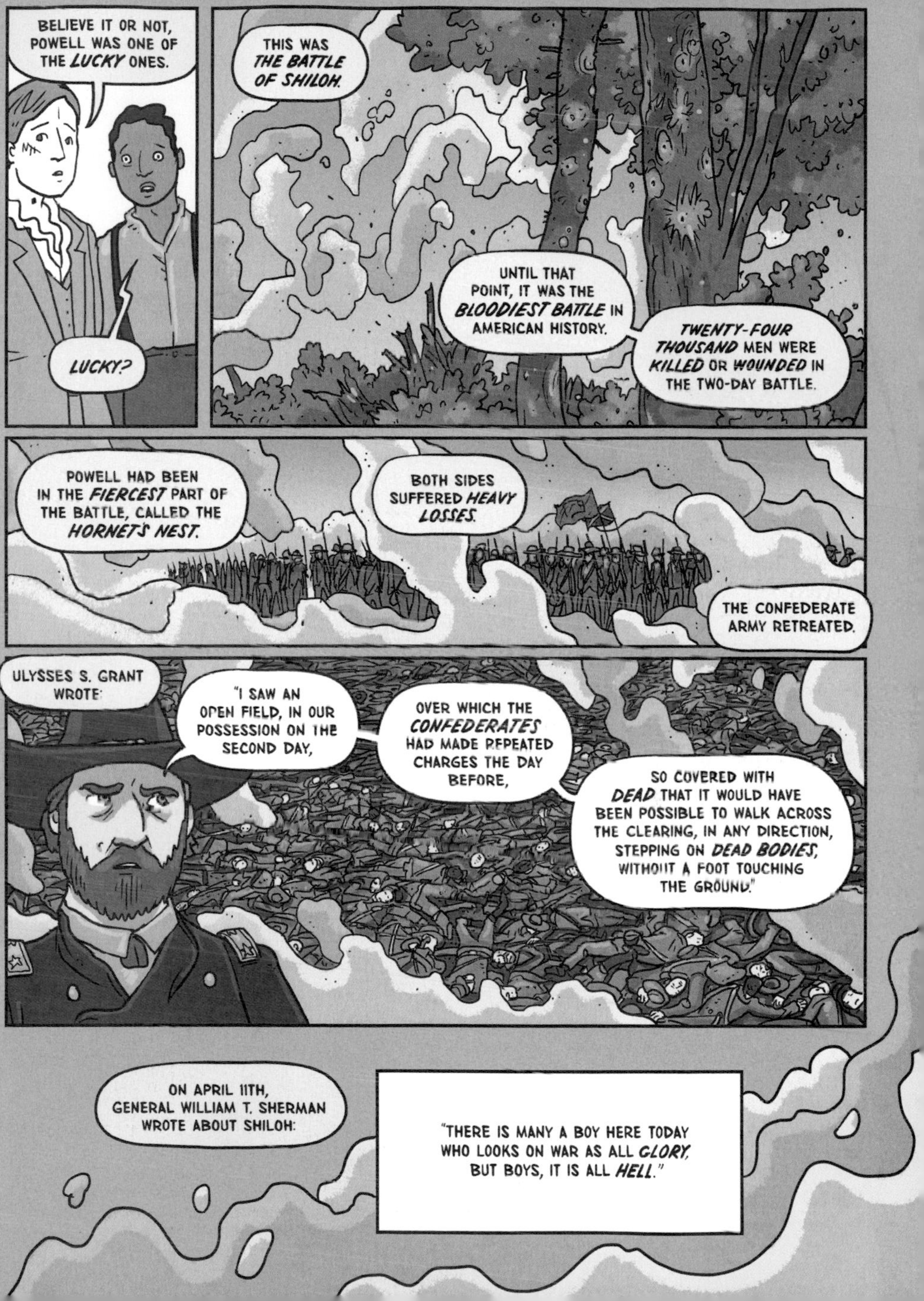
BELIEVE IT OR NOT, POWELL WAS ONE OF THE *LUCKY* ONES.
LUCKY?
THIS WAS *THE BATTLE OF SHILOH.*
UNTIL THAT POINT, IT WAS THE *BLOODIEST BATTLE* IN AMERICAN HISTORY.
TWENTY-FOUR THOUSAND MEN WERE *KILLED* OR *WOUNDED* IN THE TWO-DAY BATTLE.
POWELL HAD BEEN IN THE *FIERCEST* PART OF THE BATTLE, CALLED THE *HORNET'S NEST.*
BOTH SIDES SUFFERED *HEAVY LOSSES.*
THE CONFEDERATE ARMY RETREATED.
ULYSSES S. GRANT WROTE:
"I SAW AN OPEN FIELD, IN OUR POSSESSION ON THE SECOND DAY,
OVER WHICH THE *CONFEDERATES* HAD MADE REPEATED CHARGES THE DAY BEFORE,
SO COVERED WITH *DEAD* THAT IT WOULD HAVE BEEN POSSIBLE TO WALK ACROSS THE CLEARING, IN ANY DIRECTION, STEPPING ON *DEAD BODIES,* WITHOUT A FOOT TOUCHING THE GROUND."
ON APRIL 11TH, GENERAL WILLIAM T. SHERMAN WROTE ABOUT SHILOH:
"THERE IS MANY A BOY HERE TODAY WHO LOOKS ON WAR AS ALL *GLORY,* BUT BOYS, IT IS ALL *HELL.*"

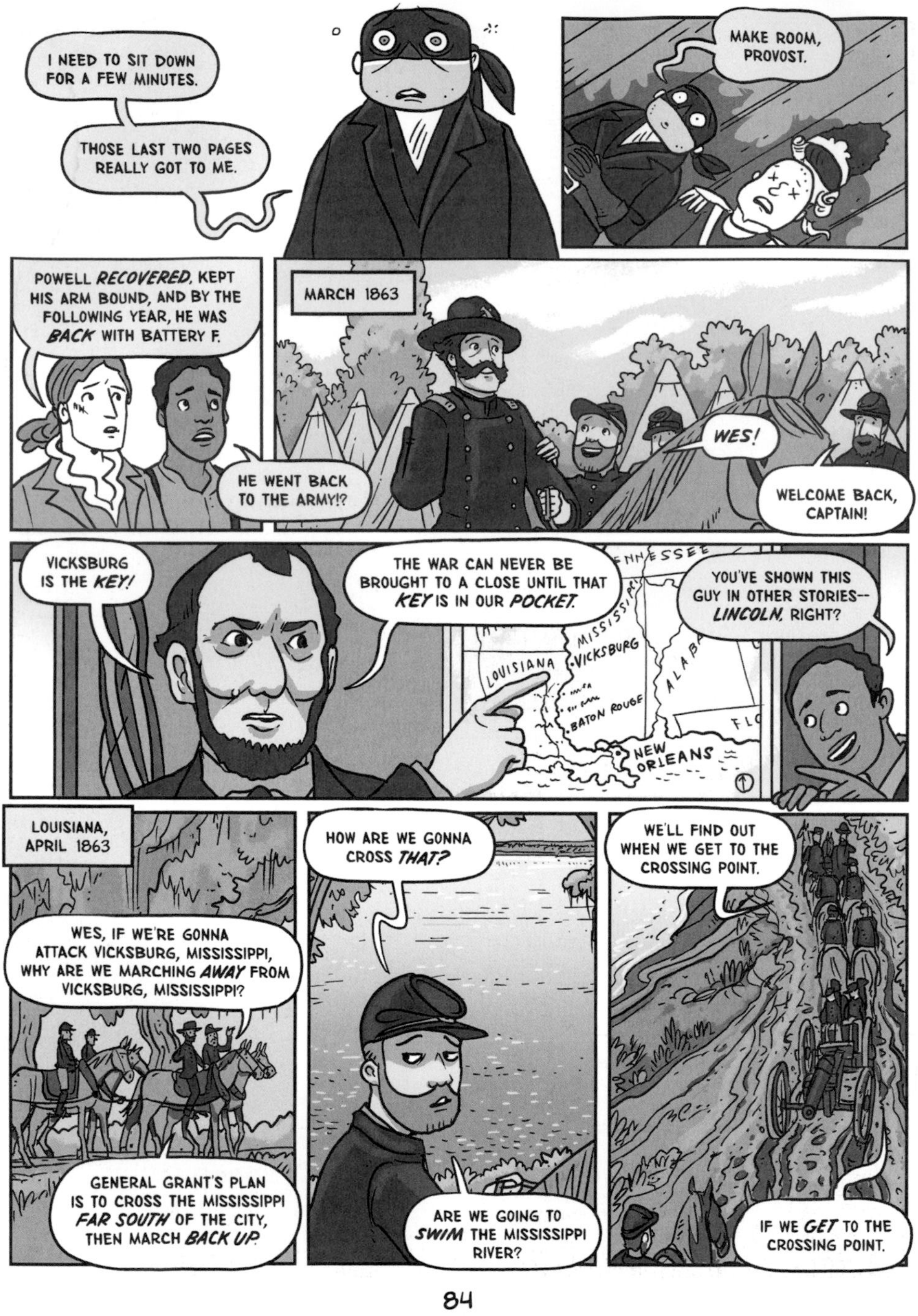

I NEED TO SIT DOWN FOR A FEW MINUTES.
THOSE LAST TWO PAGES REALLY GOT TO ME.
MAKE ROOM, PROVOST.
POWELL *RECOVERED*, KEPT HIS ARM BOUND, AND BY THE FOLLOWING YEAR, HE WAS *BACK* WITH BATTERY F.
HE WENT BACK TO THE ARMY!?
MARCH 1863
WES!
WELCOME BACK, CAPTAIN!
VICKSBURG IS THE *KEY!*
THE WAR CAN NEVER BE BROUGHT TO A CLOSE UNTIL THAT *KEY* IS IN OUR *POCKET.*
MISSISSIPPI
VICKSBURG
LOUISIANA
BATON ROUGE
NEW ORLEANS
YOU'VE SHOWN THIS GUY IN OTHER STORIES-- *LINCOLN,* RIGHT?
LOUISIANA, APRIL 1863
WES, IF WE'RE GONNA ATTACK VICKSBURG, MISSISSIPPI, WHY ARE WE MARCHING *AWAY* FROM VICKSBURG, MISSISSIPPI?
GENERAL GRANT'S PLAN IS TO CROSS THE MISSISSIPPI *FAR SOUTH* OF THE CITY, THEN MARCH *BACK UP.*
HOW ARE WE GONNA CROSS *THAT?*
ARE WE GOING TO *SWIM* THE MISSISSIPPI RIVER?
WE'LL FIND OUT WHEN WE GET TO THE CROSSING POINT.
IF WE *GET* TO THE CROSSING POINT.

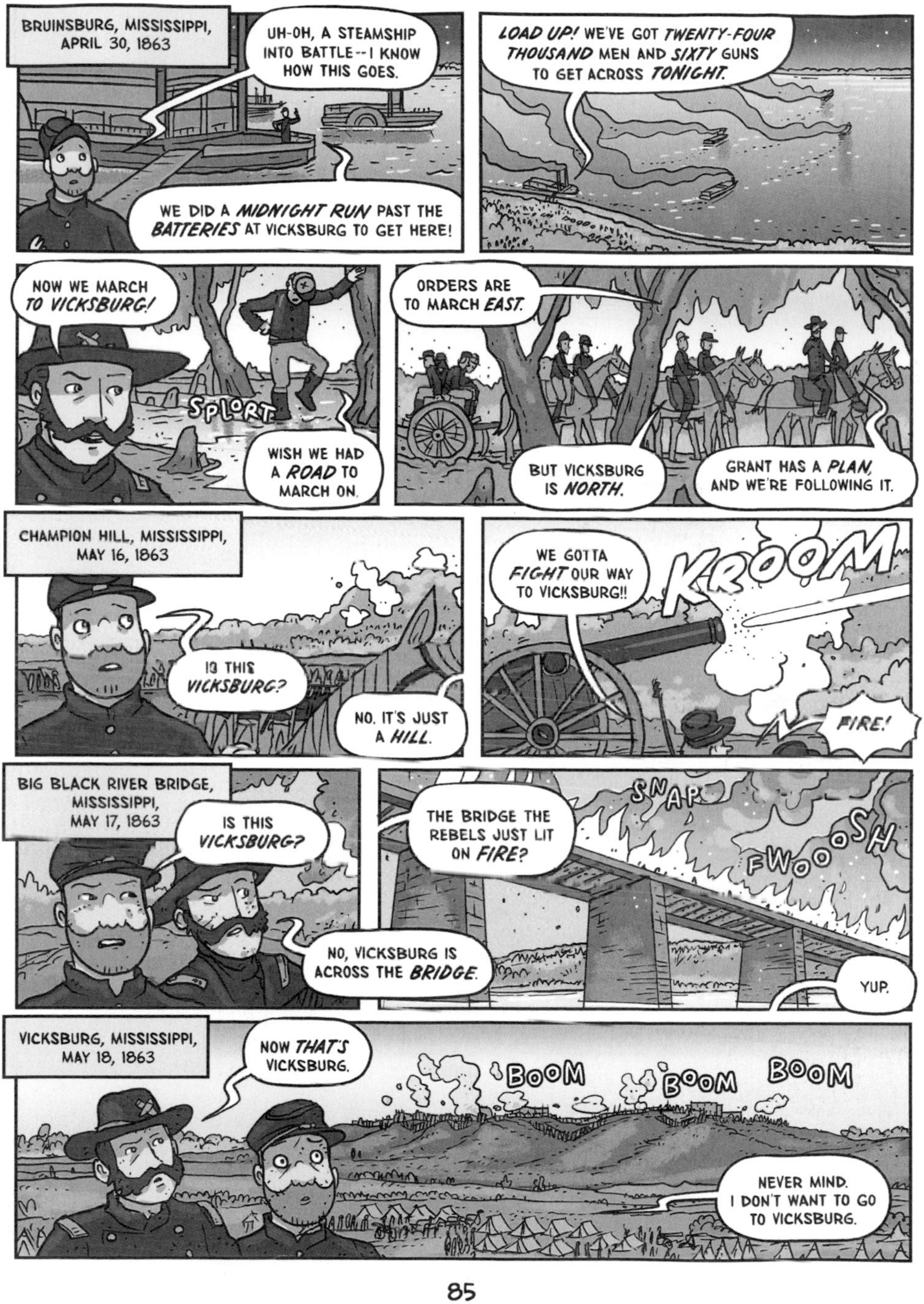
BRUINSBURG, MISSISSIPPI, APRIL 30, 1863
UH-OH, A STEAMSHIP INTO BATTLE--I KNOW HOW THIS GOES.
WE DID A MIDNIGHT RUN PAST THE BATTERIES AT VICKSBURG TO GET HERE!
LOAD UP! WE'VE GOT TWENTY-FOUR THOUSAND MEN AND SIXTY GUNS TO GET ACROSS TONIGHT.
NOW WE MARCH TO VICKSBURG!
SPLORT
WISH WE HAD A ROAD TO MARCH ON.
ORDERS ARE TO MARCH EAST.
BUT VICKSBURG IS NORTH.
GRANT HAS A PLAN, AND WE'RE FOLLOWING IT.
CHAMPION HILL, MISSISSIPPI, MAY 16, 1863
IS THIS VICKSBURG?
NO. IT'S JUST A HILL.
WE GOTTA FIGHT OUR WAY TO VICKSBURG!!
KROOM
FIRE!
BIG BLACK RIVER BRIDGE, MISSISSIPPI, MAY 17, 1863
IS THIS VICKSBURG?
NO, VICKSBURG IS ACROSS THE BRIDGE.
THE BRIDGE THE REBELS JUST LIT ON FIRE?
SNAP
FWOOOSH
YUP.
VICKSBURG, MISSISSIPPI, MAY 18, 1863
NOW THAT'S VICKSBURG.
BOOM
BOOM
BOOM
NEVER MIND. I DON'T WANT TO GO TO VICKSBURG.

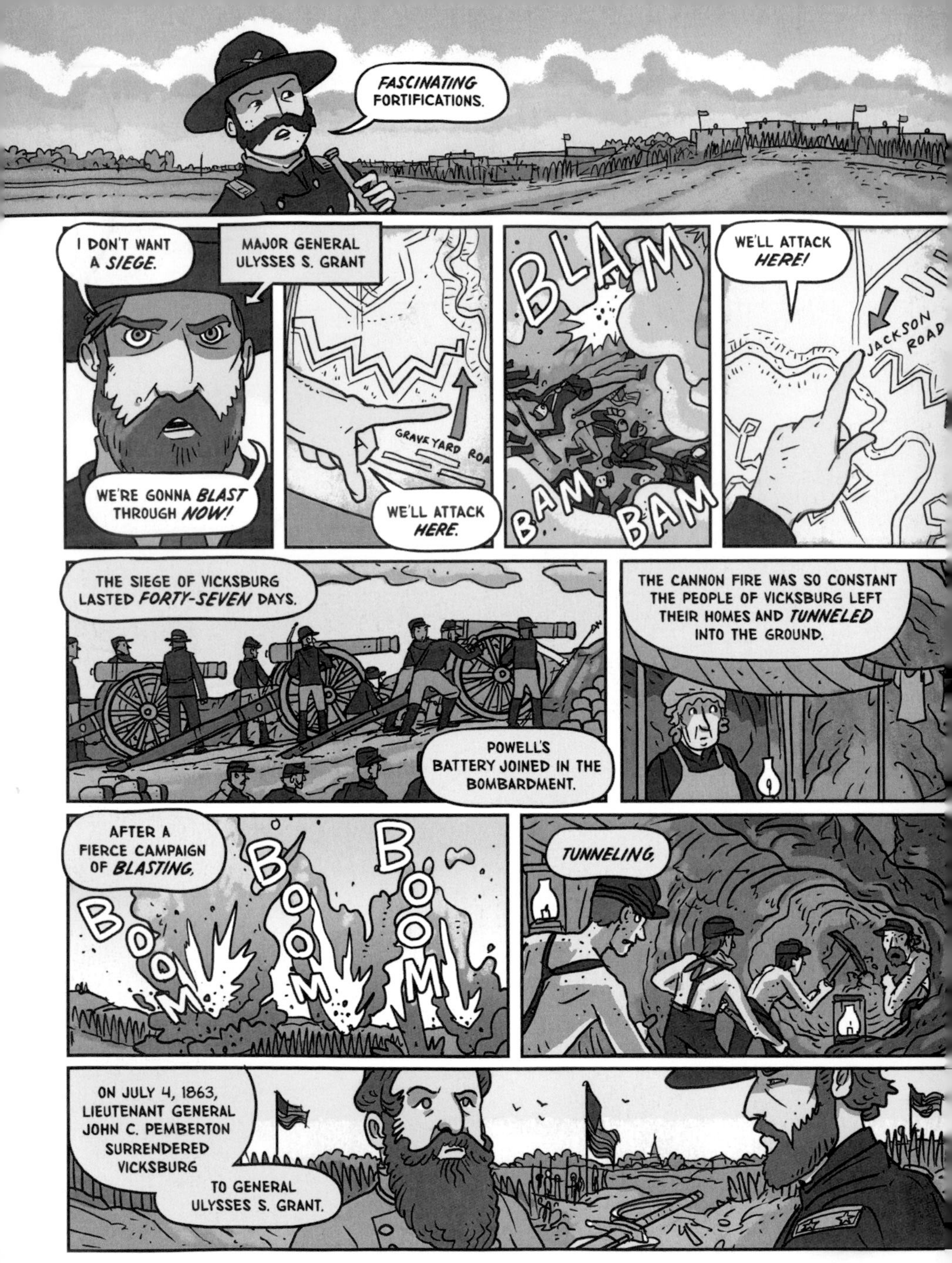
FASCINATING FORTIFICATIONS.
I DON'T WANT A *SIEGE*.
MAJOR GENERAL ULYSSES S. GRANT
WE'RE GONNA *BLAST* THROUGH *NOW!*
GRAVEYARD ROAD
WE'LL ATTACK *HERE*.
BLAM
BAM
BAM
WE'LL ATTACK *HERE!*
JACKSON ROAD
THE SIEGE OF VICKSBURG LASTED *FORTY-SEVEN* DAYS.
POWELL'S BATTERY JOINED IN THE BOMBARDMENT.
THE CANNON FIRE WAS SO CONSTANT THE PEOPLE OF VICKSBURG LEFT THEIR HOMES AND *TUNNELED* INTO THE GROUND.
AFTER A FIERCE CAMPAIGN OF *BLASTING*,
BOOOM
BOOOM
BOOOM
TUNNELING,
ON JULY 4, 1863, LIEUTENANT GENERAL JOHN C. PEMBERTON SURRENDERED VICKSBURG
TO GENERAL ULYSSES S. GRANT.

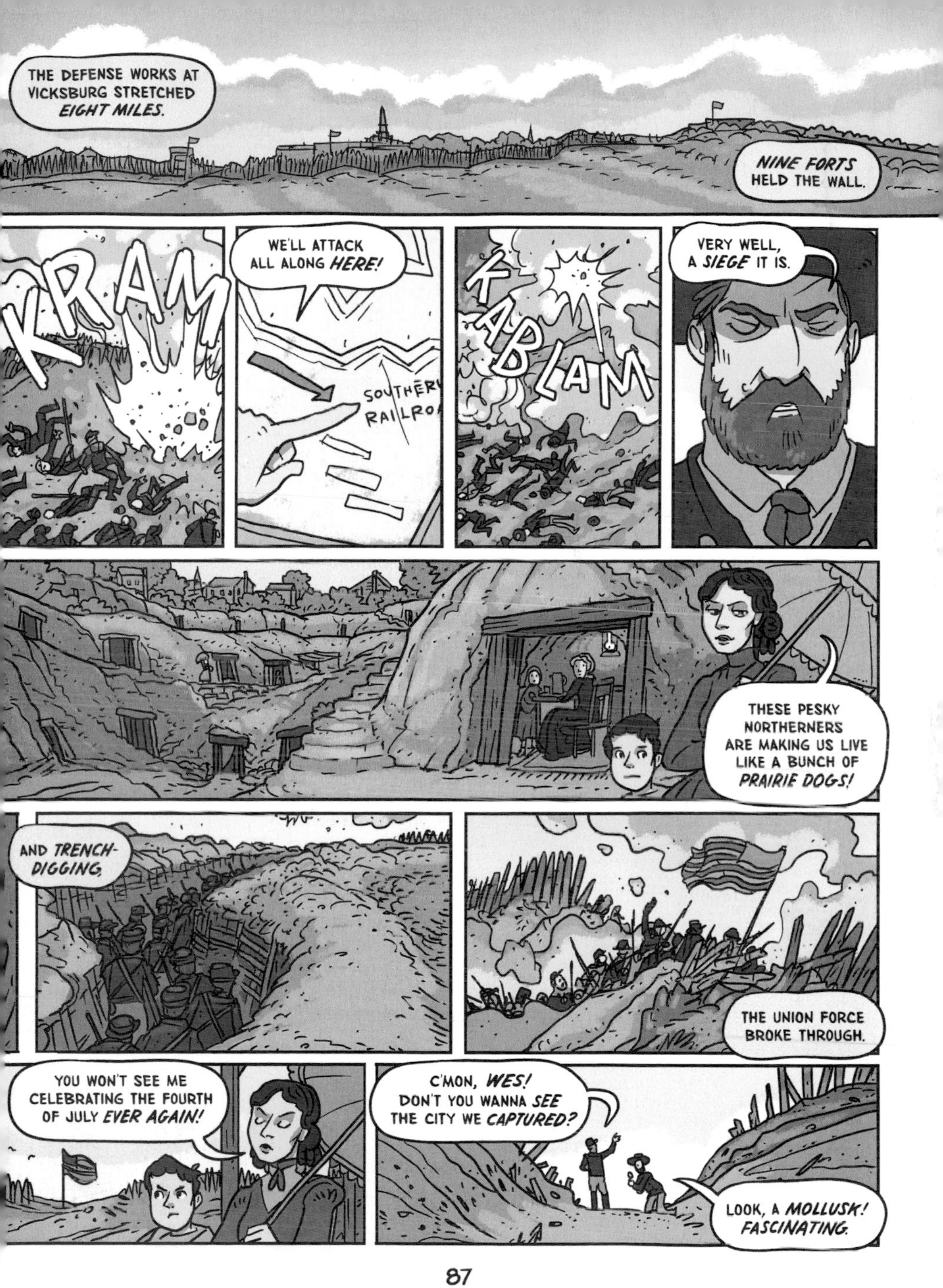
THE DEFENSE WORKS AT VICKSBURG STRETCHED *EIGHT MILES.*
NINE FORTS HELD THE WALL.
KRAM
WE'LL ATTACK ALL ALONG *HERE!*
SOUTHER
RAILRO
KABLAM
VERY WELL, A *SIEGE* IT IS.
THESE PESKY NORTHERNERS ARE MAKING US LIVE LIKE A BUNCH OF *PRAIRIE DOGS!*
AND *TRENCH-DIGGING.*
THE UNION FORCE BROKE THROUGH.
YOU WON'T SEE ME CELEBRATING THE FOURTH OF JULY *EVER AGAIN!*
C'MON, *WES!* DON'T YOU WANNA *SEE* THE CITY WE *CAPTURED?*
LOOK, A *MOLLUSK!* *FASCINATING.*

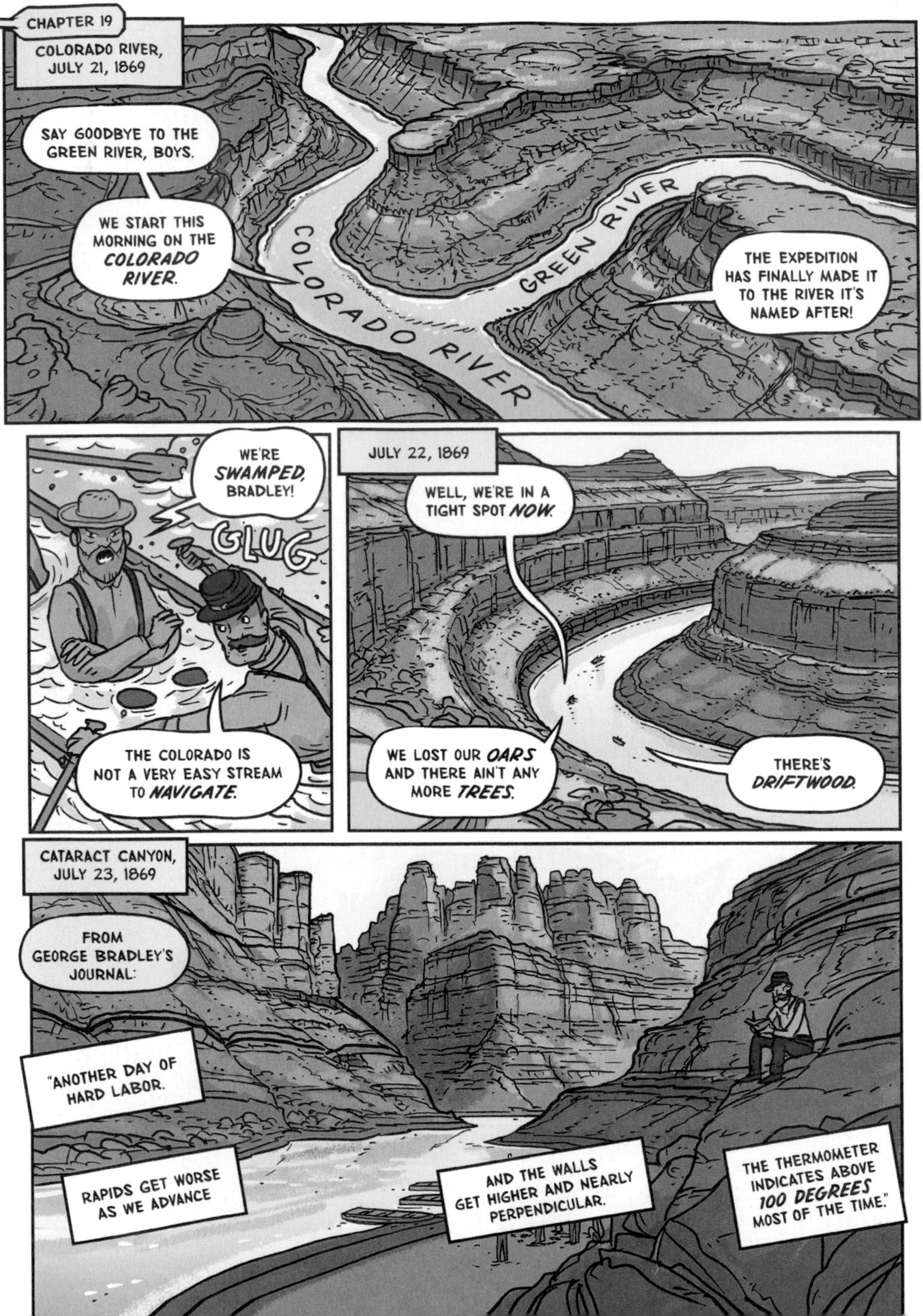
CHAPTER 19
COLORADO RIVER, JULY 21, 1869
SAY GOODBYE TO THE GREEN RIVER, BOYS.
WE START THIS MORNING ON THE *COLORADO RIVER*.
GREEN RIVER
COLORADO RIVER
THE EXPEDITION HAS FINALLY MADE IT TO THE RIVER IT'S NAMED AFTER!
WE'RE *SWAMPED*, BRADLEY!
GLUG
THE COLORADO IS NOT A VERY EASY STREAM TO *NAVIGATE*.
JULY 22, 1869
WELL, WE'RE IN A TIGHT SPOT *NOW*.
WE LOST OUR *OARS* AND THERE AIN'T ANY MORE *TREES*.
THERE'S *DRIFTWOOD*.
CATARACT CANYON, JULY 23, 1869
FROM GEORGE BRADLEY'S JOURNAL:
"ANOTHER DAY OF HARD LABOR.
RAPIDS GET WORSE AS WE ADVANCE
AND THE WALLS GET HIGHER AND NEARLY PERPENDICULAR.
THE THERMOMETER INDICATES ABOVE *100 DEGREES* MOST OF THE TIME."

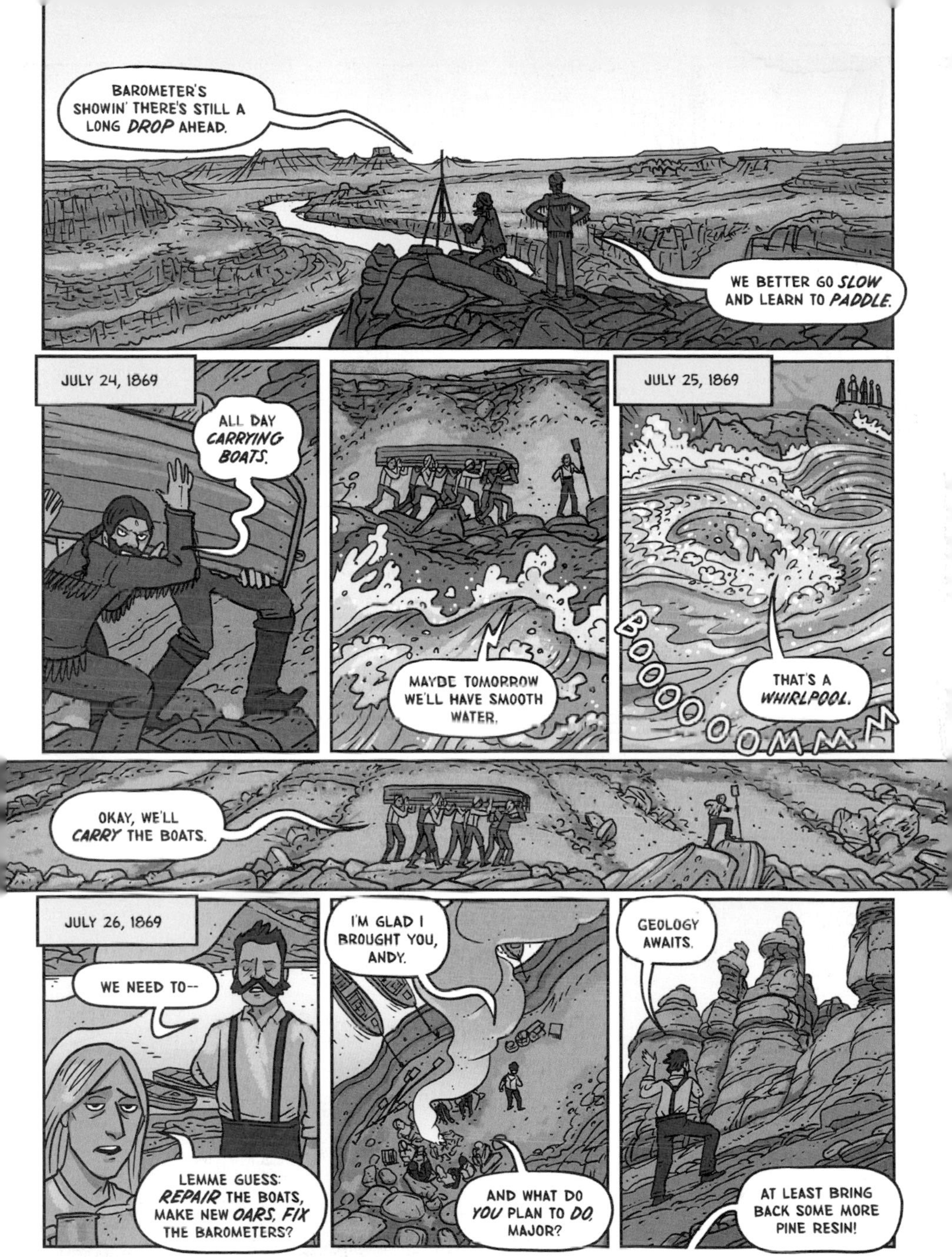
BAROMETER'S SHOWIN' THERE'S STILL A LONG *DROP* AHEAD.
WE BETTER GO *SLOW* AND LEARN TO *PADDLE.*
JULY 24, 1869
ALL DAY *CARRYING BOATS.*
MAYBE TOMORROW WE'LL HAVE SMOOTH WATER.
JULY 25, 1869
BOOOOOOMMM
THAT'S A *WHIRLPOOL.*
OKAY, WE'LL *CARRY* THE BOATS.
JULY 26, 1869
WE NEED TO--
LEMME GUESS: *REPAIR* THE BOATS, MAKE NEW *OARS, FIX* THE BAROMETERS?
I'M GLAD I BROUGHT YOU, ANDY.
AND WHAT DO *YOU* PLAN TO *DO,* MAJOR?
GEOLOGY AWAITS.
AT LEAST BRING BACK SOME MORE PINE RESIN!

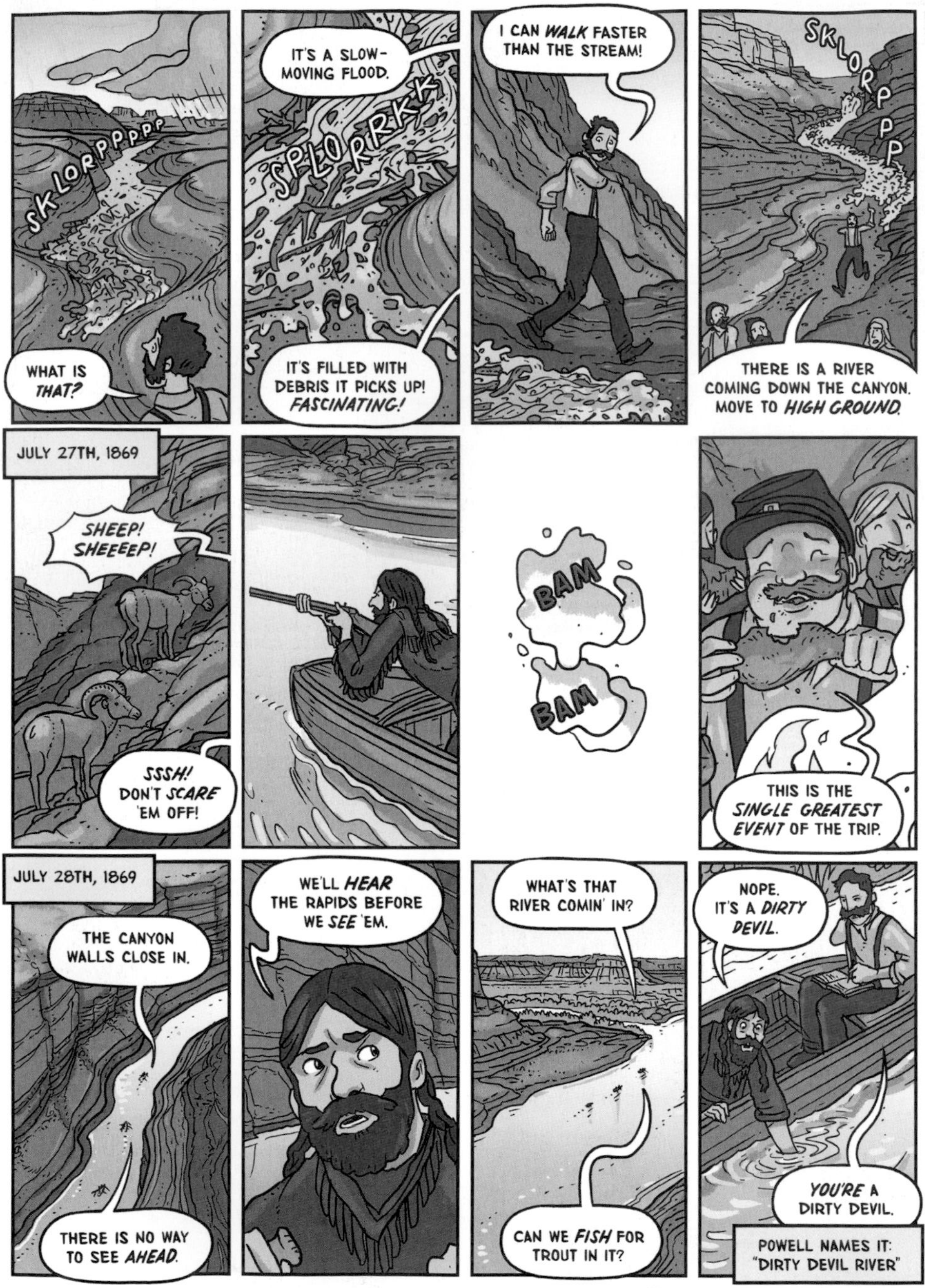
SKLORPPPPPP
WHAT IS THAT?
SPLORRKK
IT'S A SLOW-MOVING FLOOD.
IT'S FILLED WITH DEBRIS IT PICKS UP! FASCINATING!
I CAN WALK FASTER THAN THE STREAM!
SKLORPPP
THERE IS A RIVER COMING DOWN THE CANYON. MOVE TO HIGH GROUND.
JULY 27TH, 1869
SHEEP! SHEEEEP!
SSSH! DON'T SCARE 'EM OFF!
BAM
BAM
THIS IS THE SINGLE GREATEST EVENT OF THE TRIP.
JULY 28TH, 1869
THE CANYON WALLS CLOSE IN.
THERE IS NO WAY TO SEE AHEAD.
WE'LL HEAR THE RAPIDS BEFORE WE SEE 'EM.
WHAT'S THAT RIVER COMIN' IN?
CAN WE FISH FOR TROUT IN IT?
NOPE. IT'S A DIRTY DEVIL.
YOU'RE A DIRTY DEVIL.
POWELL NAMES IT: "DIRTY DEVIL RIVER"

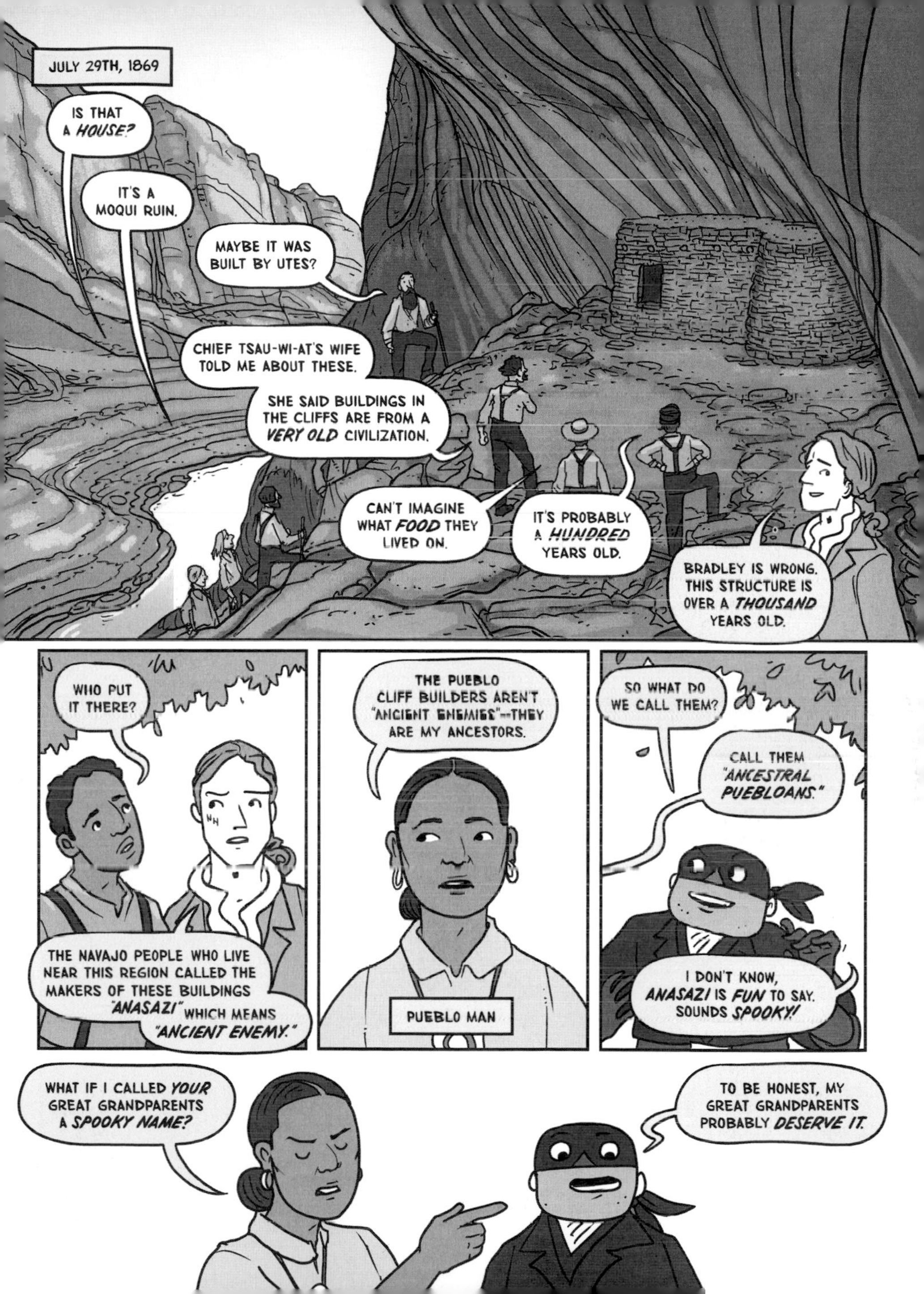

JULY 29TH, 1869
IS THAT A *HOUSE?*
IT'S A MOQUI RUIN.
MAYBE IT WAS BUILT BY UTES?
CHIEF TSAU-WI-AT'S WIFE TOLD ME ABOUT THESE.
SHE SAID BUILDINGS IN THE CLIFFS ARE FROM A *VERY OLD* CIVILIZATION.
CAN'T IMAGINE WHAT *FOOD* THEY LIVED ON.
IT'S PROBABLY A *HUNDRED* YEARS OLD.
BRADLEY IS WRONG. THIS STRUCTURE IS OVER A *THOUSAND* YEARS OLD.
WHO PUT IT THERE?
THE NAVAJO PEOPLE WHO LIVE NEAR THIS REGION CALLED THE MAKERS OF THESE BUILDINGS *"ANASAZI"* WHICH MEANS *"ANCIENT ENEMY."*
THE PUEBLO CLIFF BUILDERS AREN'T "ANCIENT ENEMIES"—THEY ARE MY ANCESTORS.
PUEBLO MAN
SO WHAT DO WE CALL THEM?
CALL THEM *"ANCESTRAL PUEBLOANS."*
I DON'T KNOW, *ANASAZI* IS *FUN* TO SAY. SOUNDS *SPOOKY!*
WHAT IF I CALLED *YOUR* GREAT GRANDPARENTS A *SPOOKY NAME?*
TO BE HONEST, MY GREAT GRANDPARENTS PROBABLY *DESERVE IT.*

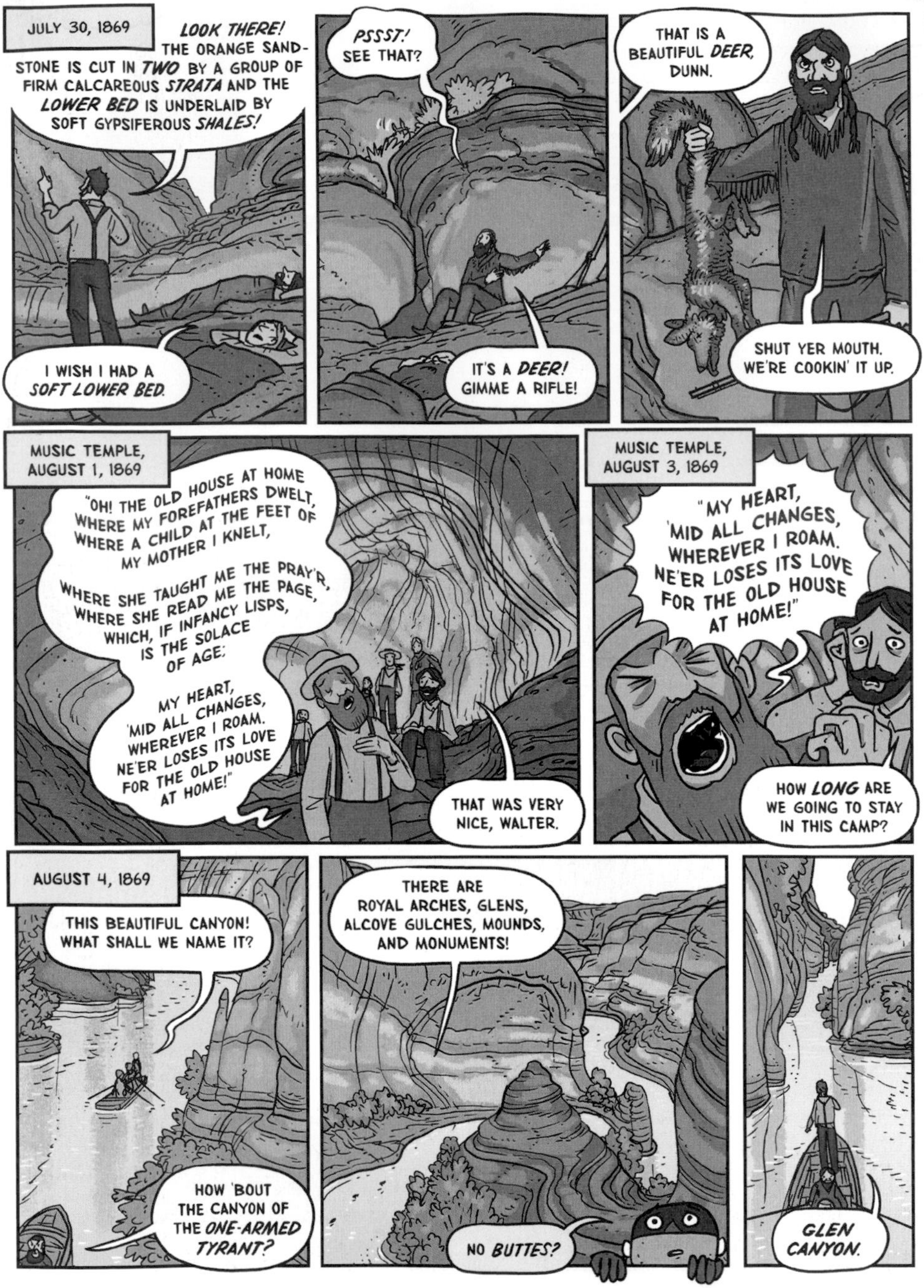
JULY 30, 1869
LOOK THERE! THE ORANGE SANDSTONE IS CUT IN TWO BY A GROUP OF FIRM CALCAREOUS STRATA AND THE LOWER BED IS UNDERLAID BY SOFT GYPSIFEROUS SHALES!
I WISH I HAD A SOFT LOWER BED.
PSSST! SEE THAT?
IT'S A DEER! GIMME A RIFLE!
THAT IS A BEAUTIFUL DEER, DUNN.
SHUT YER MOUTH. WE'RE COOKIN' IT UP.
MUSIC TEMPLE, AUGUST 1, 1869
"OH! THE OLD HOUSE AT HOME WHERE MY FOREFATHERS DWELT, WHERE A CHILD AT THE FEET OF MY MOTHER I KNELT,
WHERE SHE TAUGHT ME THE PRAY'R, WHERE SHE READ ME THE PAGE, WHICH, IF INFANCY LISPS, IS THE SOLACE OF AGE;
MY HEART, 'MID ALL CHANGES, WHEREVER I ROAM. NE'ER LOSES ITS LOVE FOR THE OLD HOUSE AT HOME!"
THAT WAS VERY NICE, WALTER.
MUSIC TEMPLE, AUGUST 3, 1869
"MY HEART, 'MID ALL CHANGES, WHEREVER I ROAM. NE'ER LOSES ITS LOVE FOR THE OLD HOUSE AT HOME!"
HOW LONG ARE WE GOING TO STAY IN THIS CAMP?
AUGUST 4, 1869
THIS BEAUTIFUL CANYON! WHAT SHALL WE NAME IT?
HOW 'BOUT THE CANYON OF THE ONE-ARMED TYRANT?
THERE ARE ROYAL ARCHES, GLENS, ALCOVE GULCHES, MOUNDS, AND MONUMENTS!
NO BUTTES?
GLEN CANYON.

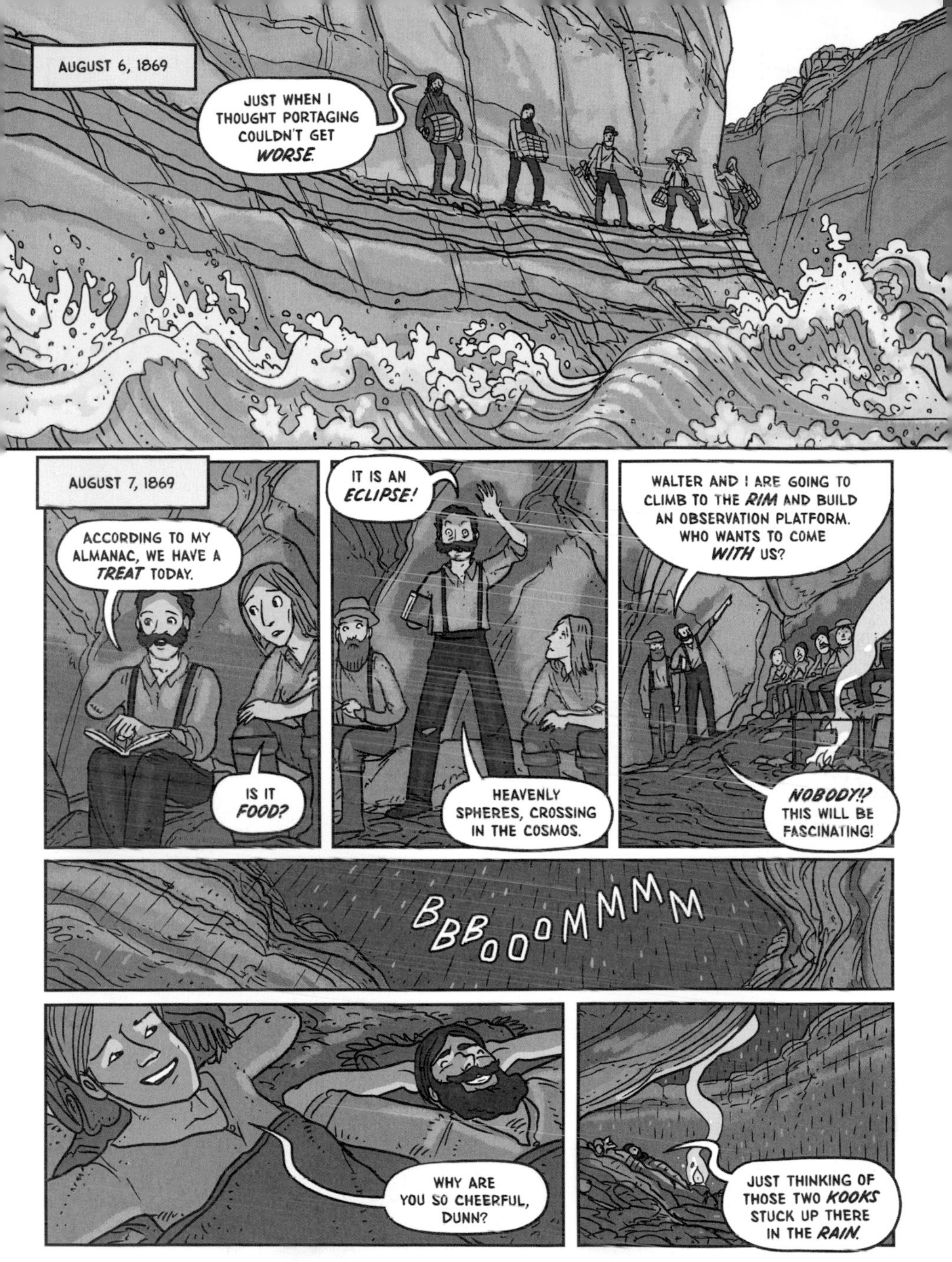
AUGUST 6, 1869
JUST WHEN I THOUGHT PORTAGING COULDN'T GET WORSE.
AUGUST 7, 1869
ACCORDING TO MY ALMANAC, WE HAVE A TREAT TODAY.
IS IT FOOD?
IT IS AN ECLIPSE!
HEAVENLY SPHERES, CROSSING IN THE COSMOS.
WALTER AND I ARE GOING TO CLIMB TO THE RIM AND BUILD AN OBSERVATION PLATFORM. WHO WANTS TO COME WITH US?
NOBODY!? THIS WILL BE FASCINATING!
BBBOOOMMMMM
WHY ARE YOU SO CHEERFUL, DUNN?
JUST THINKING OF THOSE TWO KOOKS STUCK UP THERE IN THE RAIN.

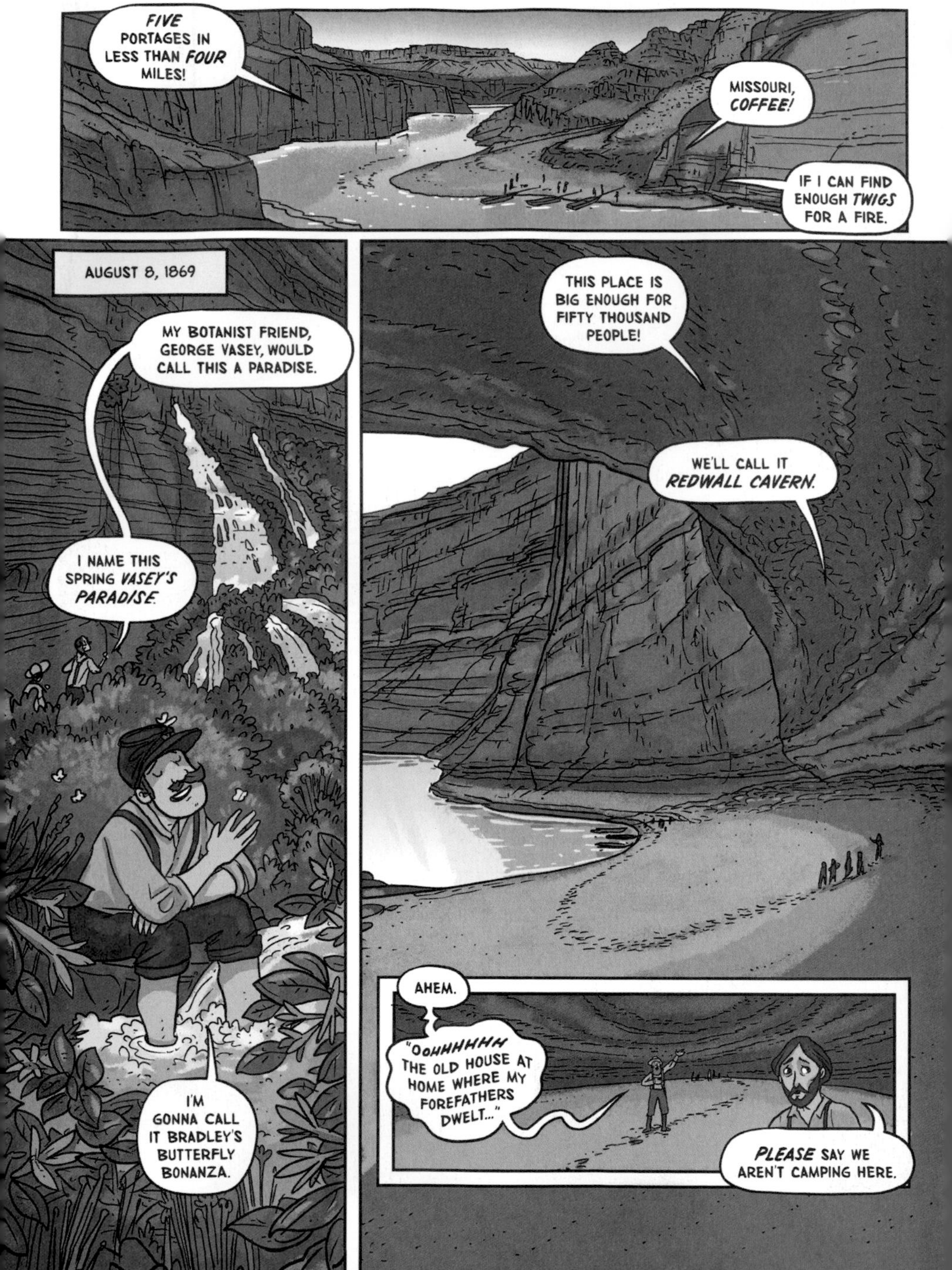

FIVE PORTAGES IN LESS THAN FOUR MILES!
MISSOURI, COFFEE!
IF I CAN FIND ENOUGH TWIGS FOR A FIRE.
AUGUST 8, 1869
MY BOTANIST FRIEND, GEORGE VASEY, WOULD CALL THIS A PARADISE.
I NAME THIS SPRING VASEY'S PARADISE.
I'M GONNA CALL IT BRADLEY'S BUTTERFLY BONANZA.
THIS PLACE IS BIG ENOUGH FOR FIFTY THOUSAND PEOPLE!
WE'LL CALL IT REDWALL CAVERN.
AHEM.
"OOHHHHHH THE OLD HOUSE AT HOME WHERE MY FOREFATHERS DWELT..."
PLEASE SAY WE AREN'T CAMPING HERE.

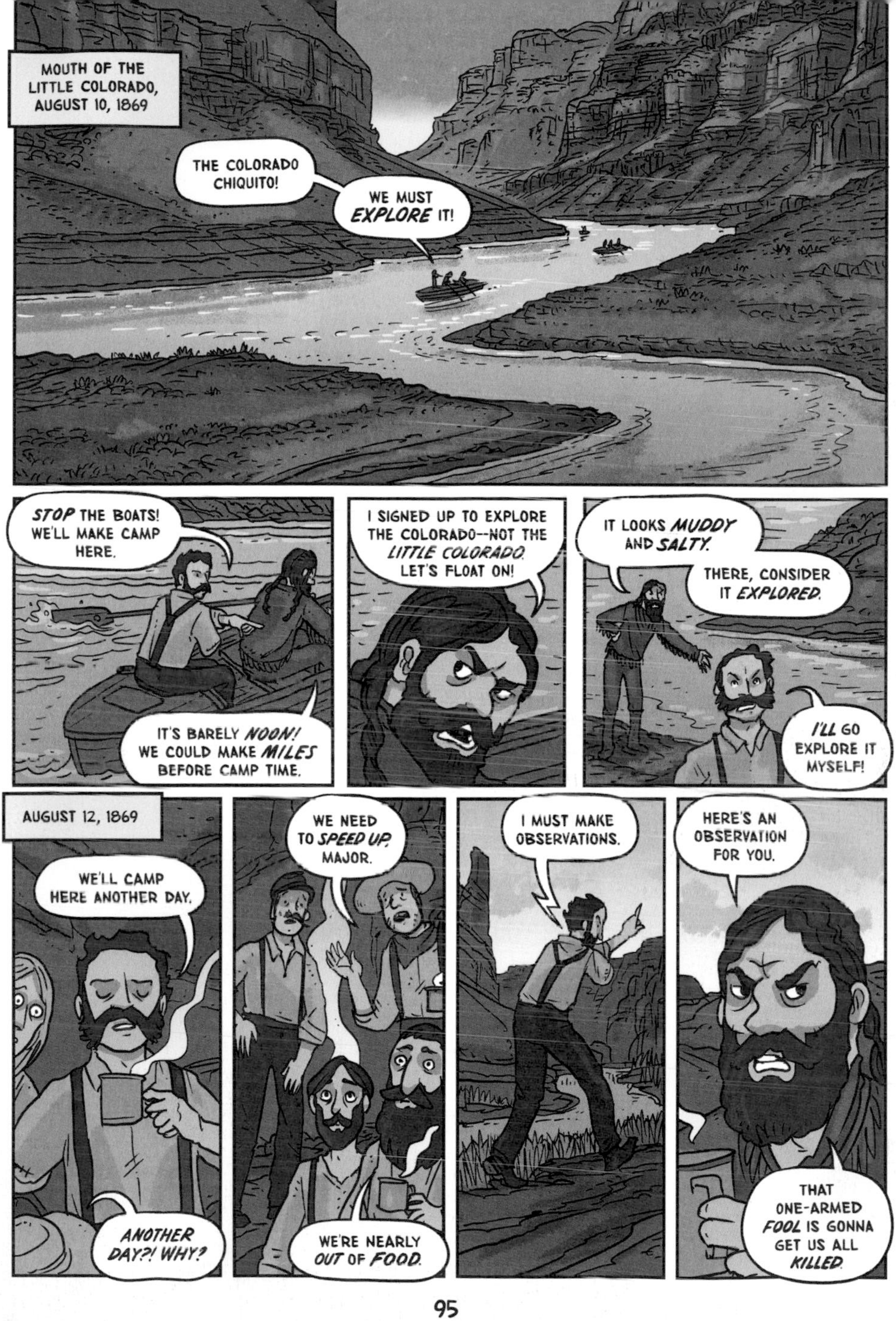
MOUTH OF THE LITTLE COLORADO, AUGUST 10, 1869
THE COLORADO CHIQUITO!
WE MUST EXPLORE IT!
STOP THE BOATS! WE'LL MAKE CAMP HERE.
IT'S BARELY NOON! WE COULD MAKE MILES BEFORE CAMP TIME.
I SIGNED UP TO EXPLORE THE COLORADO--NOT THE LITTLE COLORADO. LET'S FLOAT ON!
IT LOOKS MUDDY AND SALTY.
THERE, CONSIDER IT EXPLORED.
I'LL GO EXPLORE IT MYSELF!
AUGUST 12, 1869
WE'LL CAMP HERE ANOTHER DAY.
ANOTHER DAY?! WHY?
WE NEED TO SPEED UP, MAJOR.
WE'RE NEARLY OUT OF FOOD.
I MUST MAKE OBSERVATIONS.
HERE'S AN OBSERVATION FOR YOU.
THAT ONE-ARMED FOOL IS GONNA GET US ALL KILLED.

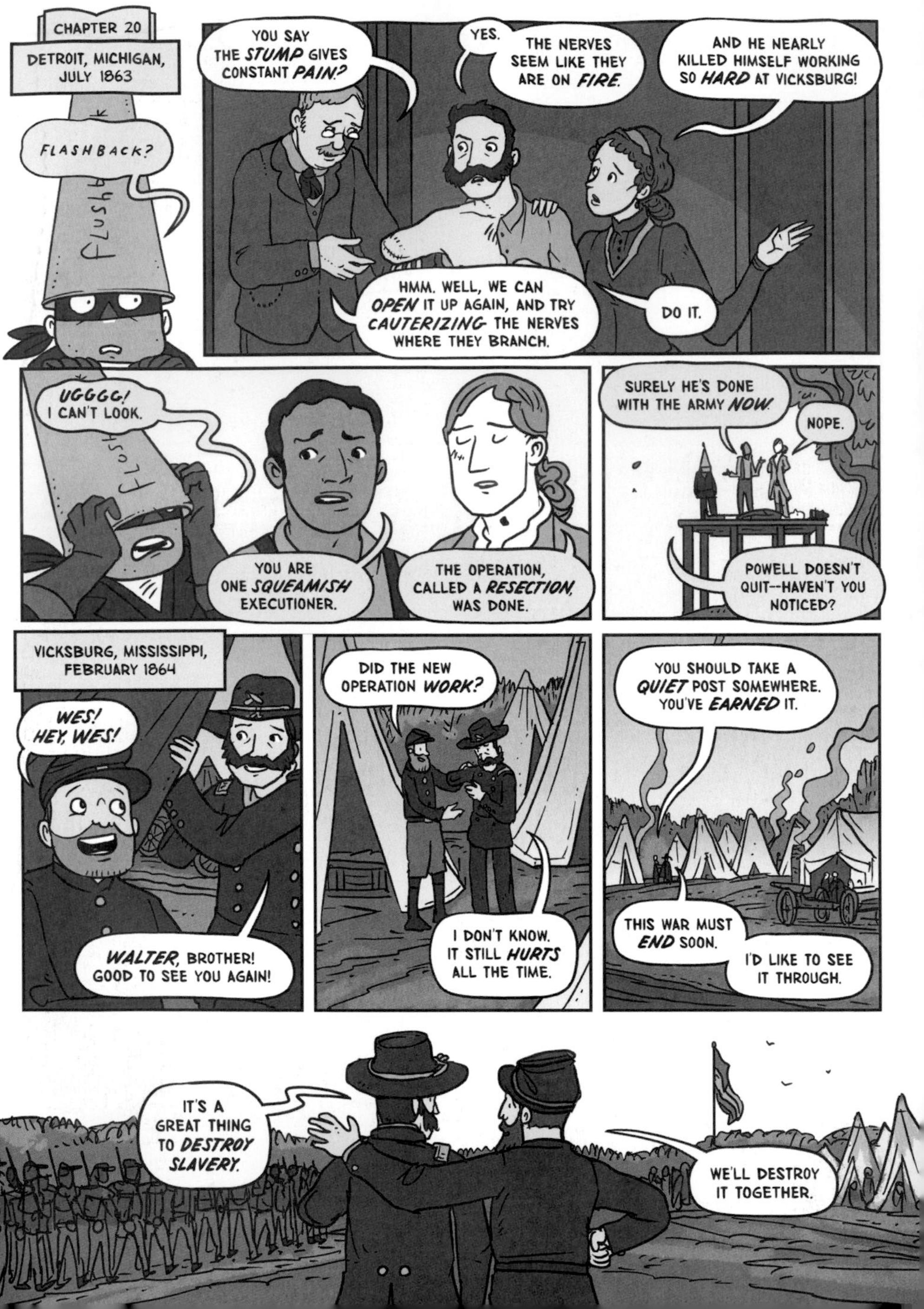
CHAPTER 20
DETROIT, MICHIGAN, JULY 1863
FLASHBACK?
Flush
YOU SAY THE STUMP GIVES CONSTANT PAIN?
YES.
THE NERVES SEEM LIKE THEY ARE ON FIRE.
AND HE NEARLY KILLED HIMSELF WORKING SO HARD AT VICKSBURG!
HMM. WELL, WE CAN OPEN IT UP AGAIN, AND TRY CAUTERIZING THE NERVES WHERE THEY BRANCH.
DO IT.
UGGGG! I CAN'T LOOK.
Flush
YOU ARE ONE SQUEAMISH EXECUTIONER.
THE OPERATION, CALLED A RESECTION, WAS DONE.
SURELY HE'S DONE WITH THE ARMY NOW.
NOPE.
POWELL DOESN'T QUIT--HAVEN'T YOU NOTICED?
VICKSBURG, MISSISSIPPI, FEBRUARY 1864
WES! HEY, WES!
WALTER, BROTHER! GOOD TO SEE YOU AGAIN!
DID THE NEW OPERATION WORK?
I DON'T KNOW. IT STILL HURTS ALL THE TIME.
YOU SHOULD TAKE A QUIET POST SOMEWHERE. YOU'VE EARNED IT.
THIS WAR MUST END SOON.
I'D LIKE TO SEE IT THROUGH.
IT'S A GREAT THING TO DESTROY SLAVERY.
WE'LL DESTROY IT TOGETHER.

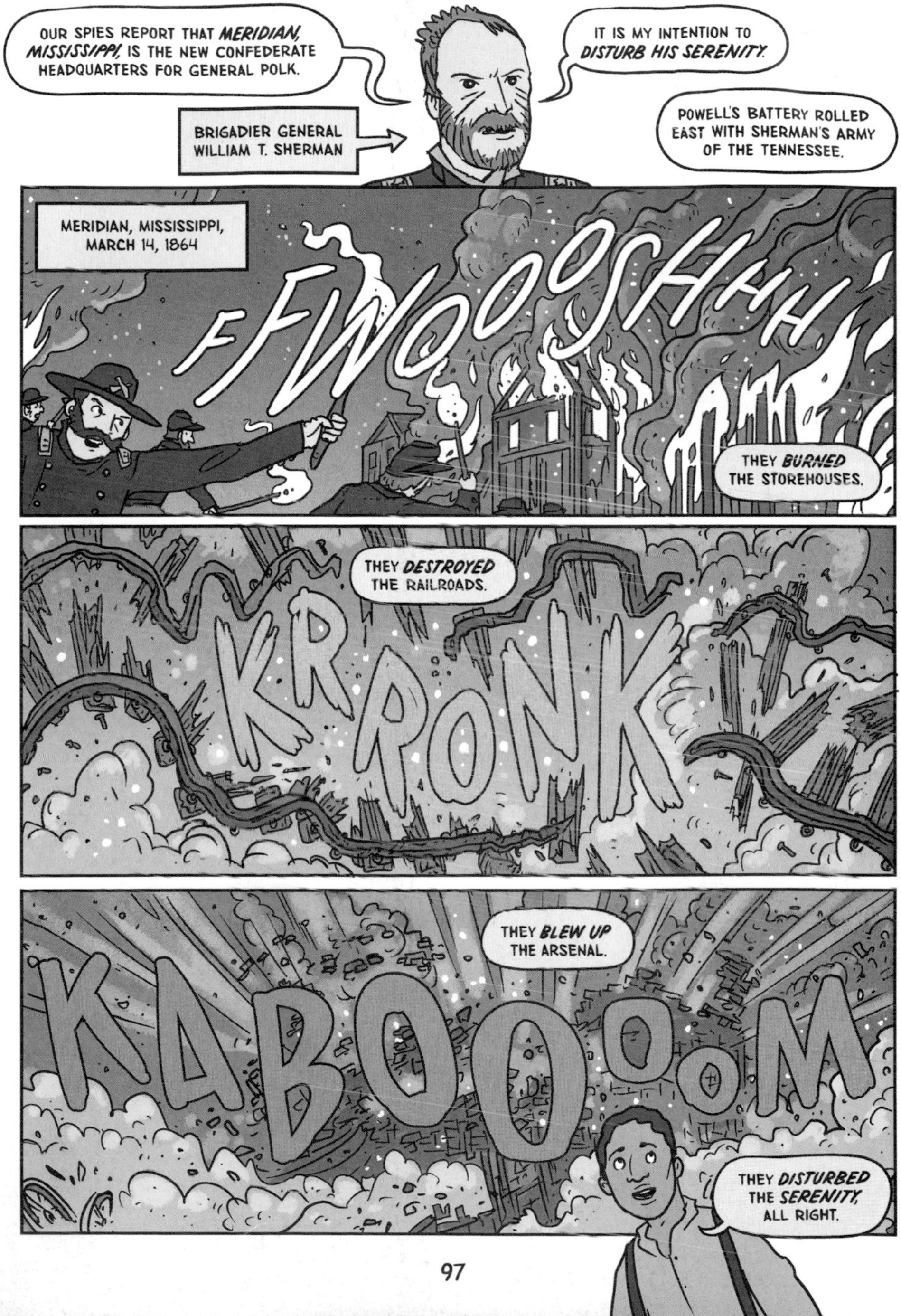
OUR SPIES REPORT THAT *MERIDIAN, MISSISSIPPI,* IS THE NEW CONFEDERATE HEADQUARTERS FOR GENERAL POLK.
BRIGADIER GENERAL WILLIAM T. SHERMAN
IT IS MY INTENTION TO *DISTURB HIS SERENITY.*
POWELL'S BATTERY ROLLED EAST WITH SHERMAN'S ARMY OF THE TENNESSEE.
MERIDIAN, MISSISSIPPI, MARCH 14, 1864
FFWOOOOSHHH
THEY *BURNED* THE STOREHOUSES.
THEY *DESTROYED* THE RAILROADS.
KRRONK
THEY *BLEW UP* THE ARSENAL.
KABOOOOM
THEY *DISTURBED* THE *SERENITY,* ALL RIGHT.

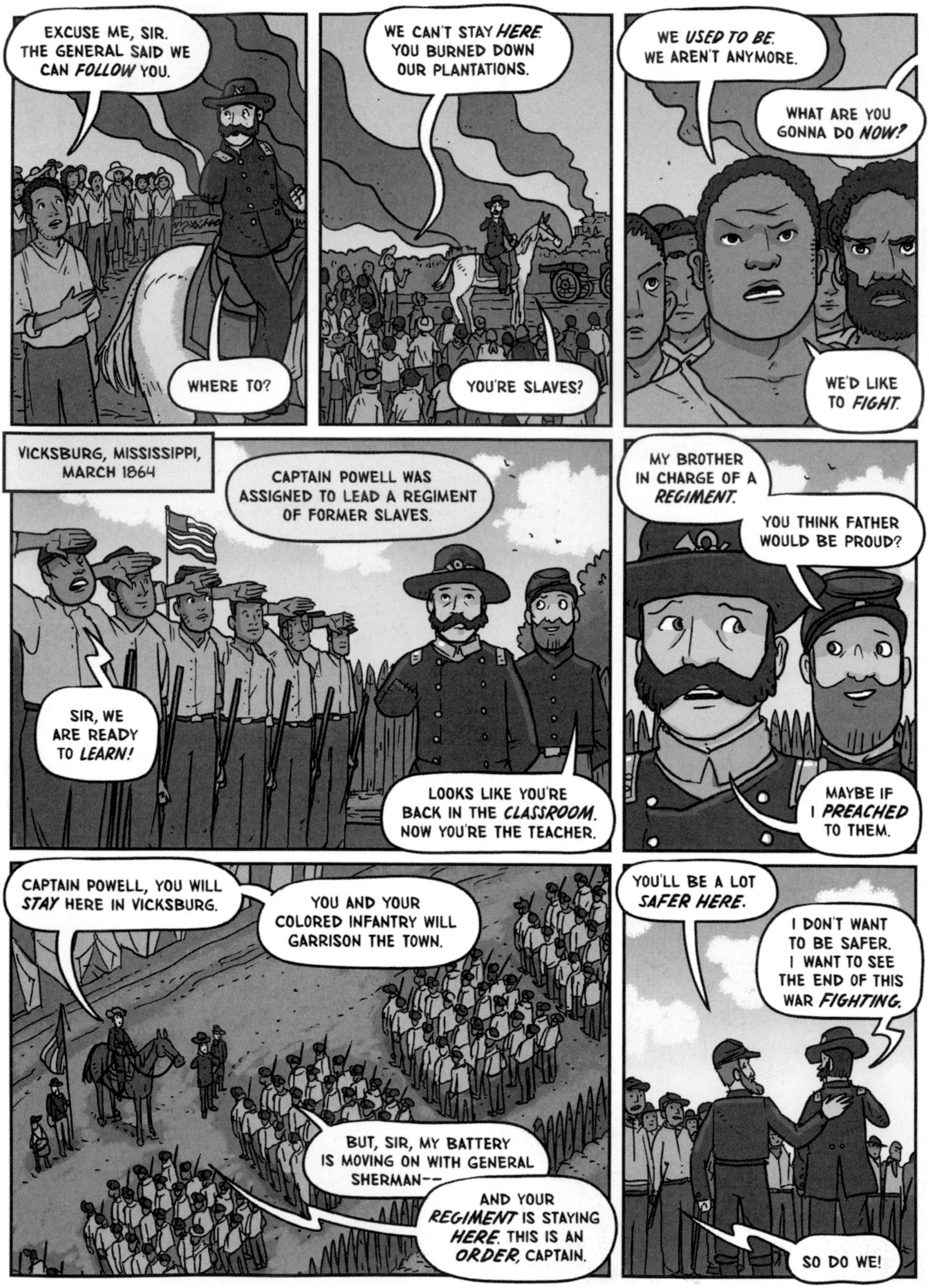
EXCUSE ME, SIR. THE GENERAL SAID WE CAN FOLLOW YOU.
WHERE TO?
WE CAN'T STAY HERE. YOU BURNED DOWN OUR PLANTATIONS.
YOU'RE SLAVES?
WE USED TO BE. WE AREN'T ANYMORE.
WHAT ARE YOU GONNA DO NOW?
WE'D LIKE TO FIGHT.
VICKSBURG, MISSISSIPPI, MARCH 1864
CAPTAIN POWELL WAS ASSIGNED TO LEAD A REGIMENT OF FORMER SLAVES.
SIR, WE ARE READY TO LEARN!
LOOKS LIKE YOU'RE BACK IN THE CLASSROOM. NOW YOU'RE THE TEACHER.
MY BROTHER IN CHARGE OF A REGIMENT.
YOU THINK FATHER WOULD BE PROUD?
MAYBE IF I PREACHED TO THEM.
CAPTAIN POWELL, YOU WILL STAY HERE IN VICKSBURG.
YOU AND YOUR COLORED INFANTRY WILL GARRISON THE TOWN.
BUT, SIR, MY BATTERY IS MOVING ON WITH GENERAL SHERMAN--
AND YOUR REGIMENT IS STAYING HERE. THIS IS AN ORDER, CAPTAIN.
YOU'LL BE A LOT SAFER HERE.
I DON'T WANT TO BE SAFER. I WANT TO SEE THE END OF THIS WAR FIGHTING.
SO DO WE!

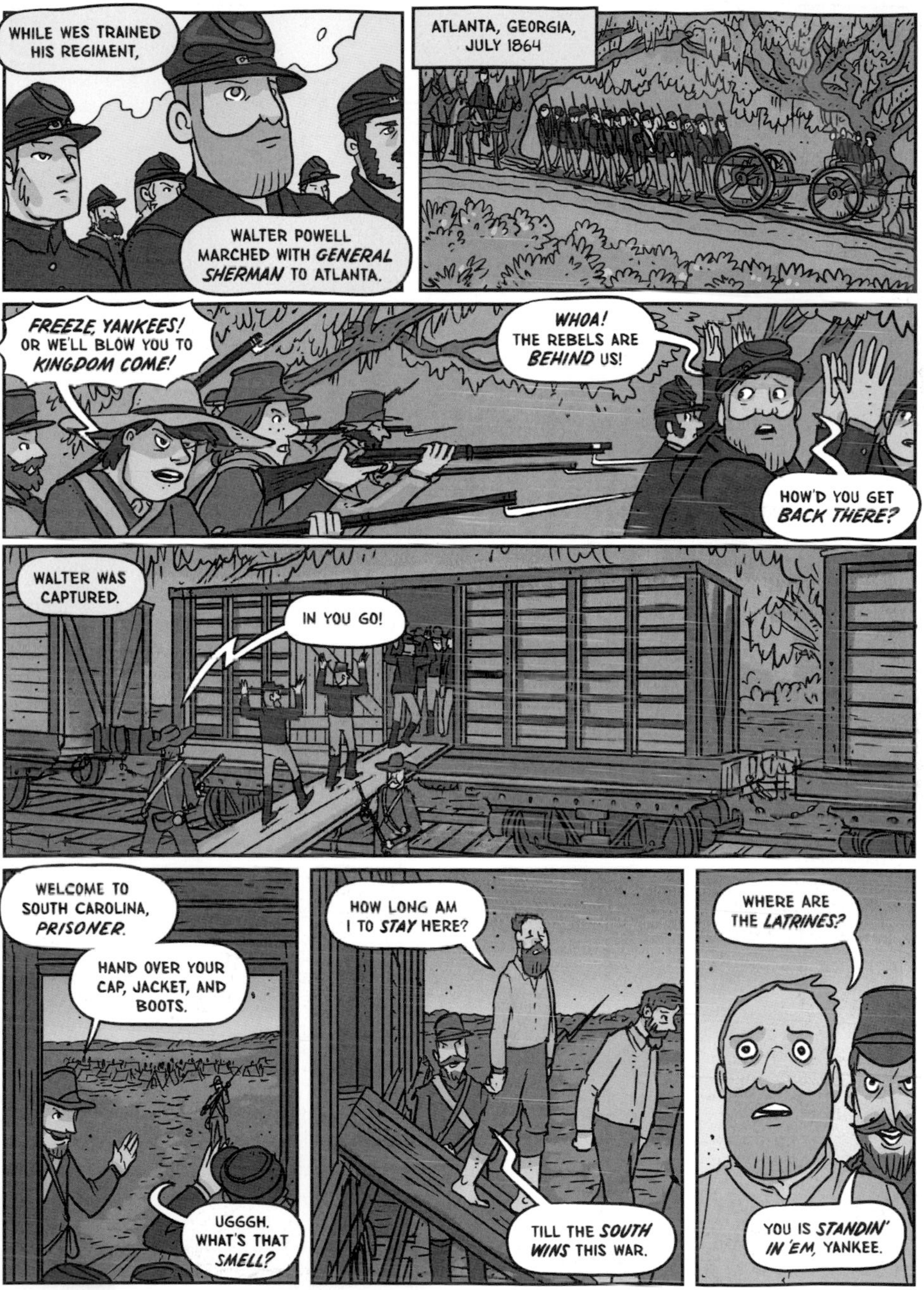
WHILE WES TRAINED HIS REGIMENT,
WALTER POWELL MARCHED WITH GENERAL SHERMAN TO ATLANTA.
ATLANTA, GEORGIA, JULY 1864
FREEZE, YANKEES! OR WE'LL BLOW YOU TO KINGDOM COME!
WHOA! THE REBELS ARE BEHIND US!
HOW'D YOU GET BACK THERE?
WALTER WAS CAPTURED.
IN YOU GO!
WELCOME TO SOUTH CAROLINA, PRISONER.
HAND OVER YOUR CAP, JACKET, AND BOOTS.
UGGGH. WHAT'S THAT SMELL?
HOW LONG AM I TO STAY HERE?
TILL THE SOUTH WINS THIS WAR.
WHERE ARE THE LATRINES?
YOU IS STANDIN' IN 'EM, YANKEE.

CHAPTER 21

AUGUST 13, 1869

FROM POWELL'S JOURNAL:

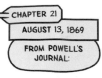

"WE ARE NOW READY TO START ON OUR WAY DOWN THE *GREAT UNKNOWN*.

OUR BOATS, TIED TO A COMMON STAKE, ARE *CHAFING* EACH OTHER, AS THEY ARE *TOSSED* BY THE *FRETFUL* RIVER.

THEY RIDE HIGH AND BUOYANT, FOR THEIR LOADS ARE *LIGHTER* THAN WE COULD DESIRE.

WE HAVE BUT A *MONTH'S* RATIONS REMAINING.

THE FLOUR HAS BEEN *RESIFTED* THROUGH THE MOSQUITO NET SIEVE;

THE SPOILED BACON HAS BEEN *DRIED*, AND THE WORST OF IT *BOILED*;

THE *FEW POUNDS* OF DRIED APPLES HAVE BEEN SPREAD IN THE SUN, AND RESHRUNKEN TO THEIR NORMAL BULK;

THE SUGAR HAS ALL *MELTED*, AND *GONE* ON ITS WAY DOWN THE RIVER;

BUT WE HAVE A LARGE SACK OF *COFFEE*.

THE LIGHTING OF THE BOATS HAS THIS ADVANTAGE:

THEY WILL *RIDE* THE WAVES BETTER,

AND WE SHALL HAVE BUT LITTLE TO *CARRY* WHEN WE MAKE A PORTAGE.

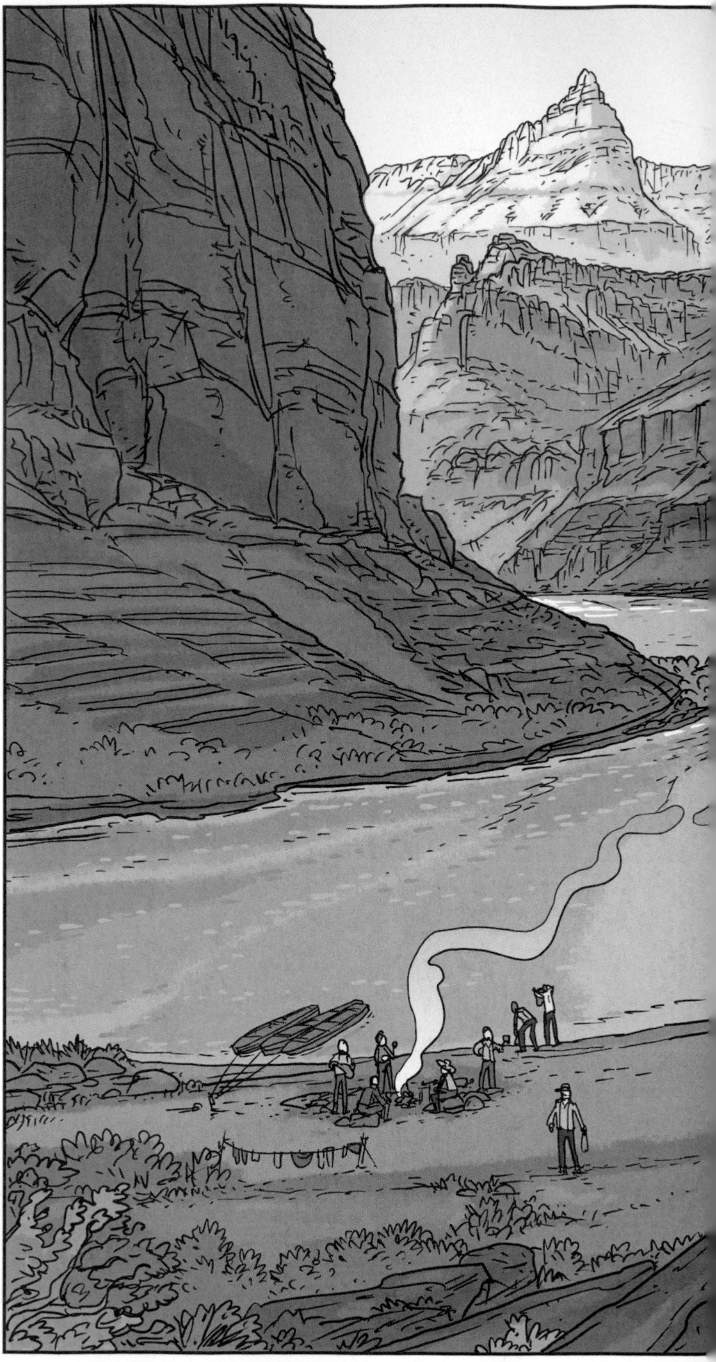

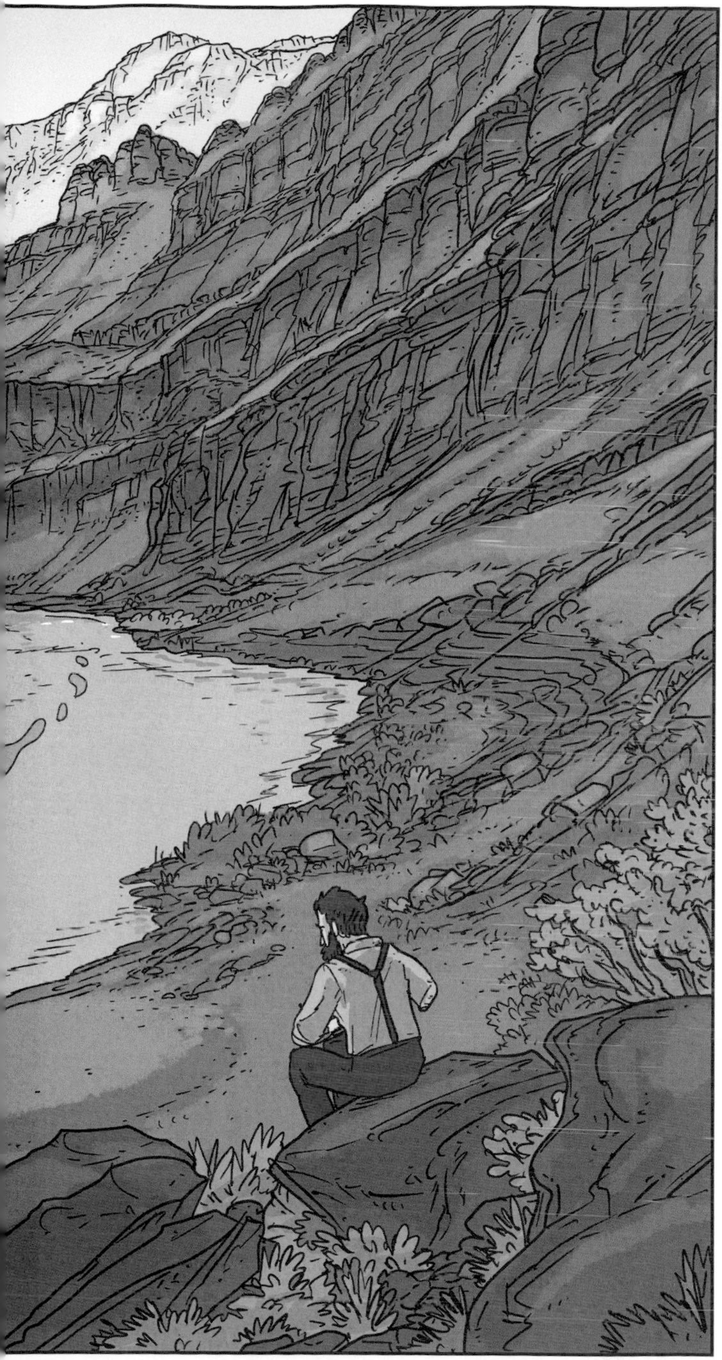

WE ARE THREE
QUARTERS OF A
MILE IN THE *DEPTHS*
OF THE EARTH,

AND THE GREAT
RIVER *SHRINKS* INTO
INSIGNIFICANCE,

AS IT DASHES ITS
ANGRY WAVES AGAINST
THE WALLS AND CLIFFS,
THAT RISE TO THE
WORLD ABOVE;

THEY ARE BUT
PUNY RIPPLES,

AND WE BUT
PYGMIES, RUNNING UP
AND DOWN THE SANDS,
OR *LOST* AMONG THE
BOULDERS."

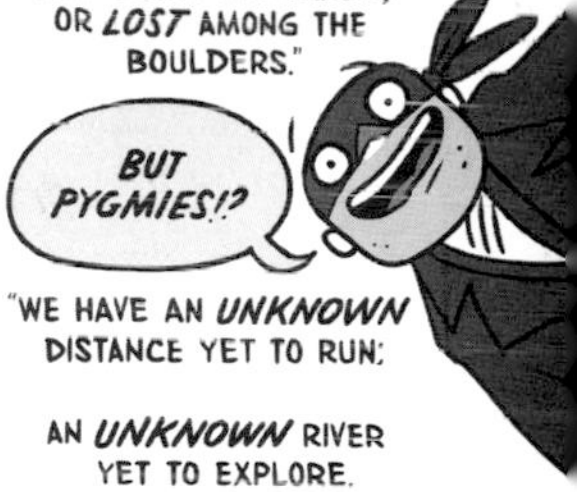
BUT PYGMIES!?

"WE HAVE AN *UNKNOWN*
DISTANCE YET TO RUN;

AN *UNKNOWN* RIVER
YET TO EXPLORE.

WHAT *FALLS*
THERE ARE,

WE KNOW NOT;

WHAT *ROCKS*
BESET THE CHANNEL,

WE KNOW NOT;

WHAT *WALLS* RISE
OVER THE RIVER,

WE KNOW NOT.

AH, WELL!

WE MAY
CONJECTURE
MANY THINGS.

THE MEN TALK AS
CHEERFULLY AS EVER;

JESTS ARE
BANDIED ABOUT FREELY
THIS MORNING;

BUT TO ME THE
CHEER IS *SOMBER*
AND THE JESTS
ARE *GHASTLY*."

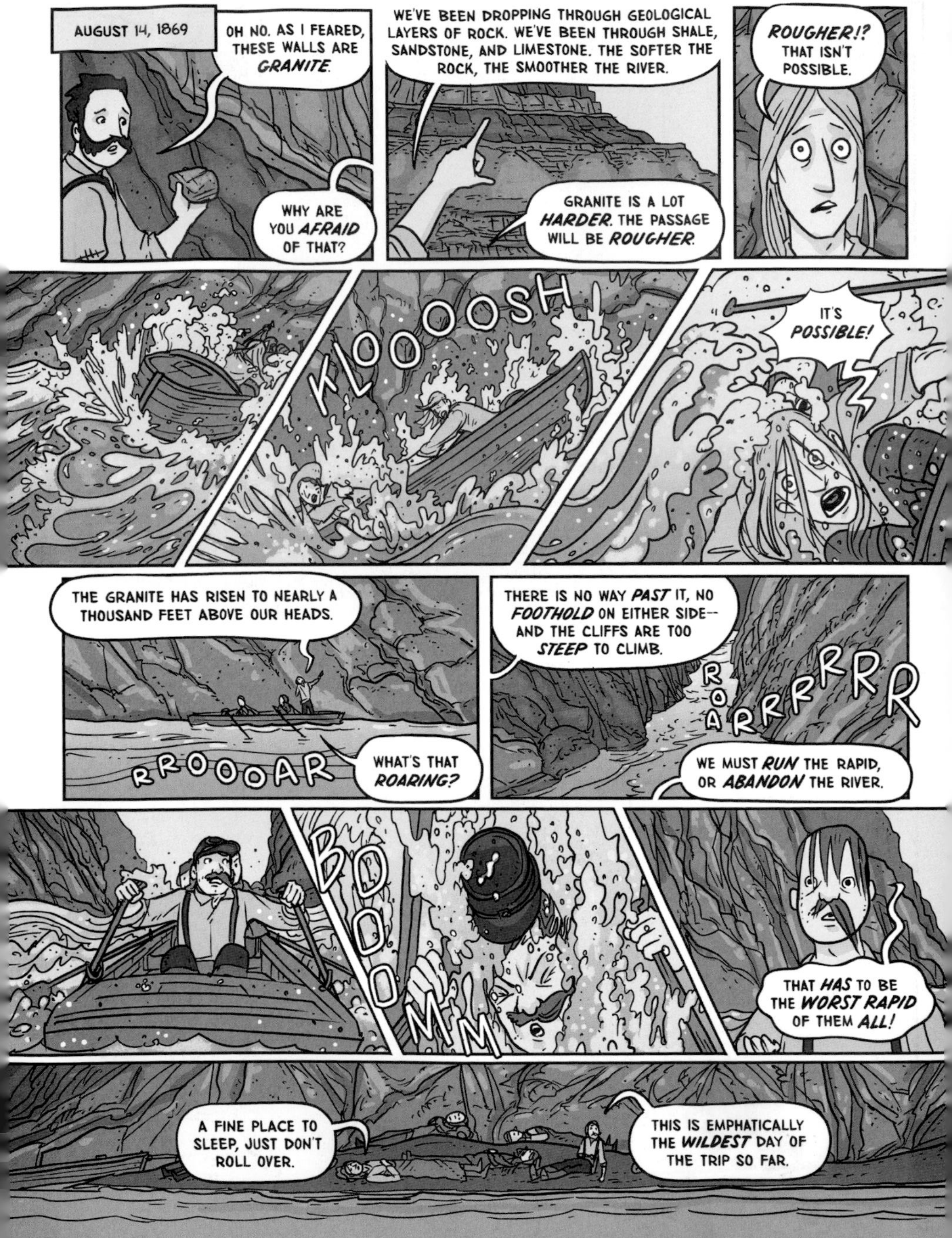
AUGUST 14, 1869
OH NO. AS I FEARED, THESE WALLS ARE *GRANITE*.
WHY ARE YOU *AFRAID* OF THAT?
WE'VE BEEN DROPPING THROUGH GEOLOGICAL LAYERS OF ROCK. WE'VE BEEN THROUGH SHALE, SANDSTONE, AND LIMESTONE. THE SOFTER THE ROCK, THE SMOOTHER THE RIVER.
GRANITE IS A LOT *HARDER*. THE PASSAGE WILL BE *ROUGHER*.
ROUGHER!? THAT ISN'T POSSIBLE.
KLOOOOSH!
IT'S *POSSIBLE!*
THE GRANITE HAS RISEN TO NEARLY A THOUSAND FEET ABOVE OUR HEADS.
RROOOOAR
WHAT'S THAT *ROARING?*
THERE IS NO WAY *PAST* IT, NO *FOOTHOLD* ON EITHER SIDE-- AND THE CLIFFS ARE TOO *STEEP* TO CLIMB.
ROARRRRRRR
WE MUST *RUN* THE RAPID, OR *ABANDON* THE RIVER.
BOOOMM
THAT *HAS* TO BE THE *WORST RAPID* OF THEM *ALL!*
A FINE PLACE TO SLEEP, JUST DON'T ROLL OVER.
THIS IS EMPHATICALLY THE *WILDEST* DAY OF THE TRIP SO FAR.

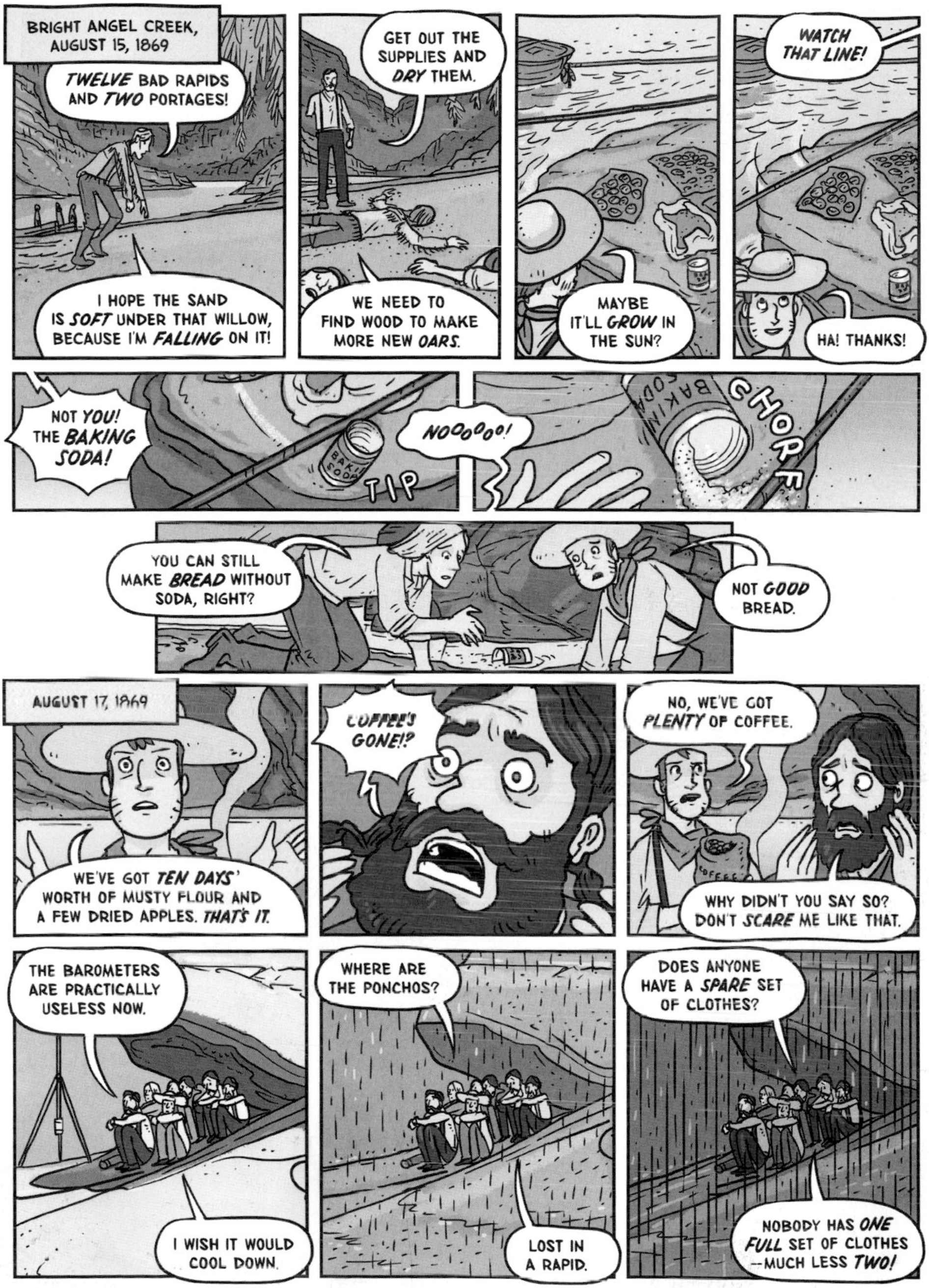
BRIGHT ANGEL CREEK, AUGUST 15, 1869
TWELVE BAD RAPIDS AND TWO PORTAGES!
I HOPE THE SAND IS SOFT UNDER THAT WILLOW, BECAUSE I'M FALLING ON IT!
GET OUT THE SUPPLIES AND DRY THEM.
WE NEED TO FIND WOOD TO MAKE MORE NEW OARS.
MAYBE IT'LL GROW IN THE SUN?
WATCH THAT LINE!
HA! THANKS!
NOT YOU! THE BAKING SODA!
NOOOOOO!
TIP
CHOMP
YOU CAN STILL MAKE BREAD WITHOUT SODA, RIGHT?
NOT GOOD BREAD.
AUGUST 17, 1869
WE'VE GOT TEN DAYS' WORTH OF MUSTY FLOUR AND A FEW DRIED APPLES. THAT'S IT.
COFFEE'S GONE!?
NO, WE'VE GOT PLENTY OF COFFEE.
WHY DIDN'T YOU SAY SO? DON'T SCARE ME LIKE THAT.
THE BAROMETERS ARE PRACTICALLY USELESS NOW.
I WISH IT WOULD COOL DOWN.
WHERE ARE THE PONCHOS?
LOST IN A RAPID.
DOES ANYONE HAVE A SPARE SET OF CLOTHES?
NOBODY HAS ONE FULL SET OF CLOTHES --MUCH LESS TWO!

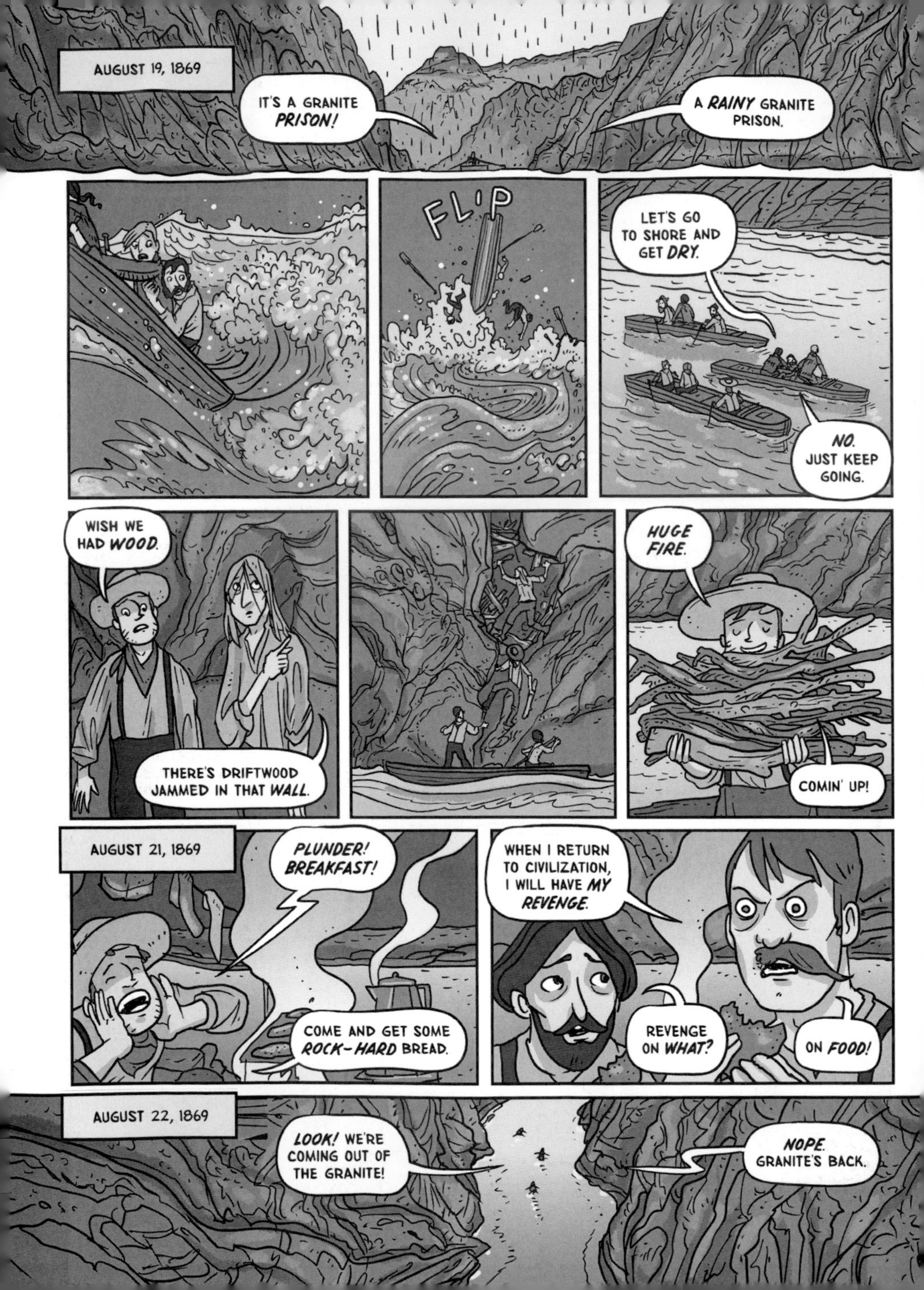
AUGUST 19, 1869
IT'S A GRANITE PRISON!
A RAINY GRANITE PRISON.
FLIP
LET'S GO TO SHORE AND GET DRY.
NO. JUST KEEP GOING.
WISH WE HAD WOOD.
THERE'S DRIFTWOOD JAMMED IN THAT WALL.
HUGE FIRE.
COMIN' UP!
AUGUST 21, 1869
PLUNDER! BREAKFAST!
COME AND GET SOME ROCK-HARD BREAD.
WHEN I RETURN TO CIVILIZATION, I WILL HAVE MY REVENGE.
REVENGE ON WHAT?
ON FOOD!
AUGUST 22, 1869
LOOK! WE'RE COMING OUT OF THE GRANITE!
NOPE. GRANITE'S BACK.

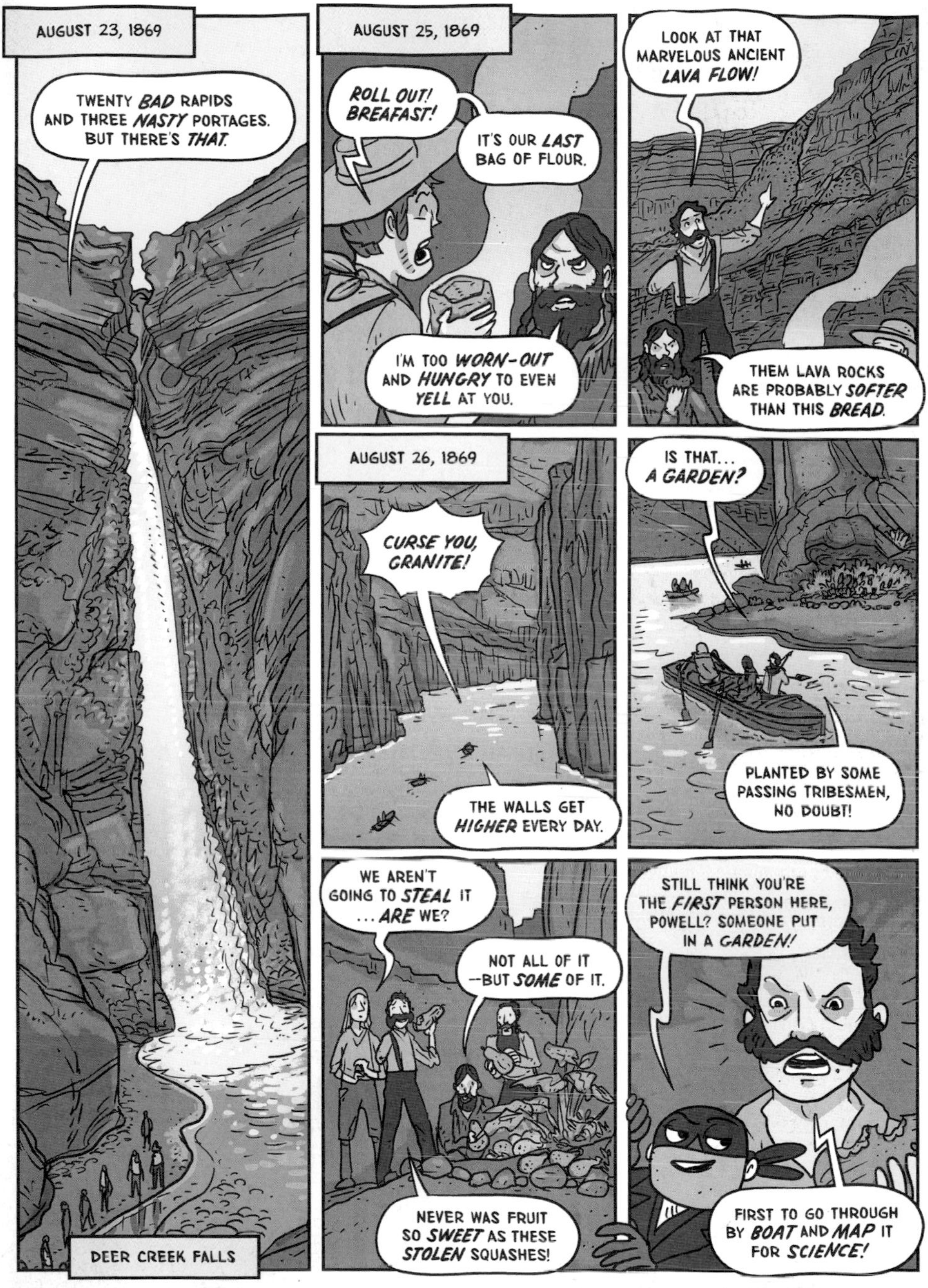
AUGUST 23, 1869
TWENTY BAD RAPIDS AND THREE NASTY PORTAGES. BUT THERE'S THAT.
DEER CREEK FALLS
AUGUST 25, 1869
ROLL OUT! BREAFAST!
IT'S OUR LAST BAG OF FLOUR.
I'M TOO WORN-OUT AND HUNGRY TO EVEN YELL AT YOU.
LOOK AT THAT MARVELOUS ANCIENT LAVA FLOW!
THEM LAVA ROCKS ARE PROBABLY SOFTER THAN THIS BREAD.
AUGUST 26, 1869
CURSE YOU, GRANITE!
THE WALLS GET HIGHER EVERY DAY.
IS THAT... A GARDEN?
PLANTED BY SOME PASSING TRIBESMEN, NO DOUBT!
WE AREN'T GOING TO STEAL IT ...ARE WE?
NOT ALL OF IT --BUT SOME OF IT.
NEVER WAS FRUIT SO SWEET AS THESE STOLEN SQUASHES!
STILL THINK YOU'RE THE FIRST PERSON HERE, POWELL? SOMEONE PUT IN A GARDEN!
FIRST TO GO THROUGH BY BOAT AND MAP IT FOR SCIENCE!

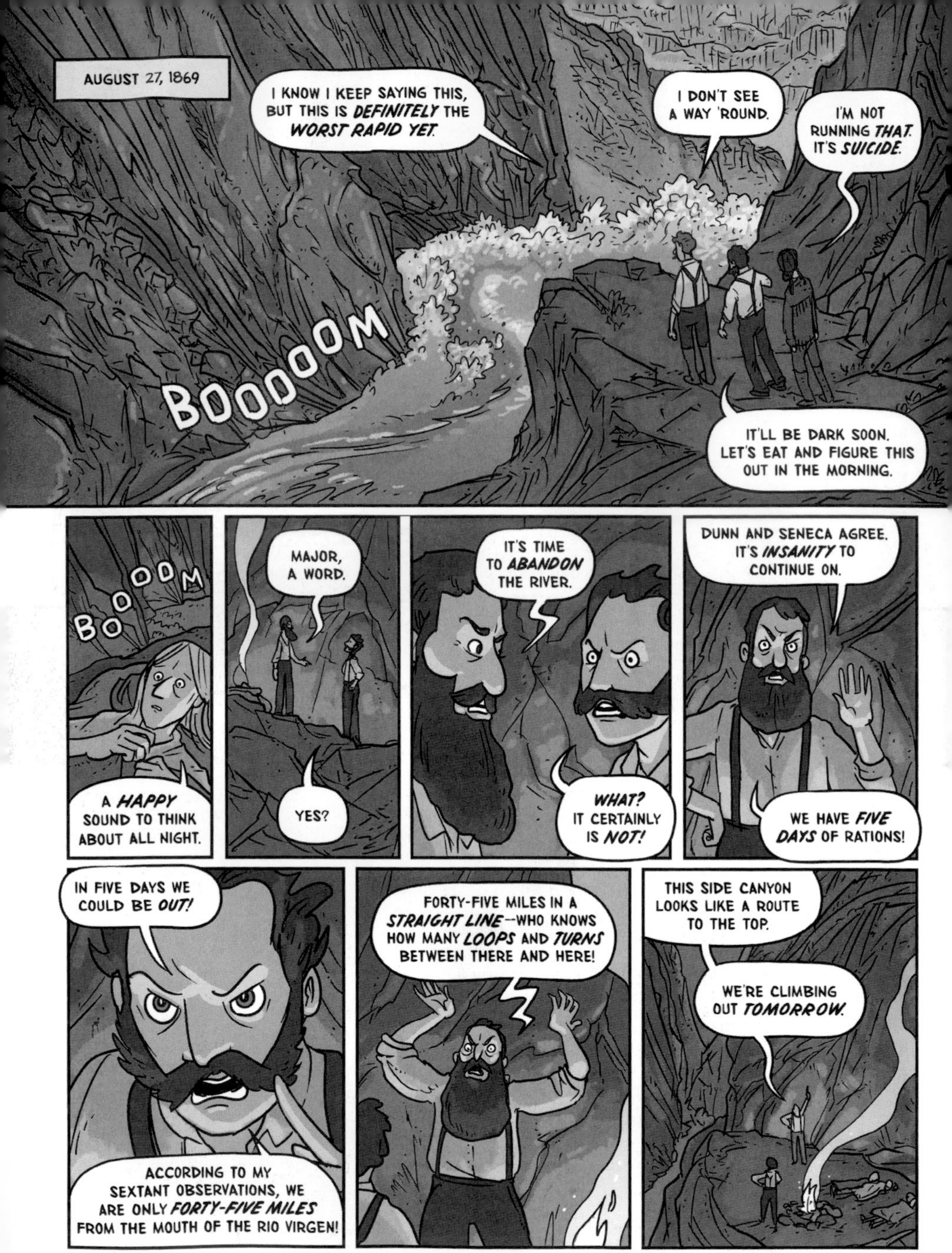
AUGUST 27, 1869
I KNOW I KEEP SAYING THIS, BUT THIS IS DEFINITELY THE WORST RAPID YET.
I DON'T SEE A WAY 'ROUND.
I'M NOT RUNNING THAT. IT'S SUICIDE.
BOOOOOM
IT'LL BE DARK SOON. LET'S EAT AND FIGURE THIS OUT IN THE MORNING.
BOOOOM
A HAPPY SOUND TO THINK ABOUT ALL NIGHT.
MAJOR, A WORD.
YES?
IT'S TIME TO ABANDON THE RIVER.
WHAT? IT CERTAINLY IS NOT!
DUNN AND SENECA AGREE. IT'S INSANITY TO CONTINUE ON.
WE HAVE FIVE DAYS OF RATIONS!
IN FIVE DAYS WE COULD BE OUT!
ACCORDING TO MY SEXTANT OBSERVATIONS, WE ARE ONLY FORTY-FIVE MILES FROM THE MOUTH OF THE RIO VIRGEN!
FORTY-FIVE MILES IN A STRAIGHT LINE--WHO KNOWS HOW MANY LOOPS AND TURNS BETWEEN THERE AND HERE!
THIS SIDE CANYON LOOKS LIKE A ROUTE TO THE TOP.
WE'RE CLIMBING OUT TOMORROW.

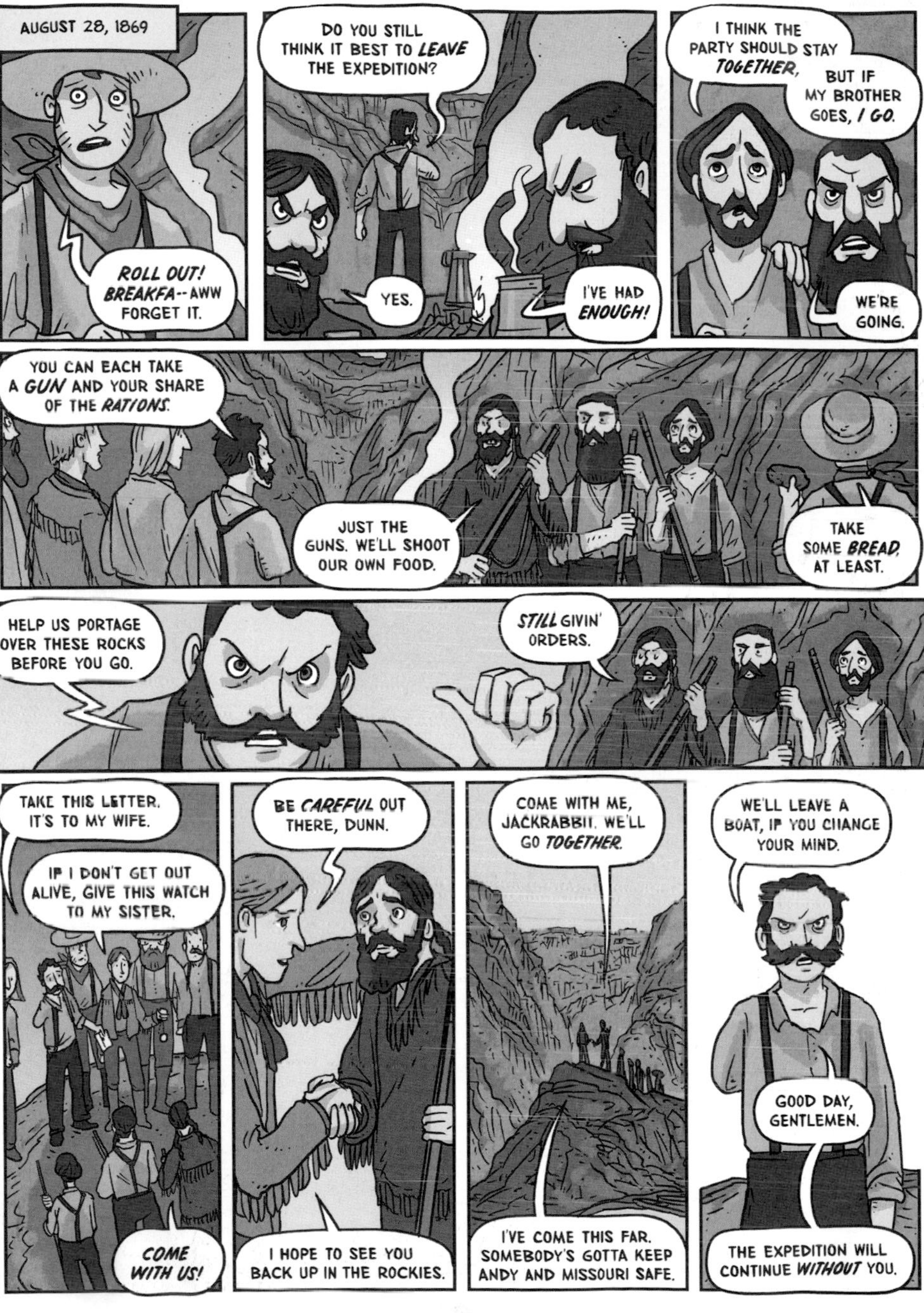
AUGUST 28, 1869
ROLL OUT! BREAKFA--AWW FORGET IT.
DO YOU STILL THINK IT BEST TO LEAVE THE EXPEDITION?
YES.
I'VE HAD ENOUGH!
I THINK THE PARTY SHOULD STAY TOGETHER,
BUT IF MY BROTHER GOES, I GO.
WE'RE GOING.
YOU CAN EACH TAKE A GUN AND YOUR SHARE OF THE RATIONS.
JUST THE GUNS. WE'LL SHOOT OUR OWN FOOD.
TAKE SOME BREAD, AT LEAST.
HELP US PORTAGE OVER THESE ROCKS BEFORE YOU GO.
STILL GIVIN' ORDERS.
TAKE THIS LETTER. IT'S TO MY WIFE.
IF I DON'T GET OUT ALIVE, GIVE THIS WATCH TO MY SISTER.
COME WITH US!
BE CAREFUL OUT THERE, DUNN.
I HOPE TO SEE YOU BACK UP IN THE ROCKIES.
COME WITH ME, JACKRABBIT. WE'LL GO TOGETHER.
I'VE COME THIS FAR. SOMEBODY'S GOTTA KEEP ANDY AND MISSOURI SAFE.
WE'LL LEAVE A BOAT, IF YOU CHANGE YOUR MIND.
GOOD DAY, GENTLEMEN.
THE EXPEDITION WILL CONTINUE WITHOUT YOU.

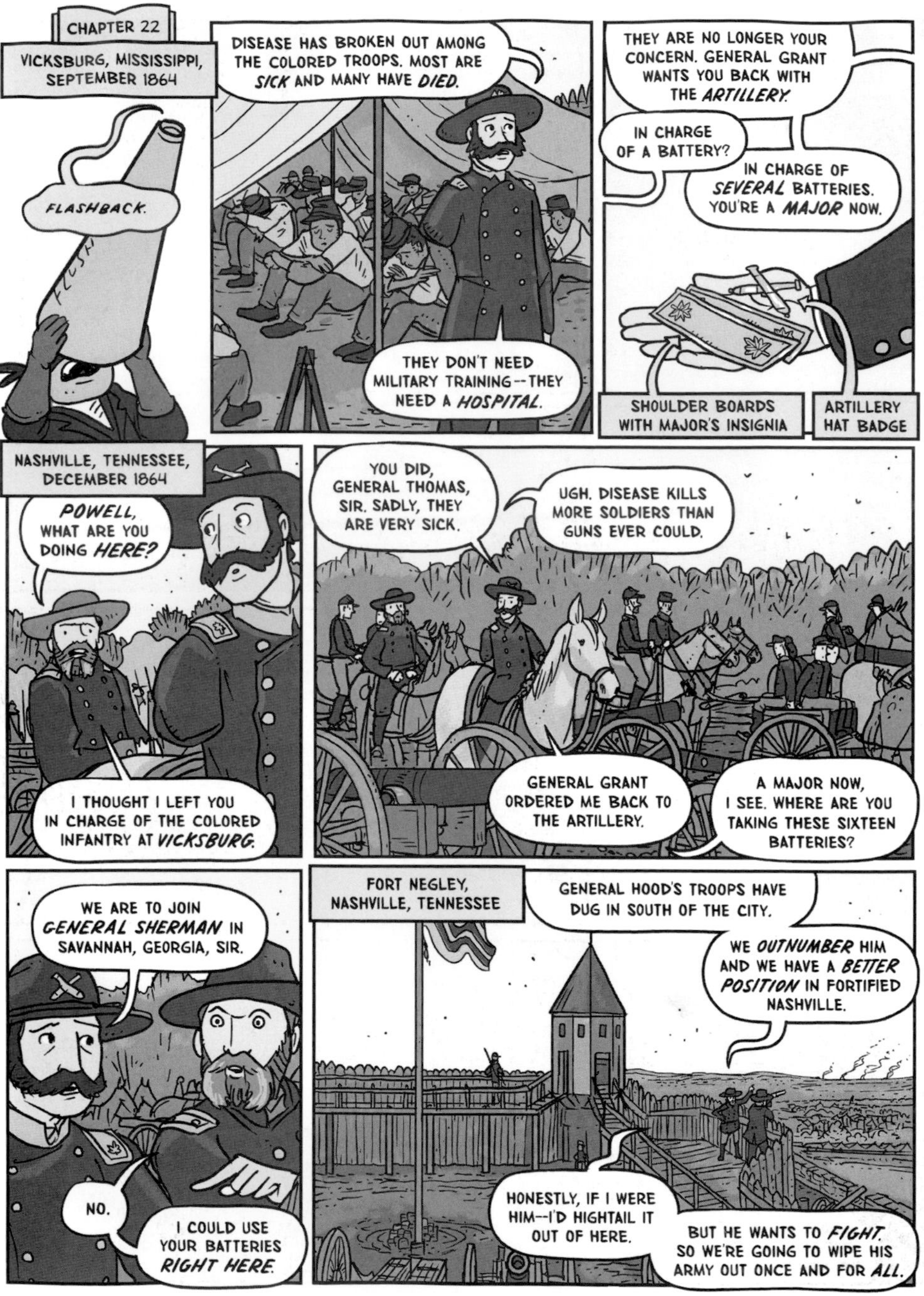
CHAPTER 22
VICKSBURG, MISSISSIPPI, SEPTEMBER 1864
FLASHBACK.
DISEASE HAS BROKEN OUT AMONG THE COLORED TROOPS. MOST ARE SICK AND MANY HAVE DIED.
THEY DON'T NEED MILITARY TRAINING--THEY NEED A HOSPITAL.
THEY ARE NO LONGER YOUR CONCERN. GENERAL GRANT WANTS YOU BACK WITH THE ARTILLERY.
IN CHARGE OF A BATTERY?
IN CHARGE OF SEVERAL BATTERIES. YOU'RE A MAJOR NOW.
SHOULDER BOARDS WITH MAJOR'S INSIGNIA
ARTILLERY HAT BADGE
NASHVILLE, TENNESSEE, DECEMBER 1864
POWELL, WHAT ARE YOU DOING HERE?
I THOUGHT I LEFT YOU IN CHARGE OF THE COLORED INFANTRY AT VICKSBURG.
YOU DID, GENERAL THOMAS, SIR. SADLY, THEY ARE VERY SICK.
UGH. DISEASE KILLS MORE SOLDIERS THAN GUNS EVER COULD.
GENERAL GRANT ORDERED ME BACK TO THE ARTILLERY.
A MAJOR NOW, I SEE. WHERE ARE YOU TAKING THESE SIXTEEN BATTERIES?
WE ARE TO JOIN GENERAL SHERMAN IN SAVANNAH, GEORGIA, SIR.
NO.
I COULD USE YOUR BATTERIES RIGHT HERE.
FORT NEGLEY, NASHVILLE, TENNESSEE
GENERAL HOOD'S TROOPS HAVE DUG IN SOUTH OF THE CITY.
WE OUTNUMBER HIM AND WE HAVE A BETTER POSITION IN FORTIFIED NASHVILLE.
HONESTLY, IF I WERE HIM--I'D HIGHTAIL IT OUT OF HERE.
BUT HE WANTS TO FIGHT, SO WE'RE GOING TO WIPE HIS ARMY OUT ONCE AND FOR ALL.

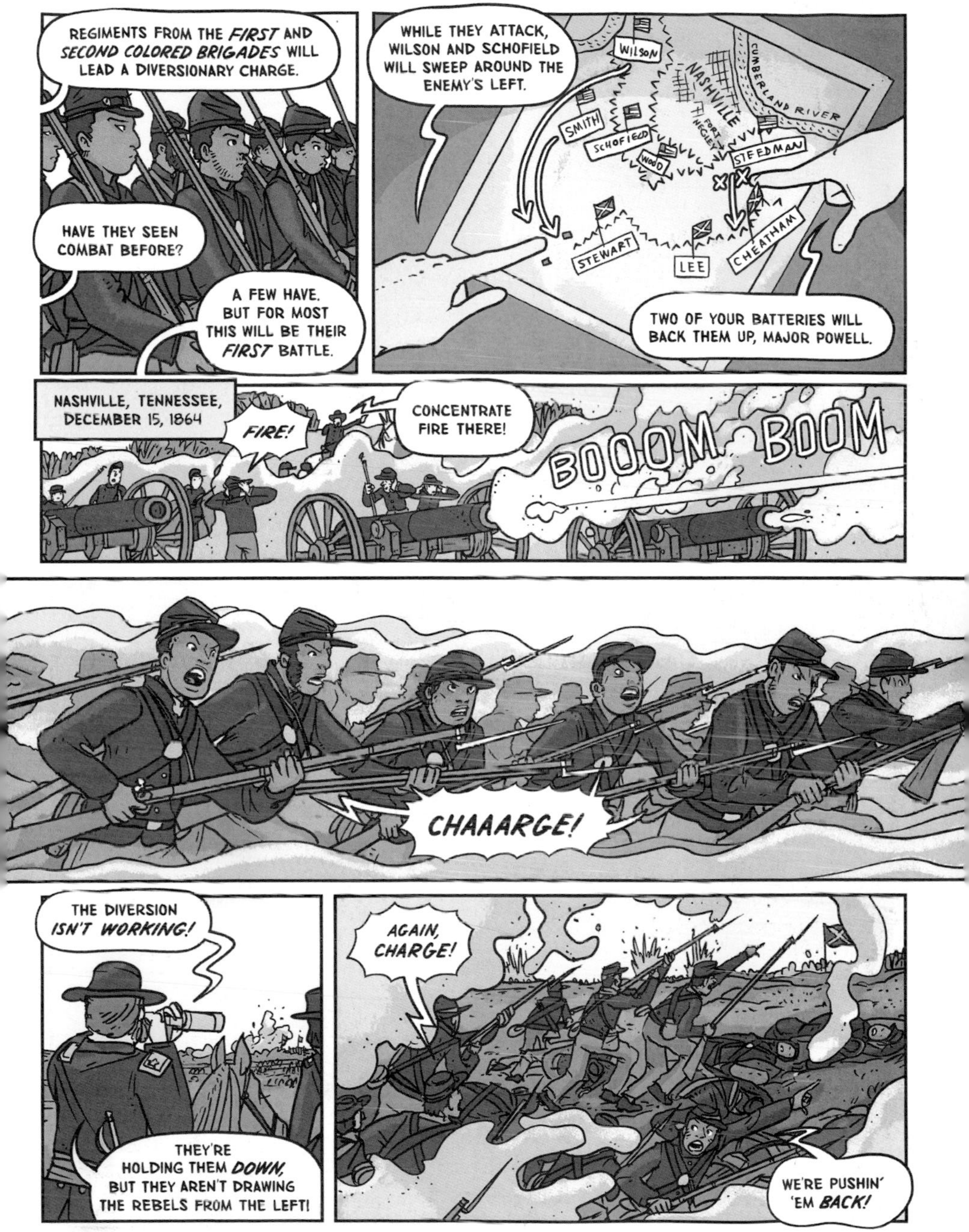
REGIMENTS FROM THE FIRST AND SECOND COLORED BRIGADES WILL LEAD A DIVERSIONARY CHARGE.
HAVE THEY SEEN COMBAT BEFORE?
A FEW HAVE. BUT FOR MOST THIS WILL BE THEIR FIRST BATTLE.
WHILE THEY ATTACK, WILSON AND SCHOFIELD WILL SWEEP AROUND THE ENEMY'S LEFT.
WILSON
NASHVILLE
CUMBERLAND RIVER
SMITH
SCHOFIELD
FORT NEGLEY
WOOD
STEEDMAN
STEWART
LEE
CHEATHAM
TWO OF YOUR BATTERIES WILL BACK THEM UP, MAJOR POWELL.
NASHVILLE, TENNESSEE, DECEMBER 15, 1864
FIRE!
CONCENTRATE FIRE THERE!
BOOOM BOOM
CHAAARGE!
THE DIVERSION ISN'T WORKING!
THEY'RE HOLDING THEM DOWN, BUT THEY AREN'T DRAWING THE REBELS FROM THE LEFT!
AGAIN, CHARGE!
WE'RE PUSHIN' 'EM BACK!

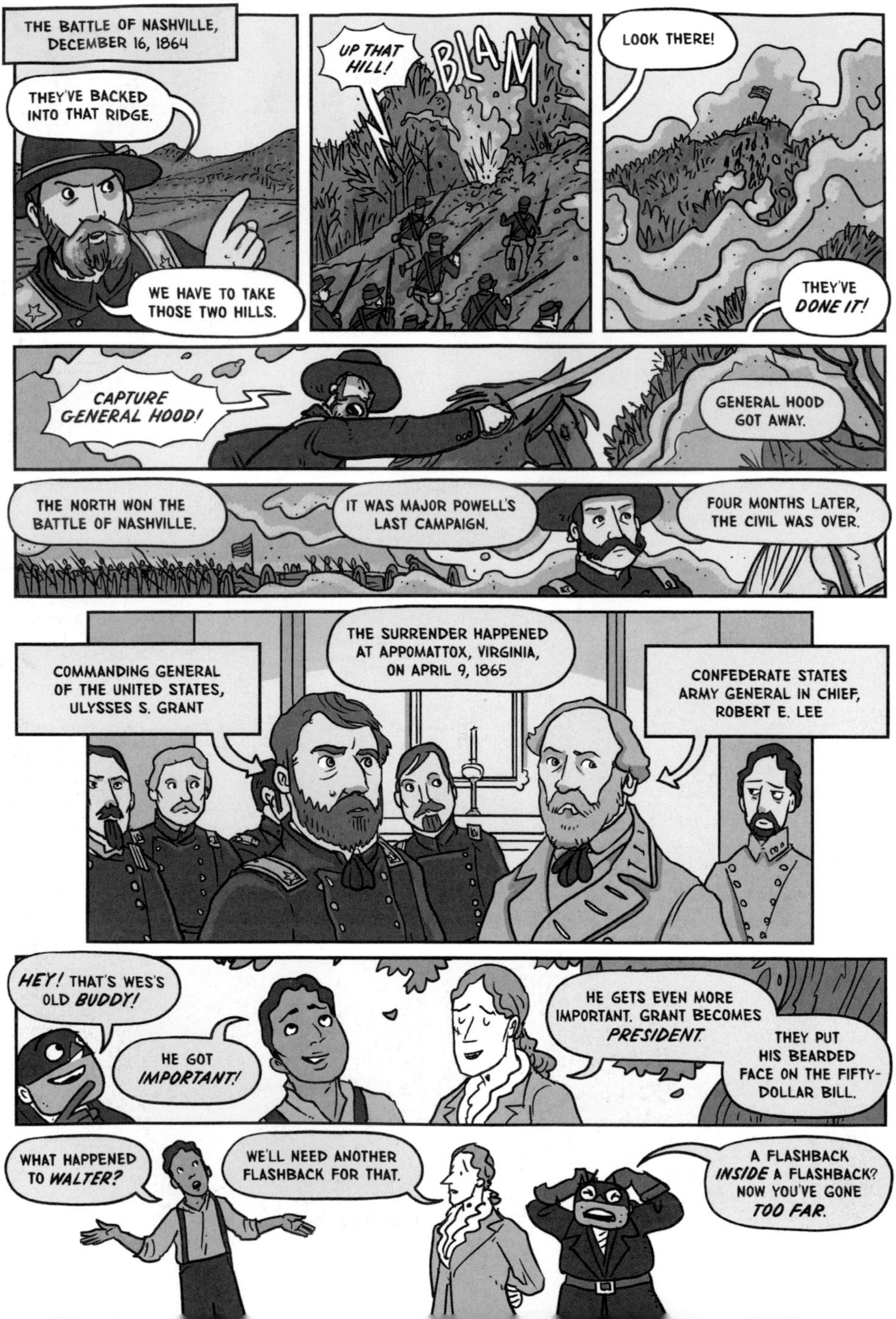
THE BATTLE OF NASHVILLE, DECEMBER 16, 1864
THEY'VE BACKED INTO THAT RIDGE.
WE HAVE TO TAKE THOSE TWO HILLS.
UP THAT HILL!
BLAM
LOOK THERE!
THEY'VE DONE IT!
CAPTURE GENERAL HOOD!
GENERAL HOOD GOT AWAY.
THE NORTH WON THE BATTLE OF NASHVILLE.
IT WAS MAJOR POWELL'S LAST CAMPAIGN.
FOUR MONTHS LATER, THE CIVIL WAS OVER.
THE SURRENDER HAPPENED AT APPOMATTOX, VIRGINIA, ON APRIL 9, 1865
COMMANDING GENERAL OF THE UNITED STATES, ULYSSES S. GRANT
CONFEDERATE STATES ARMY GENERAL IN CHIEF, ROBERT E. LEE
HEY! THAT'S WES'S OLD BUDDY!
HE GOT IMPORTANT!
HE GETS EVEN MORE IMPORTANT. GRANT BECOMES PRESIDENT.
THEY PUT HIS BEARDED FACE ON THE FIFTY-DOLLAR BILL.
WHAT HAPPENED TO WALTER?
WE'LL NEED ANOTHER FLASHBACK FOR THAT.
A FLASHBACK INSIDE A FLASHBACK? NOW YOU'VE GONE TOO FAR.

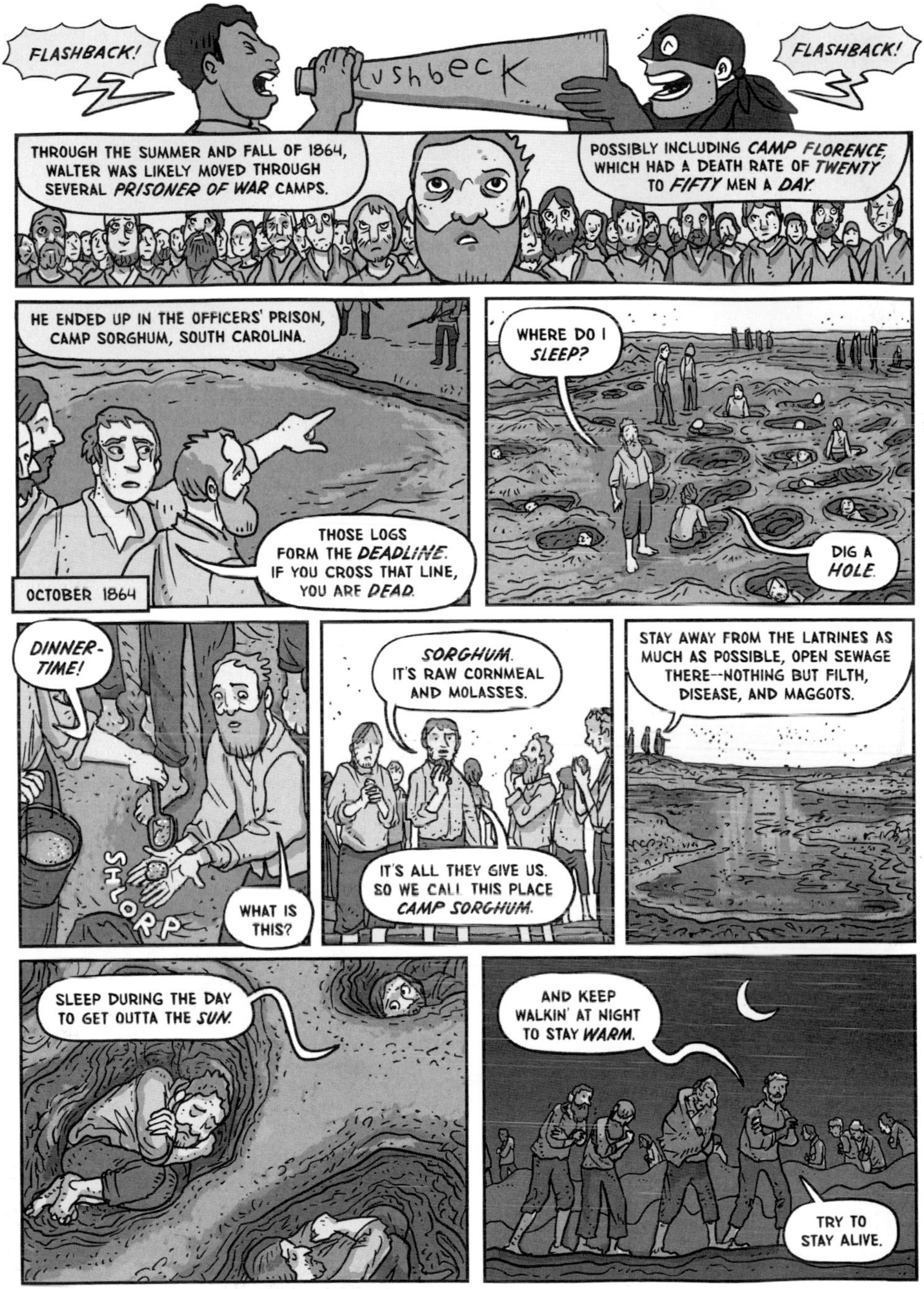
FLASHBACK!
LUSHBECK
FLASHBACK!
THROUGH THE SUMMER AND FALL OF 1864, WALTER WAS LIKELY MOVED THROUGH SEVERAL PRISONER OF WAR CAMPS.
POSSIBLY INCLUDING CAMP FLORENCE, WHICH HAD A DEATH RATE OF TWENTY TO FIFTY MEN A DAY.
HE ENDED UP IN THE OFFICERS' PRISON, CAMP SORGHUM, SOUTH CAROLINA.
OCTOBER 1864
THOSE LOGS FORM THE DEADLINE. IF YOU CROSS THAT LINE, YOU ARE DEAD.
WHERE DO I SLEEP?
DIG A HOLE.
DINNER-TIME!
SHLORP
WHAT IS THIS?
SORGHUM. IT'S RAW CORNMEAL AND MOLASSES.
IT'S ALL THEY GIVE US. SO WE CALL THIS PLACE CAMP SORGHUM.
STAY AWAY FROM THE LATRINES AS MUCH AS POSSIBLE, OPEN SEWAGE THERE--NOTHING BUT FILTH, DISEASE, AND MAGGOTS.
SLEEP DURING THE DAY TO GET OUTTA THE SUN.
AND KEEP WALKIN' AT NIGHT TO STAY WARM.
TRY TO STAY ALIVE.

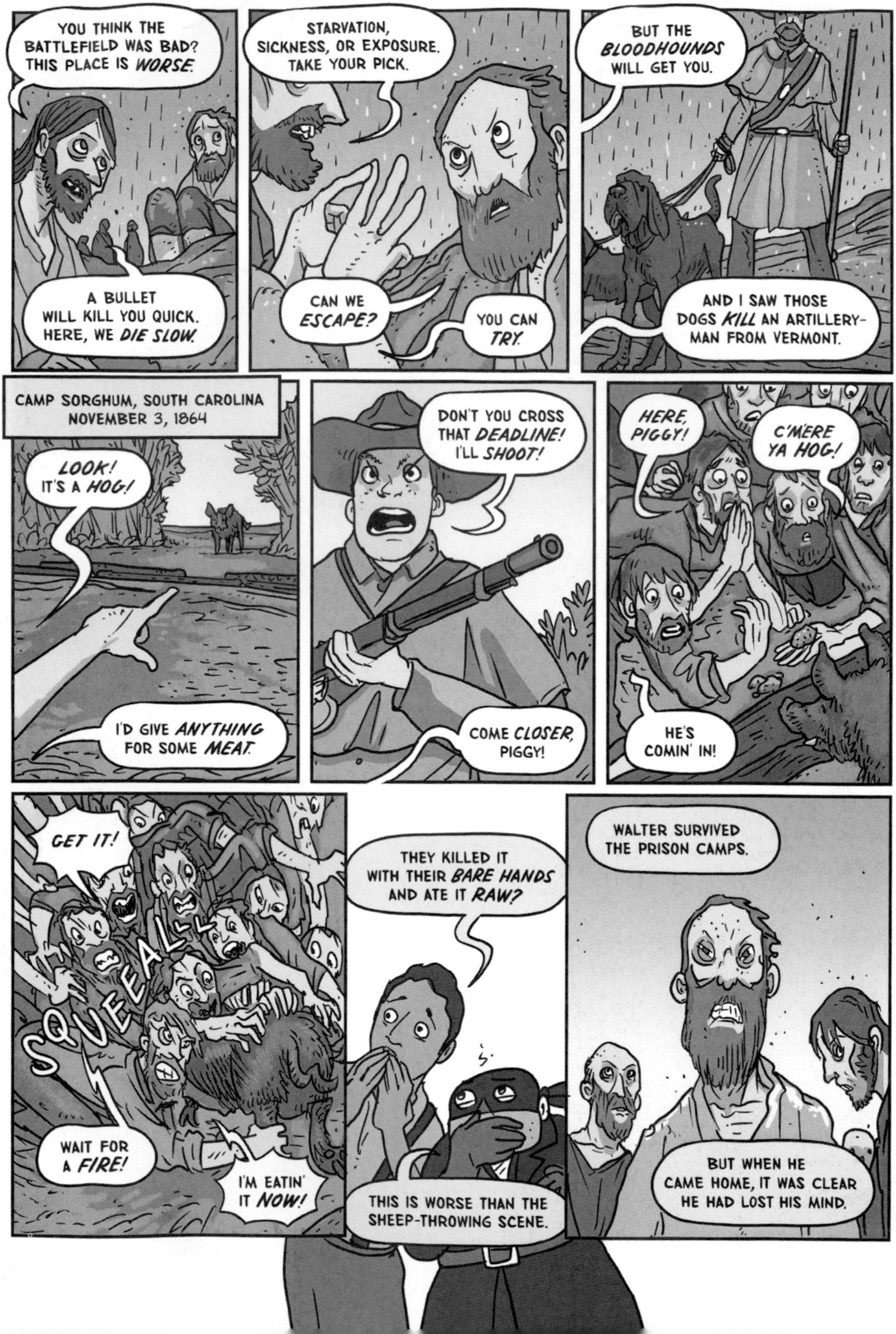

YOU THINK THE BATTLEFIELD WAS BAD? THIS PLACE IS WORSE.
A BULLET WILL KILL YOU QUICK. HERE, WE DIE SLOW.
STARVATION, SICKNESS, OR EXPOSURE. TAKE YOUR PICK.
CAN WE ESCAPE?
YOU CAN TRY.
BUT THE BLOODHOUNDS WILL GET YOU.
AND I SAW THOSE DOGS KILL AN ARTILLERY-MAN FROM VERMONT.
CAMP SORGHUM, SOUTH CAROLINA NOVEMBER 3, 1864
LOOK! IT'S A HOG!
I'D GIVE ANYTHING FOR SOME MEAT.
DON'T YOU CROSS THAT DEADLINE! I'LL SHOOT!
COME CLOSER, PIGGY!
HERE, PIGGY!
C'MERE YA HOG!
HE'S COMIN' IN!
GET IT!
SQUEEALLL
WAIT FOR A FIRE!
I'M EATIN' IT NOW!
THEY KILLED IT WITH THEIR BARE HANDS AND ATE IT RAW?
THIS IS WORSE THAN THE SHEEP-THROWING SCENE.
WALTER SURVIVED THE PRISON CAMPS.
BUT WHEN HE CAME HOME, IT WAS CLEAR HE HAD LOST HIS MIND.

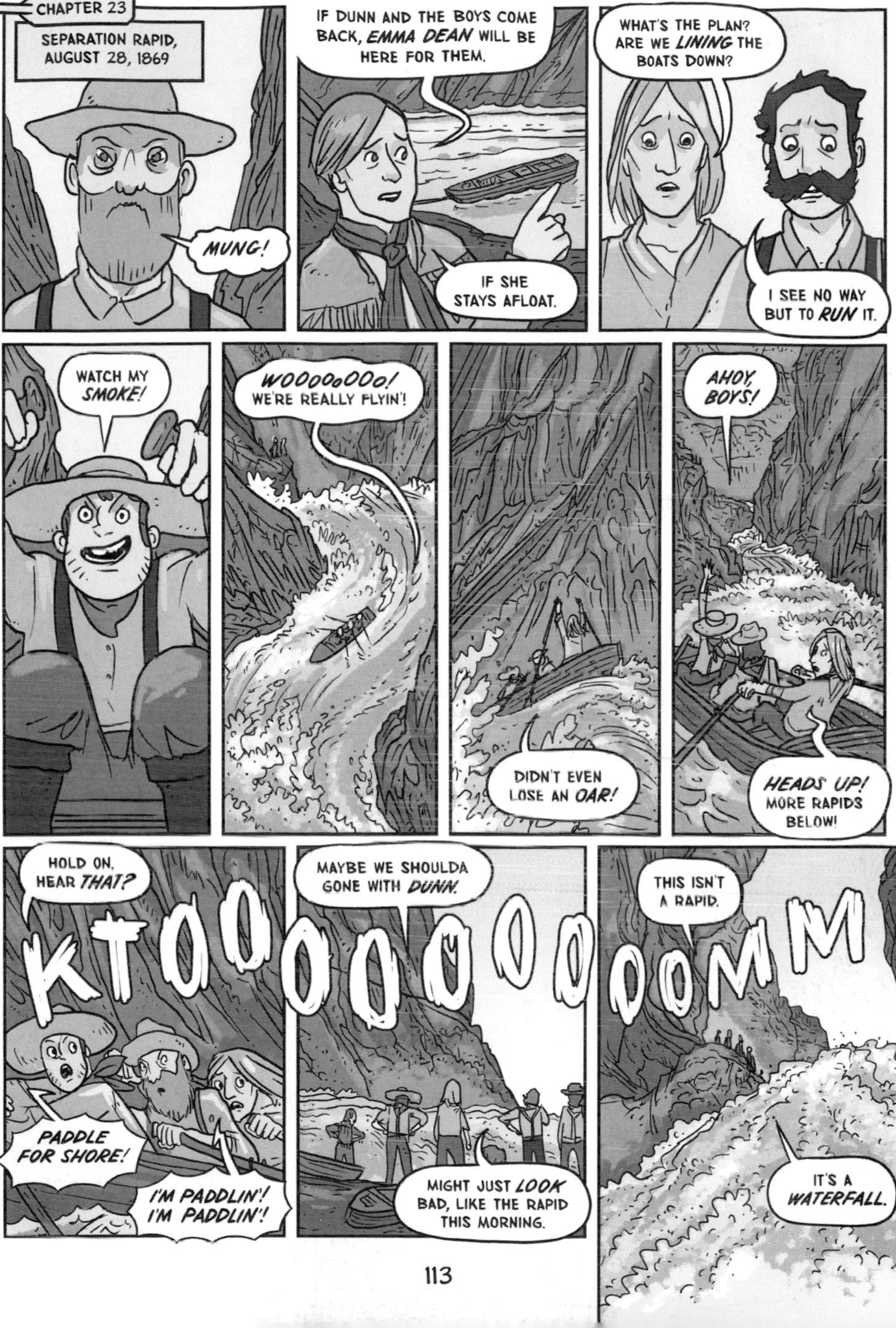
CHAPTER 23
SEPARATION RAPID, AUGUST 28, 1869
MUNG!
IF DUNN AND THE BOYS COME BACK, EMMA DEAN WILL BE HERE FOR THEM.
IF SHE STAYS AFLOAT.
WHAT'S THE PLAN? ARE WE LINING THE BOATS DOWN?
I SEE NO WAY BUT TO RUN IT.
WATCH MY SMOKE!
WOOOOoOOo! WE'RE REALLY FLYIN'!
DIDN'T EVEN LOSE AN OAR!
AHOY, BOYS!
HEADS UP! MORE RAPIDS BELOW!
HOLD ON. HEAR THAT?
KTOOOOOOOOOMM
PADDLE FOR SHORE!
I'M PADDLIN'! I'M PADDLIN'!
MAYBE WE SHOULDA GONE WITH DUNN.
MIGHT JUST LOOK BAD, LIKE THE RAPID THIS MORNING.
THIS ISN'T A RAPID.
IT'S A WATERFALL.

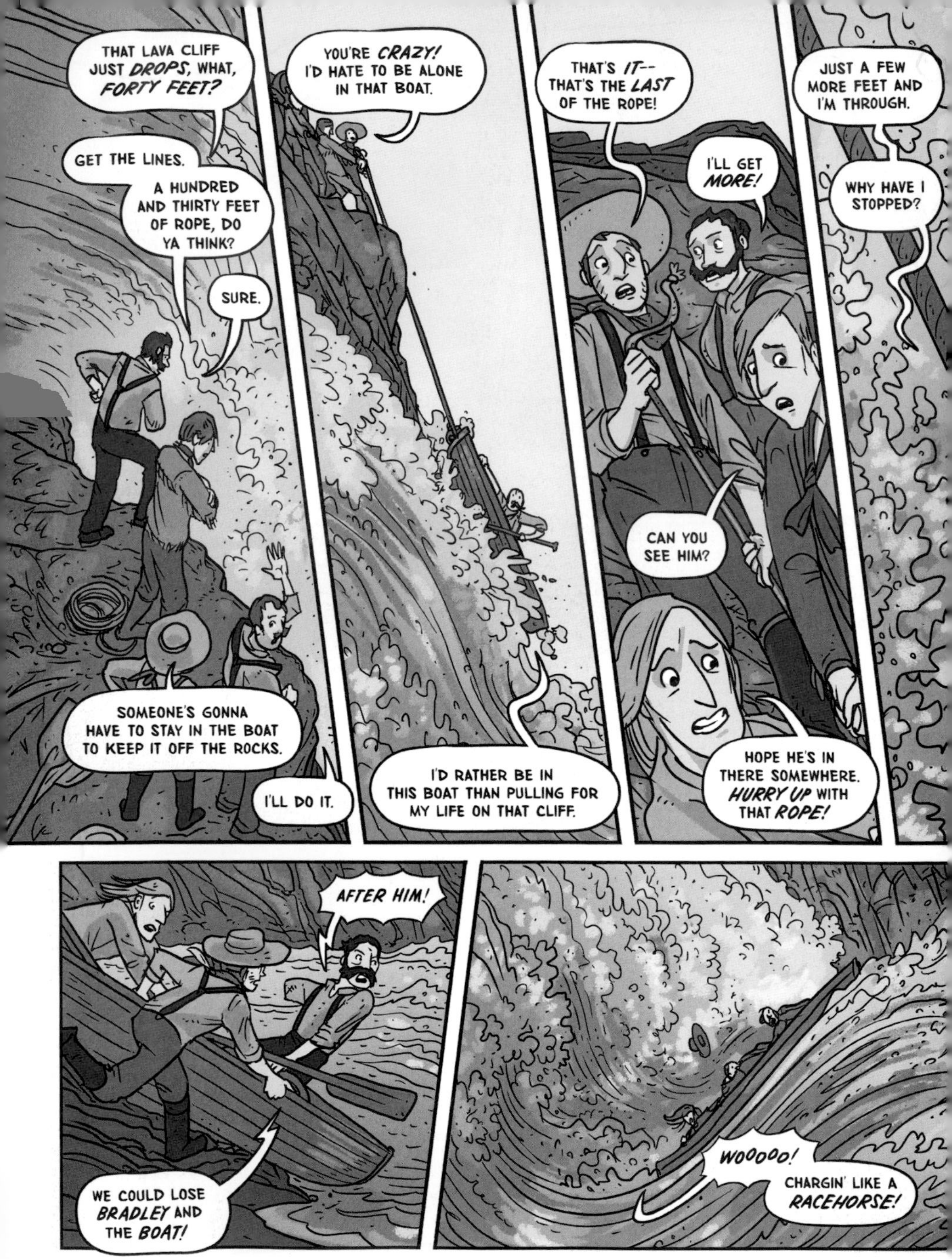
THAT LAVA CLIFF JUST DROPS, WHAT, FORTY FEET?
GET THE LINES.
A HUNDRED AND THIRTY FEET OF ROPE, DO YA THINK?
SURE.
SOMEONE'S GONNA HAVE TO STAY IN THE BOAT TO KEEP IT OFF THE ROCKS.
I'LL DO IT.
YOU'RE CRAZY! I'D HATE TO BE ALONE IN THAT BOAT.
I'D RATHER BE IN THIS BOAT THAN PULLING FOR MY LIFE ON THAT CLIFF.
THAT'S IT-- THAT'S THE LAST OF THE ROPE!
I'LL GET MORE!
CAN YOU SEE HIM?
HOPE HE'S IN THERE SOMEWHERE. HURRY UP WITH THAT ROPE!
JUST A FEW MORE FEET AND I'M THROUGH.
WHY HAVE I STOPPED?
AFTER HIM!
WE COULD LOSE BRADLEY AND THE BOAT!
WOOOOO!
CHARGIN' LIKE A RACEHORSE!

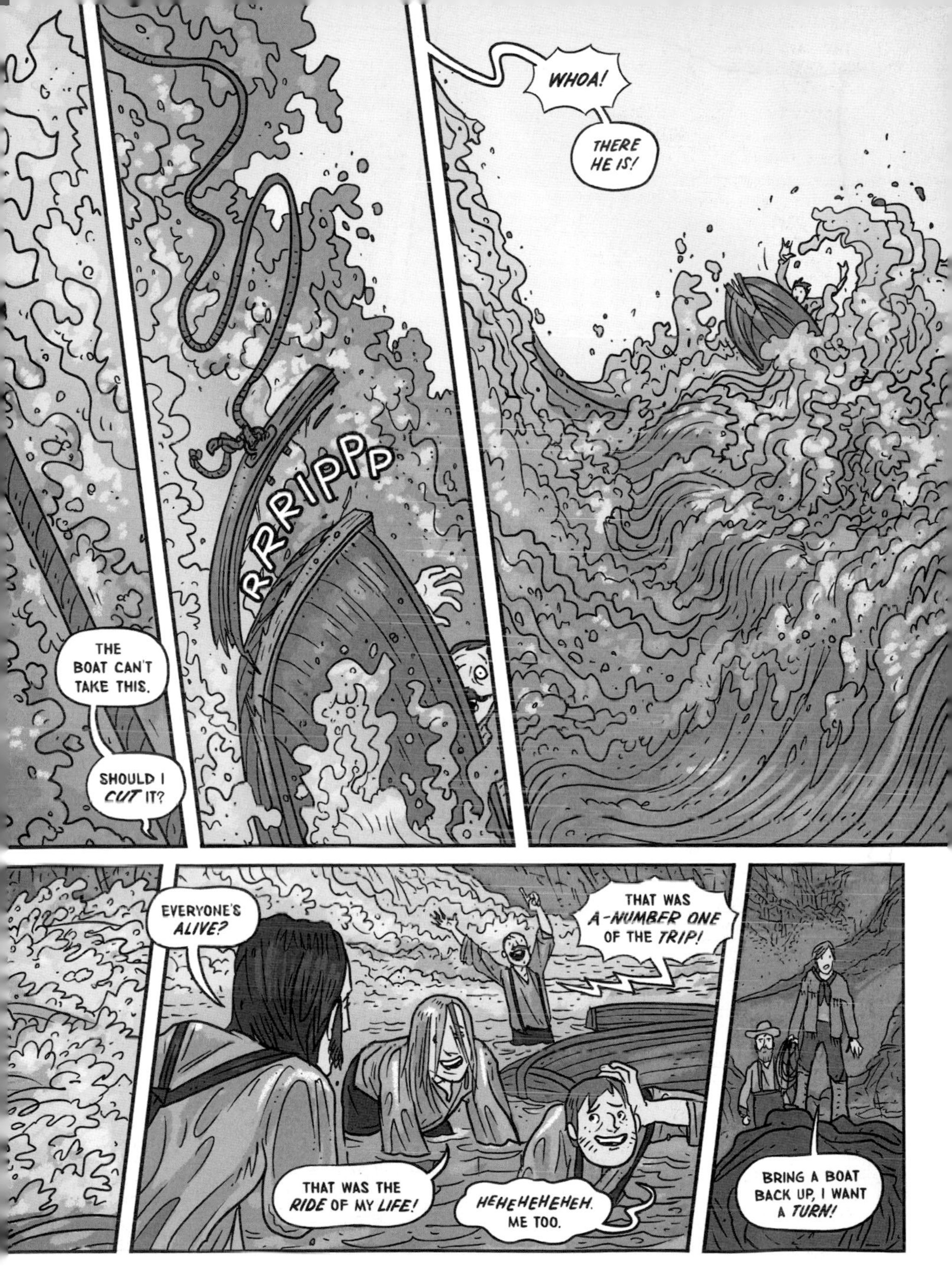
THE BOAT CAN'T TAKE THIS.
SHOULD I CUT IT?
RRRIPPP
WHOA!
THERE HE IS!
EVERYONE'S ALIVE?
THAT WAS A-NUMBER ONE OF THE TRIP!
THAT WAS THE RIDE OF MY LIFE!
HEHEHEHEHEH. ME TOO.
BRING A BOAT BACK UP, I WANT A TURN!

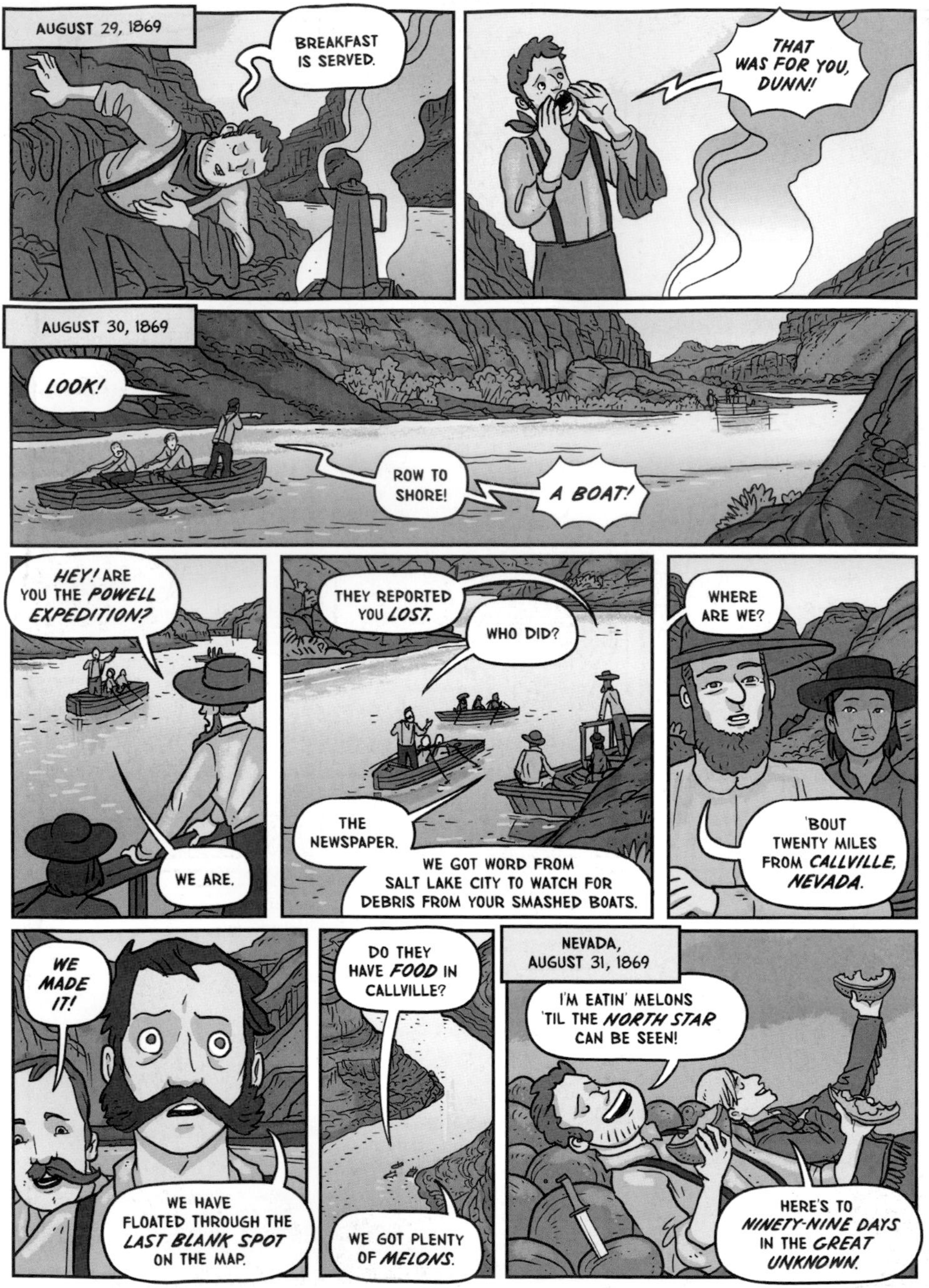
AUGUST 29, 1869
BREAKFAST IS SERVED.
THAT WAS FOR YOU, DUNN!
AUGUST 30, 1869
LOOK!
ROW TO SHORE!
A BOAT!
HEY! ARE YOU THE POWELL EXPEDITION?
WE ARE.
THEY REPORTED YOU LOST.
WHO DID?
THE NEWSPAPER.
WE GOT WORD FROM SALT LAKE CITY TO WATCH FOR DEBRIS FROM YOUR SMASHED BOATS.
WHERE ARE WE?
'BOUT TWENTY MILES FROM CALLVILLE, NEVADA.
WE MADE IT!
WE HAVE FLOATED THROUGH THE LAST BLANK SPOT ON THE MAP.
DO THEY HAVE FOOD IN CALLVILLE?
WE GOT PLENTY OF MELONS.
NEVADA, AUGUST 31, 1869
I'M EATIN' MELONS 'TIL THE NORTH STAR CAN BE SEEN!
HERE'S TO NINETY-NINE DAYS IN THE GREAT UNKNOWN.

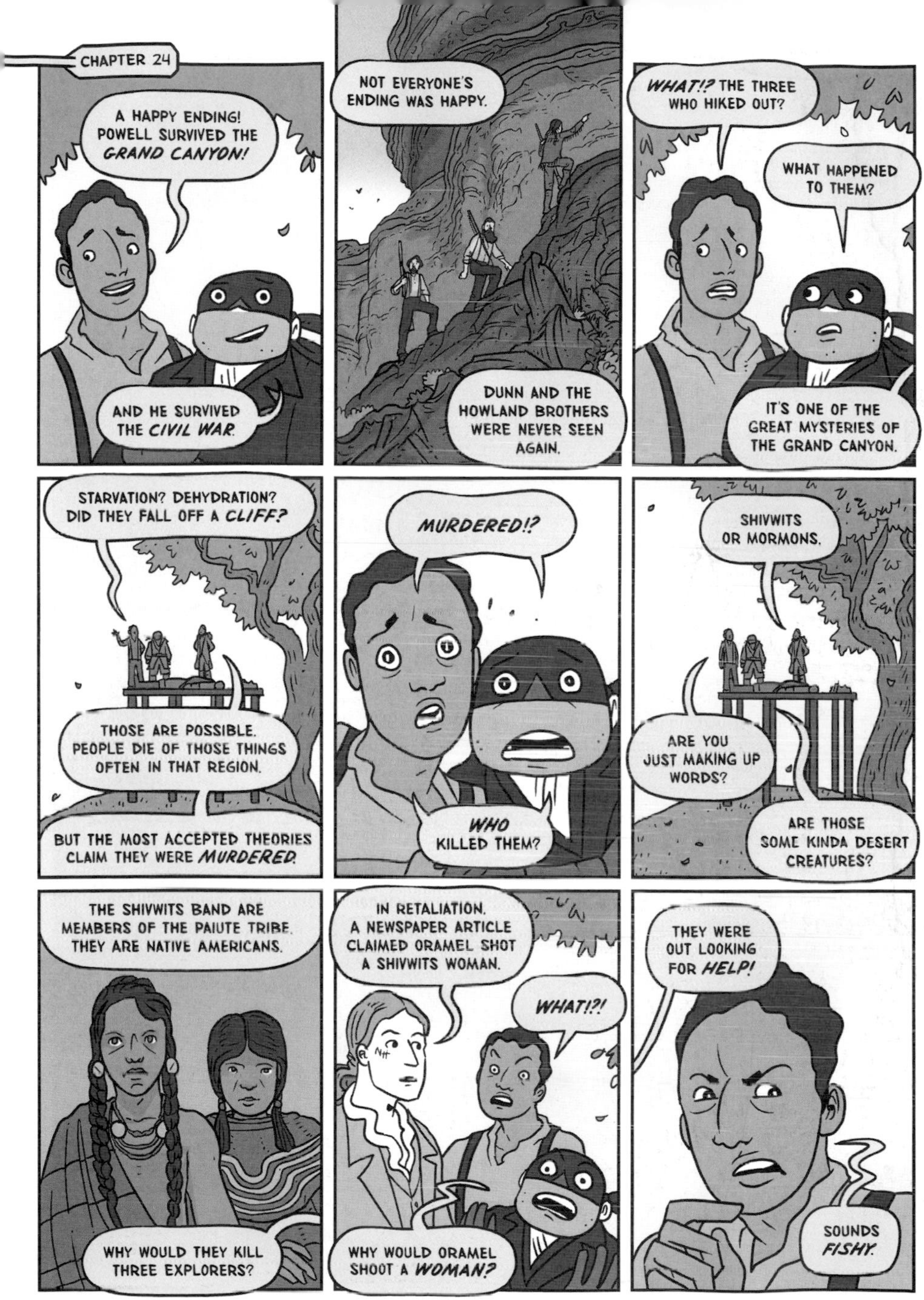
CHAPTER 24
A HAPPY ENDING! POWELL SURVIVED THE GRAND CANYON!
AND HE SURVIVED THE CIVIL WAR.
NOT EVERYONE'S ENDING WAS HAPPY.
DUNN AND THE HOWLAND BROTHERS WERE NEVER SEEN AGAIN.
WHAT!? THE THREE WHO HIKED OUT?
WHAT HAPPENED TO THEM?
IT'S ONE OF THE GREAT MYSTERIES OF THE GRAND CANYON.
STARVATION? DEHYDRATION? DID THEY FALL OFF A CLIFF?
THOSE ARE POSSIBLE. PEOPLE DIE OF THOSE THINGS OFTEN IN THAT REGION.
BUT THE MOST ACCEPTED THEORIES CLAIM THEY WERE MURDERED.
MURDERED!?
WHO KILLED THEM?
SHIVWITS OR MORMONS.
ARE YOU JUST MAKING UP WORDS?
ARE THOSE SOME KINDA DESERT CREATURES?
THE SHIVWITS BAND ARE MEMBERS OF THE PAIUTE TRIBE. THEY ARE NATIVE AMERICANS.
WHY WOULD THEY KILL THREE EXPLORERS?
IN RETALIATION. A NEWSPAPER ARTICLE CLAIMED ORAMEL SHOT A SHIVWITS WOMAN.
WHAT!?!
WHY WOULD ORAMEL SHOOT A WOMAN?
THEY WERE OUT LOOKING FOR HELP!
SOUNDS FISHY.

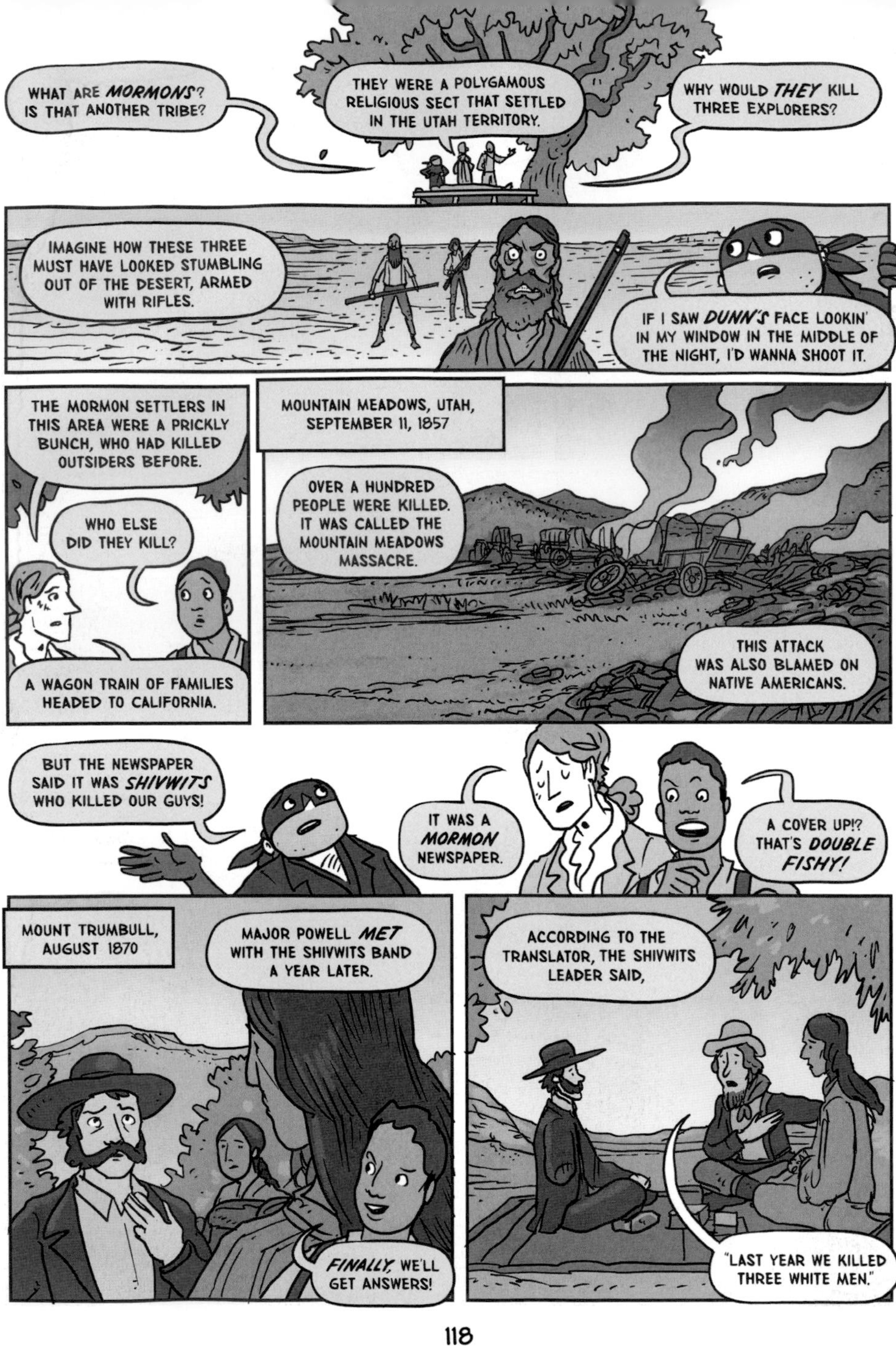
WHAT ARE MORMONS? IS THAT ANOTHER TRIBE?
THEY WERE A POLYGAMOUS RELIGIOUS SECT THAT SETTLED IN THE UTAH TERRITORY.
WHY WOULD THEY KILL THREE EXPLORERS?
IMAGINE HOW THESE THREE MUST HAVE LOOKED STUMBLING OUT OF THE DESERT, ARMED WITH RIFLES.
IF I SAW DUNN'S FACE LOOKIN' IN MY WINDOW IN THE MIDDLE OF THE NIGHT, I'D WANNA SHOOT IT.
THE MORMON SETTLERS IN THIS AREA WERE A PRICKLY BUNCH, WHO HAD KILLED OUTSIDERS BEFORE.
WHO ELSE DID THEY KILL?
A WAGON TRAIN OF FAMILIES HEADED TO CALIFORNIA.
MOUNTAIN MEADOWS, UTAH, SEPTEMBER 11, 1857
OVER A HUNDRED PEOPLE WERE KILLED. IT WAS CALLED THE MOUNTAIN MEADOWS MASSACRE.
THIS ATTACK WAS ALSO BLAMED ON NATIVE AMERICANS.
BUT THE NEWSPAPER SAID IT WAS SHIVWITS WHO KILLED OUR GUYS!
IT WAS A MORMON NEWSPAPER.
A COVER UP!? THAT'S DOUBLE FISHY!
MOUNT TRUMBULL, AUGUST 1870
MAJOR POWELL MET WITH THE SHIVWITS BAND A YEAR LATER.
FINALLY, WE'LL GET ANSWERS!
ACCORDING TO THE TRANSLATOR, THE SHIVWITS LEADER SAID,
"LAST YEAR WE KILLED THREE WHITE MEN."

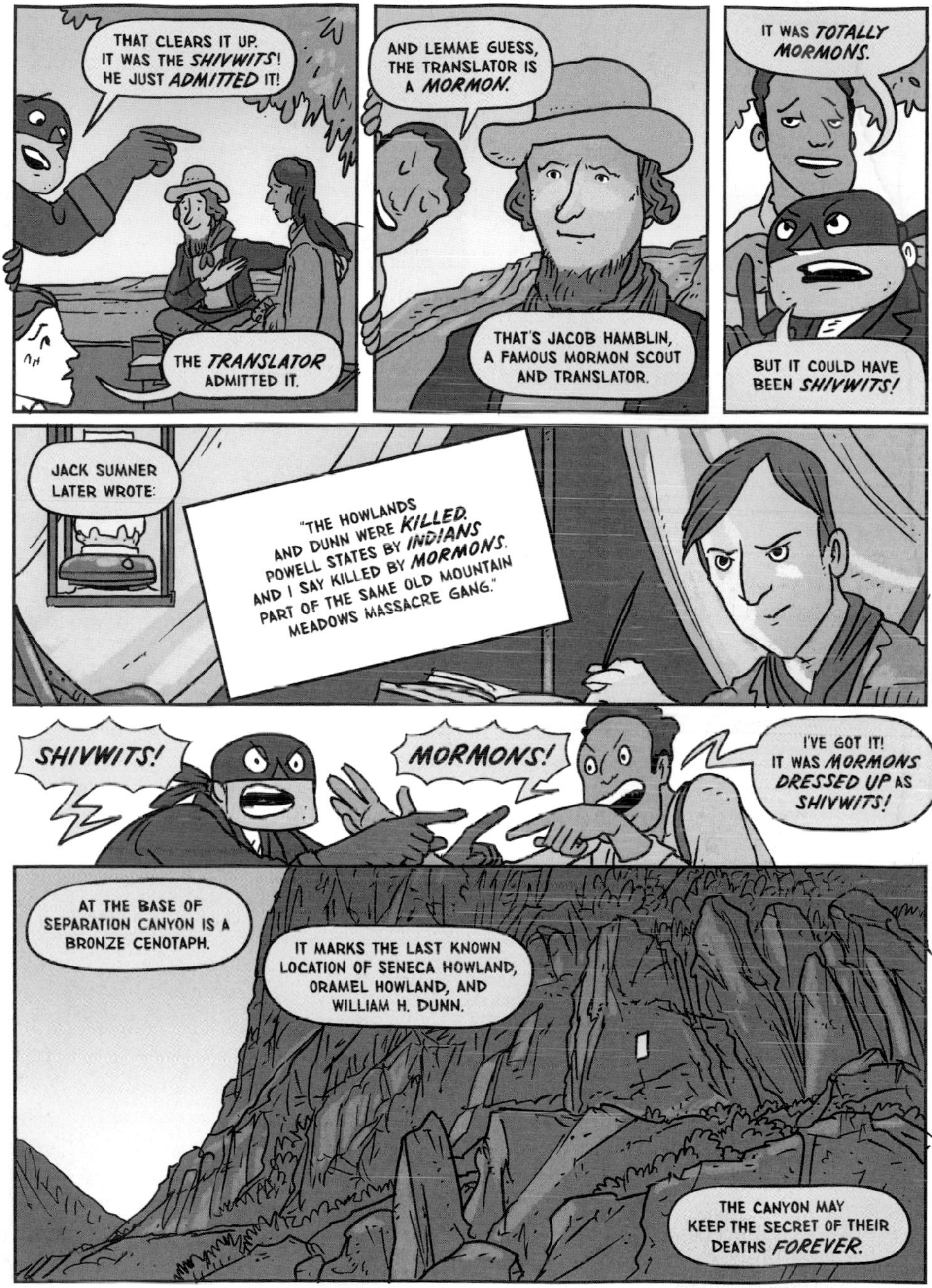
THAT CLEARS IT UP. IT WAS THE SHIVWITS! HE JUST ADMITTED IT!
THE TRANSLATOR ADMITTED IT.
AND LEMME GUESS, THE TRANSLATOR IS A MORMON.
THAT'S JACOB HAMBLIN, A FAMOUS MORMON SCOUT AND TRANSLATOR.
IT WAS TOTALLY MORMONS.
BUT IT COULD HAVE BEEN SHIVWITS!
JACK SUMNER LATER WROTE:
"THE HOWLANDS AND DUNN WERE KILLED. POWELL STATES BY INDIANS AND I SAY KILLED BY MORMONS. PART OF THE SAME OLD MOUNTAIN MEADOWS MASSACRE GANG."
SHIVWITS!
MORMONS!
I'VE GOT IT! IT WAS MORMONS DRESSED UP AS SHIVWITS!
AT THE BASE OF SEPARATION CANYON IS A BRONZE CENOTAPH.
IT MARKS THE LAST KNOWN LOCATION OF SENECA HOWLAND, ORAMEL HOWLAND, AND WILLIAM H. DUNN.
THE CANYON MAY KEEP THE SECRET OF THEIR DEATHS FOREVER.

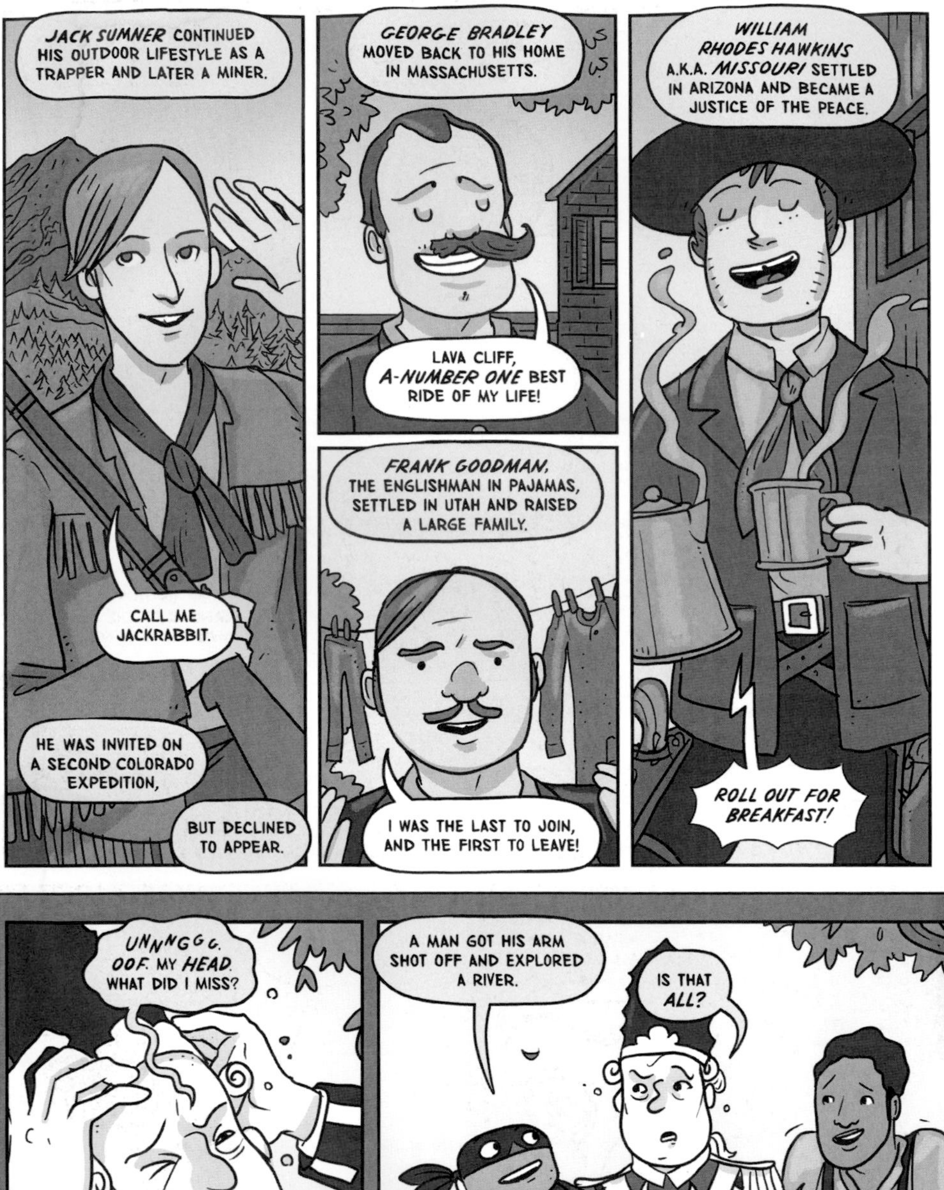
JACK SUMNER CONTINUED HIS OUTDOOR LIFESTYLE AS A TRAPPER AND LATER A MINER.
CALL ME JACKRABBIT.
HE WAS INVITED ON A SECOND COLORADO EXPEDITION,
BUT DECLINED TO APPEAR.
GEORGE BRADLEY MOVED BACK TO HIS HOME IN MASSACHUSETTS.
LAVA CLIFF, A-NUMBER ONE BEST RIDE OF MY LIFE!
FRANK GOODMAN, THE ENGLISHMAN IN PAJAMAS, SETTLED IN UTAH AND RAISED A LARGE FAMILY.
I WAS THE LAST TO JOIN, AND THE FIRST TO LEAVE!
WILLIAM RHODES HAWKINS A.K.A. MISSOURI SETTLED IN ARIZONA AND BECAME A JUSTICE OF THE PEACE.
ROLL OUT FOR BREAKFAST!
UNNNGGG. OOF. MY HEAD. WHAT DID I MISS?
A MAN GOT HIS ARM SHOT OFF AND EXPLORED A RIVER.
IS THAT ALL?
PRETTY MUCH.

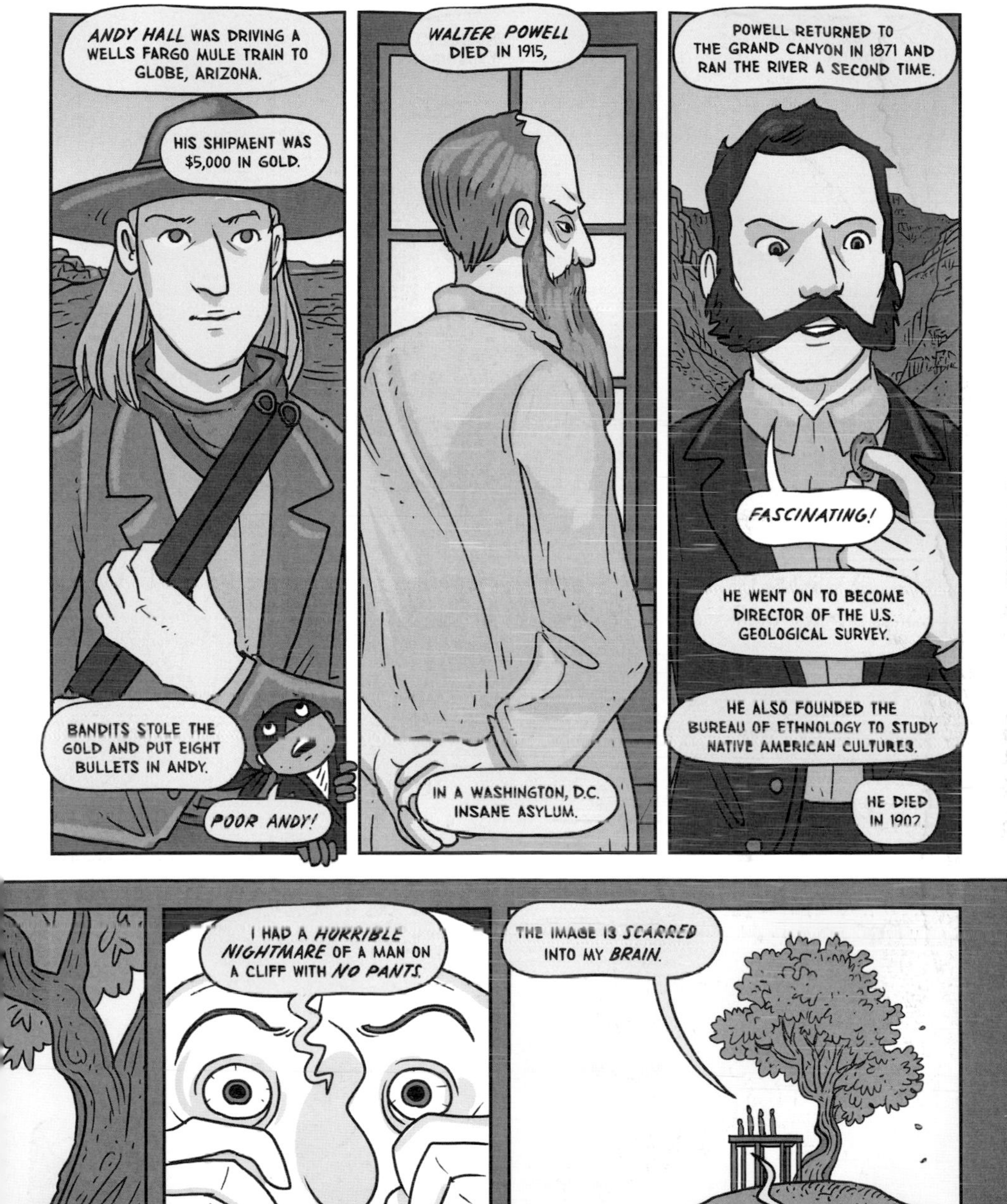

ANDY HALL WAS DRIVING A WELLS FARGO MULE TRAIN TO GLOBE, ARIZONA.
HIS SHIPMENT WAS $5,000 IN GOLD.
BANDITS STOLE THE GOLD AND PUT EIGHT BULLETS IN ANDY.
POOR ANDY!
WALTER POWELL DIED IN 1915,
IN A WASHINGTON, D.C. INSANE ASYLUM.
POWELL RETURNED TO THE GRAND CANYON IN 1871 AND RAN THE RIVER A SECOND TIME.
FASCINATING!
HE WENT ON TO BECOME DIRECTOR OF THE U.S. GEOLOGICAL SURVEY.
HE ALSO FOUNDED THE BUREAU OF ETHNOLOGY TO STUDY NATIVE AMERICAN CULTURES.
HE DIED IN 1902.
I HAD A HORRIBLE NIGHTMARE OF A MAN ON A CLIFF WITH NO PANTS.
THE IMAGE IS SCARRED INTO MY BRAIN.
TEE HEE.
THE END

ONE LAST QUOTE FROM
THE MAJOR:

"THE WONDERS OF THE GRAND CANYON
CANNOT BE ADEQUATELY REPRESENTED IN
SYMBOLS OF SPEECH, NOR BY SPEECH ITSELF.

THE RESOURCES OF THE GRAPHIC ART
ARE TAXED BEYOND THEIR POWERS IN
ATTEMPTING TO PORTRAY ITS FEATURES.

LANGUAGE AND ILLUSTRATION
COMBINED MUST *FAIL*."

—JOHN WESLEY POWELL

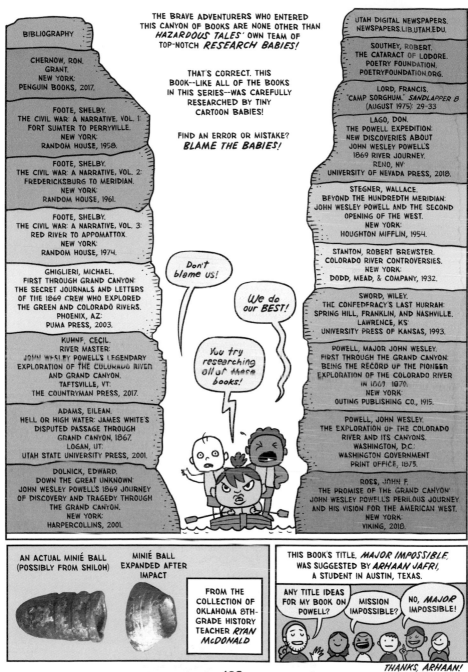

THE BRAVE ADVENTURERS WHO ENTERED THIS CANYON OF BOOKS ARE NONE OTHER THAN *HAZARDOUS TALES'* OWN TEAM OF TOP-NOTCH *RESEARCH BABIES!*

THAT'S CORRECT. THIS BOOK--LIKE ALL OF THE BOOKS IN THIS SERIES--WAS CAREFULLY RESEARCHED BY TINY CARTOON BABIES!

FIND AN ERROR OR MISTAKE? ***BLAME THE BABIES!***

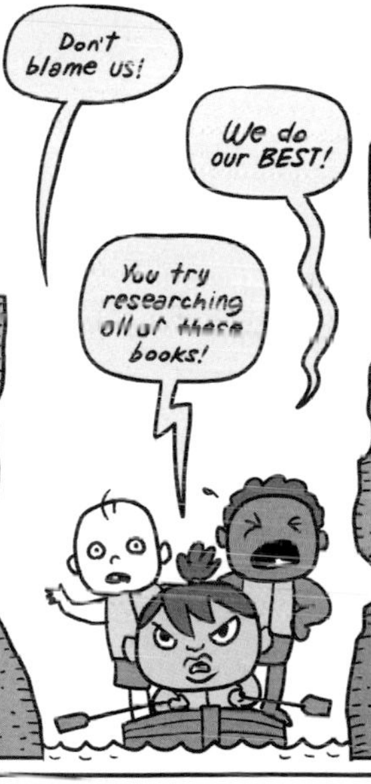
Don't blame us!
We do our *BEST!*
You try researching all of these books!

BIBLIOGRAPHY

CHERNOW, RON. GRANT. NEW YORK: PENGUIN BOOKS, 2017.

FOOTE, SHELBY. THE CIVIL WAR: A NARRATIVE, VOL. 1: FORT SUMTER TO PERRYVILLE. NEW YORK: RANDOM HOUSE, 1958.

FOOTE, SHELBY. THE CIVIL WAR: A NARRATIVE, VOL. 2: FREDERICKSBURG TO MERIDIAN. NEW YORK: RANDOM HOUSE, 1961.

FOOTE, SHELBY. THE CIVIL WAR: A NARRATIVE, VOL. 3: RED RIVER TO APPOMATTOX. NEW YORK: RANDOM HOUSE, 1974.

GHIGLIERI, MICHAEL. FIRST THROUGH GRAND CANYON: THE SECRET JOURNALS AND LETTERS OF THE 1869 CREW WHO EXPLORED THE GREEN AND COLORADO RIVERS. PHOENIX, AZ: PUMA PRESS, 2003.

KUHNE, CECIL. RIVER MASTER: JOHN WESLEY POWELL'S LEGENDARY EXPLORATION OF THE COLORADO RIVER AND GRAND CANYON. TAFTSVILLE, VT: THE COUNTRYMAN PRESS, 2017.

ADAMS, EILEAN. HELL OR HIGH WATER: JAMES WHITE'S DISPUTED PASSAGE THROUGH GRAND CANYON, 1867. LOGAN, UT: UTAH STATE UNIVERSITY PRESS, 2001.

DOLNICK, EDWARD. DOWN THE GREAT UNKNOWN: JOHN WESLEY POWELL'S 1869 JOURNEY OF DISCOVERY AND TRAGEDY THROUGH THE GRAND CANYON. NEW YORK: HARPERCOLLINS, 2001.

UTAH DIGITAL NEWSPAPERS. NEWSPAPERS.LIB.UTAH.EDU.

SOUTHEY, ROBERT. THE CATARACT OF LODORE. POETRY FOUNDATION. POETRYFOUNDATION.ORG.

LORD, FRANCIS. "CAMP SORGHUM." *SANDLAPPER 8* (AUGUST 1975): 29-33

LAGO, DON. THE POWELL EXPEDITION: NEW DISCOVERIES ABOUT JOHN WESLEY POWELL'S 1869 RIVER JOURNEY. RENO, NV: UNIVERSITY OF NEVADA PRESS, 2018.

STEGNER, WALLACE. BEYOND THE HUNDREDTH MERIDIAN: JOHN WESLEY POWELL AND THE SECOND OPENING OF THE WEST. NEW YORK: HOUGHTON MIFFLIN, 1954.

STANTON, ROBERT BREWSTER. COLORADO RIVER CONTROVERSIES. NEW YORK: DODD, MEAD, & COMPANY, 1932.

SWORD, WILEY. THE CONFEDERACY'S LAST HURRAH: SPRING HILL, FRANKLIN, AND NASHVILLE. LAWRENCE, KS: UNIVERSITY PRESS OF KANSAS, 1993.

POWELL, MAJOR JOHN WESLEY. FIRST THROUGH THE GRAND CANYON: BEING THE RECORD OF THE PIONEER EXPLORATION OF THE COLORADO RIVER IN 1869-1870. NEW YORK: OUTING PUBLISHING CO., 1915.

POWELL, JOHN WESLEY. THE EXPLORATION OF THE COLORADO RIVER AND ITS CANYONS. WASHINGTON, D.C.: WASHINGTON GOVERNMENT PRINT OFFICE, 1875.

ROSS, JOHN F. THE PROMISE OF THE GRAND CANYON: JOHN WESLEY POWELL'S PERILOUS JOURNEY AND HIS VISION FOR THE AMERICAN WEST. NEW YORK: VIKING, 2018.

AN ACTUAL MINIÉ BALL (POSSIBLY FROM SHILOH)

MINIÉ BALL EXPANDED AFTER IMPACT

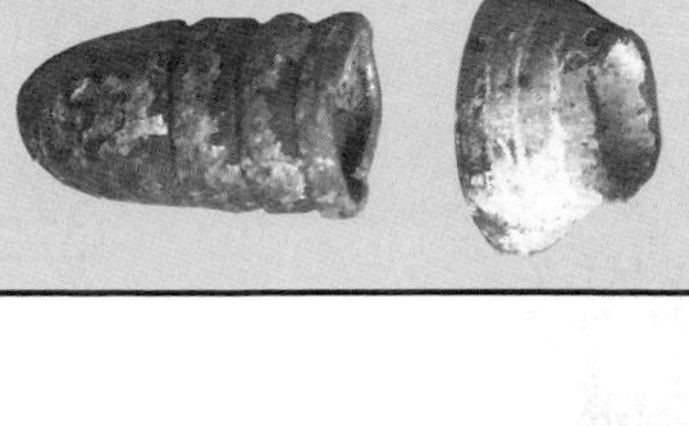

FROM THE COLLECTION OF OKLAHOMA 8TH-GRADE HISTORY TEACHER *RYAN McDONALD*

THIS BOOK'S TITLE, *MAJOR IMPOSSIBLE*, WAS SUGGESTED BY *ARHAAN JAFRI*, A STUDENT IN AUSTIN, TEXAS.

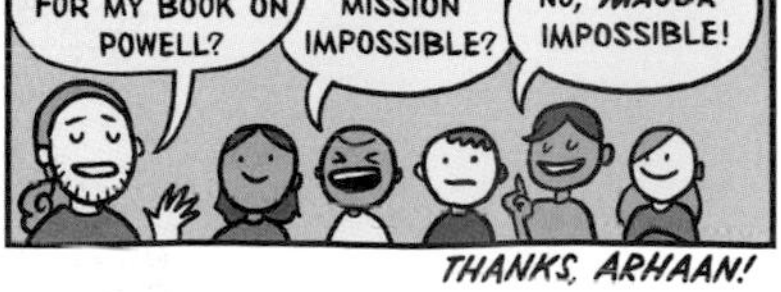
ANY TITLE IDEAS FOR MY BOOK ON POWELL?
MISSION IMPOSSIBLE?
NO, *MAJOR* IMPOSSIBLE!

THANKS, ARHAAN!

NAVIGATION OF THE BIG CANON: A TERRIBLE VOYAGE

THE PERILOUS JOURNEY OF JAMES WHITE--IN HIS OWN WORDS AND *SPELLING*

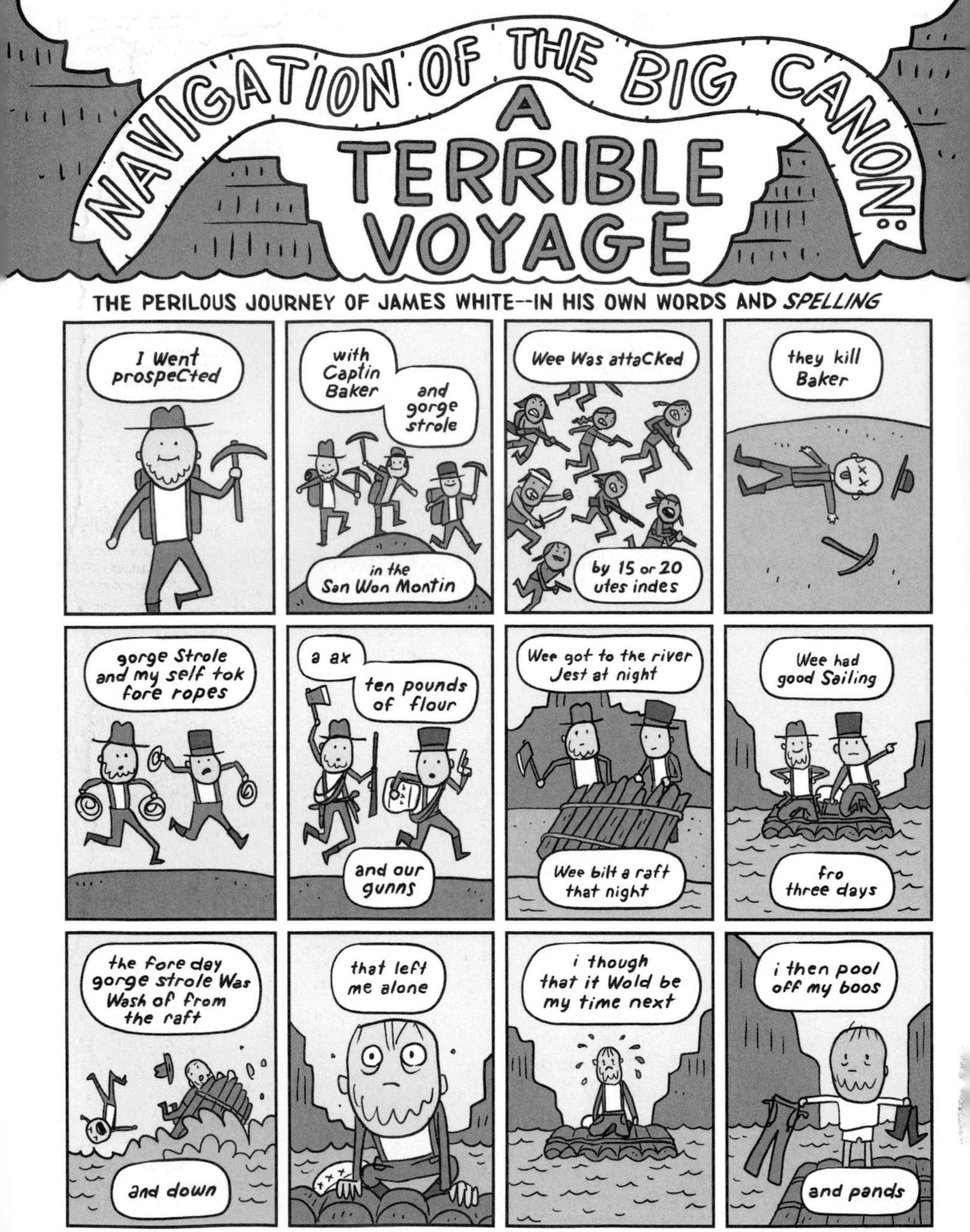

I Went prospeCted
with Captin Baker
and gorge strole
in the San Won Montin
Wee Was attaCKed
by 15 or 20 utes indes
they kill Baker
gorge Strole and my self tok fore ropes
a ax
ten pounds of flour
and our gunns
Wee got to the river Jest at night
Wee bilt a raft that night
Wee had good Sailing
fro three days
the fore day gorge strole Was Wash of from the raft
and down
that left me alone
i though that it Wold be my time next
i then pool off my boos
and pands

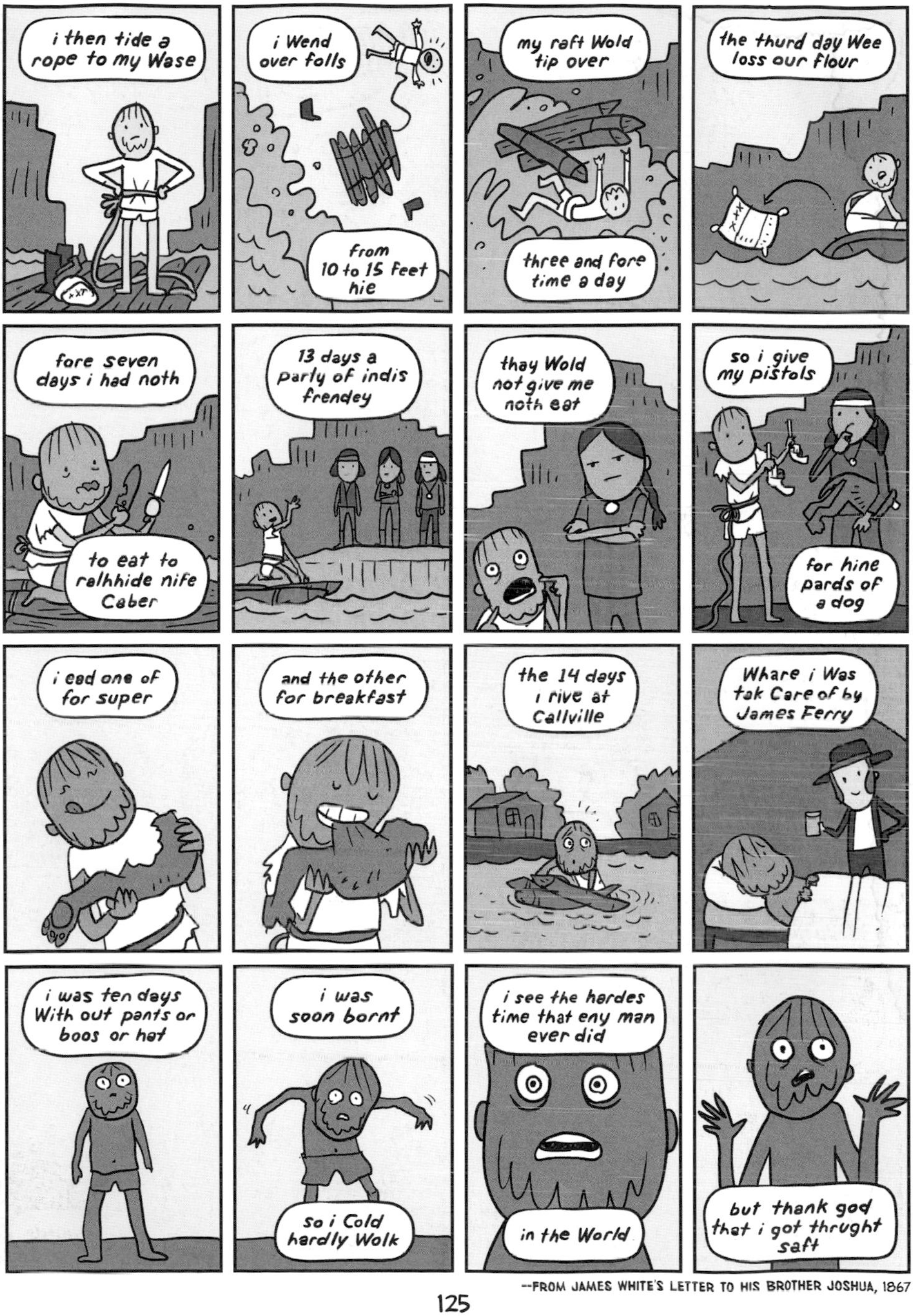

i then tide a rope to my Wase
i Wend over folls
from 10 to 15 feet hie
my raft Wold tip over
three and fore time a day
the thurd day Wee loss our flour
fore seven days i had noth
to eat to ralhhide nife Caber
13 days a parly of indis frendey
thay Wold not give me noth eat
so i give my pistols
for hine pards of a dog
i ead one of for super
and the other for breakfast
the 14 days i rive at Callville
Whare i Was tak Care of by James Ferry
i was ten days With out pants or boos or hat
i was soon bornt
so i Cold hardly Wolk
i see the hardes time that eny man ever did
in the World
but thank god that i got thrught saft

--FROM JAMES WHITE'S LETTER TO HIS BROTHER JOSHUA, 1867

AUTHOR NATHAN HALE HAS FLOATED THE GRAND CANYON *FIVE TIMES* AND HE ALWAYS TAKES HIS *WATERCOLOR* KIT. HERE ARE SOME PAINTINGS CREATED ON LOCATION.

THIS PRECARIOUS PERCH OVERLOOKS THE SCENE ON THE BOTTOM RIGHT--ABOVE DEER CREEK.

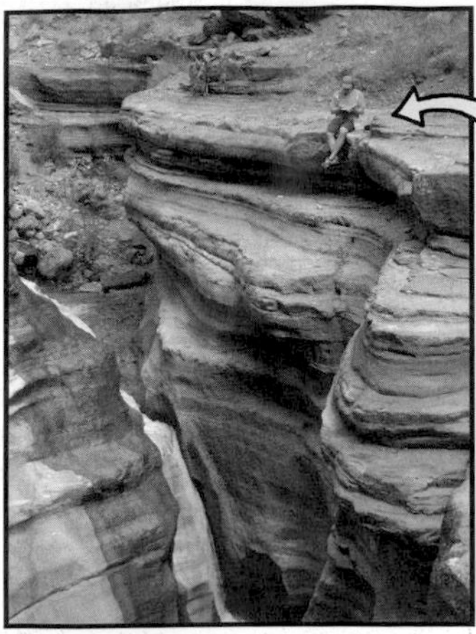

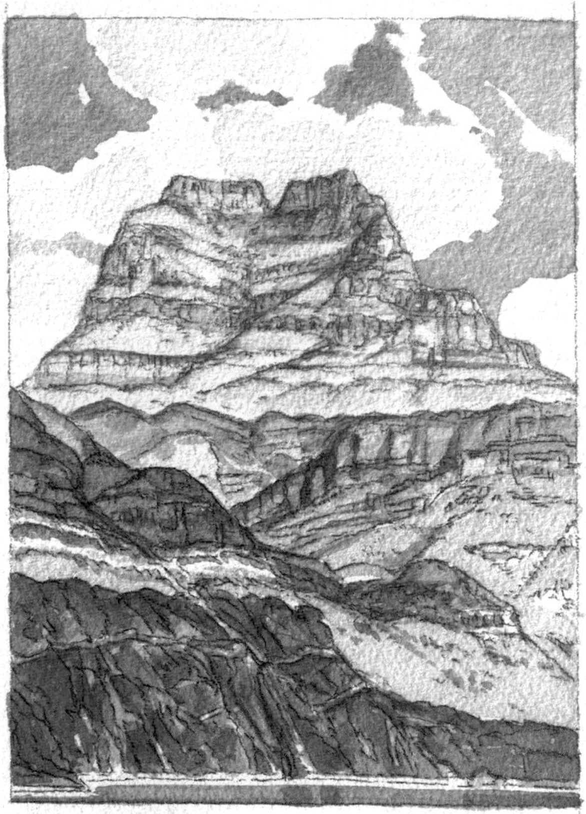

BASS UPSTREAM

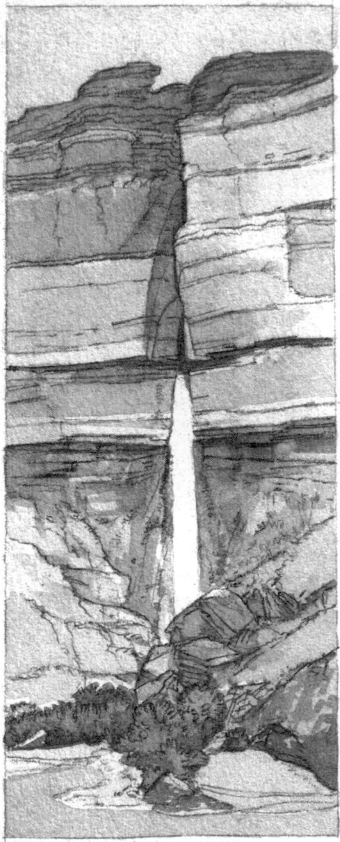

DEER CREEK FALLS

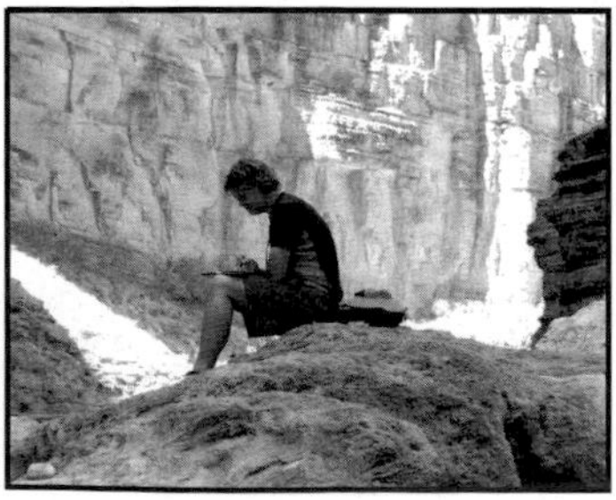

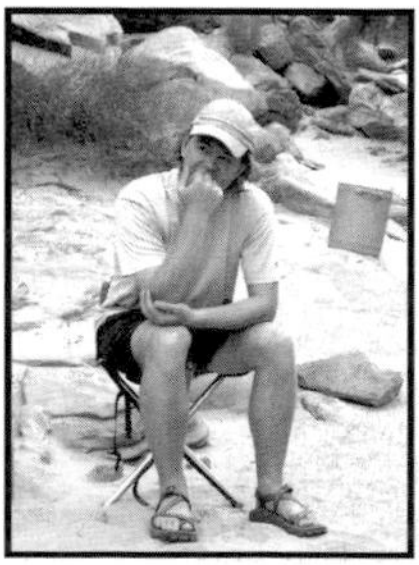

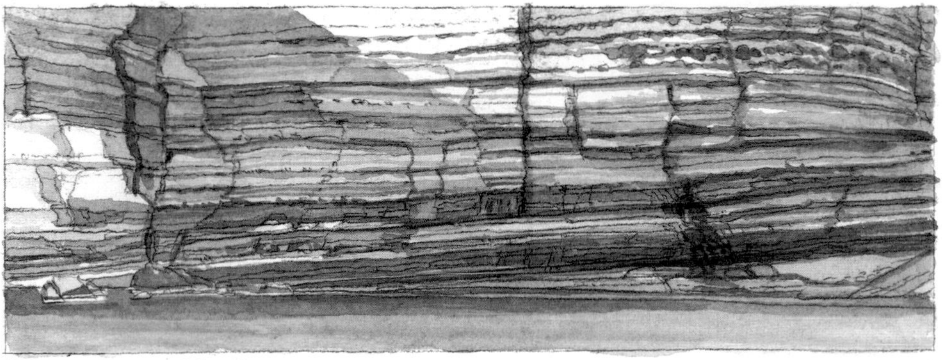
SPRING ACROSS FROM DORIS CAMP

MUCH OF THE GRAND CANYON'S SCENERY IS IDENTICAL TO WHAT POWELL SAW, BUT NOT ALL OF IT:

SEPARATION RAPID HAS CHANGED SO MUCH IT'S BARELY CONSIDERED A RAPID NOW.

LAVA CLIFF IS NOW BURIED UNDER THE WATERS OF *LAKE MEAD*. THE BIGGEST RAPID IN THE CANYON TODAY IS *LAVA FALLS*—SIMILAR-SOUNDING NAME, DIFFERENT RAPID.

THE COLORADO WAS DAMMED IN THE 1960S, FILLING *GLEN CANYON* WITH TONS OF WATER AND SILT. IT IS NOW A MAN-MADE LAKE NAMED *LAKE POWELL*, AFTER THE HERO OF THIS BOOK.

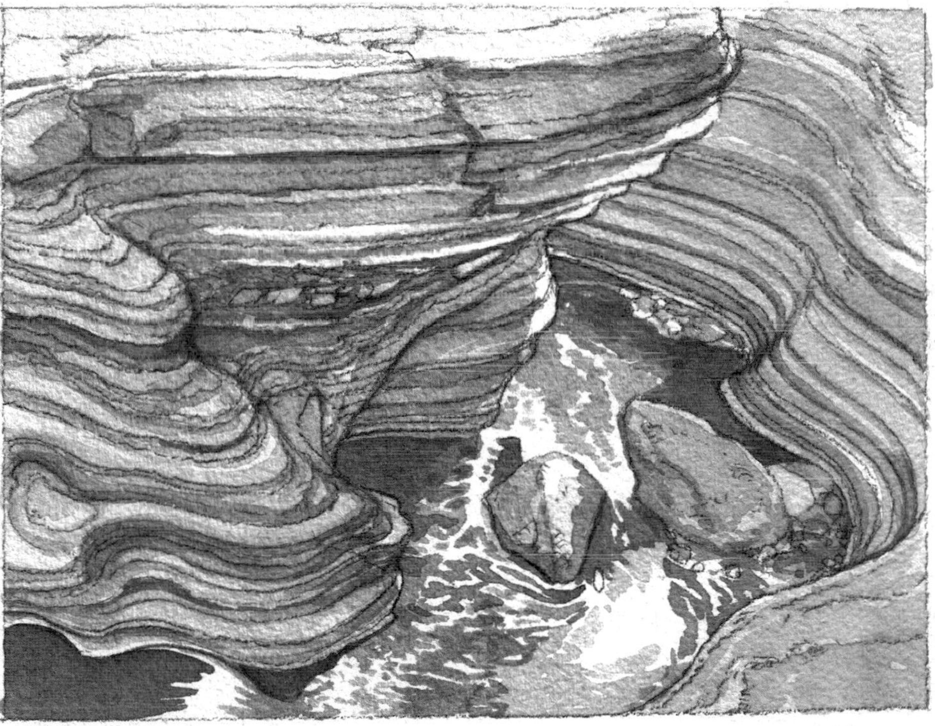
ABOVE DEER CREEK

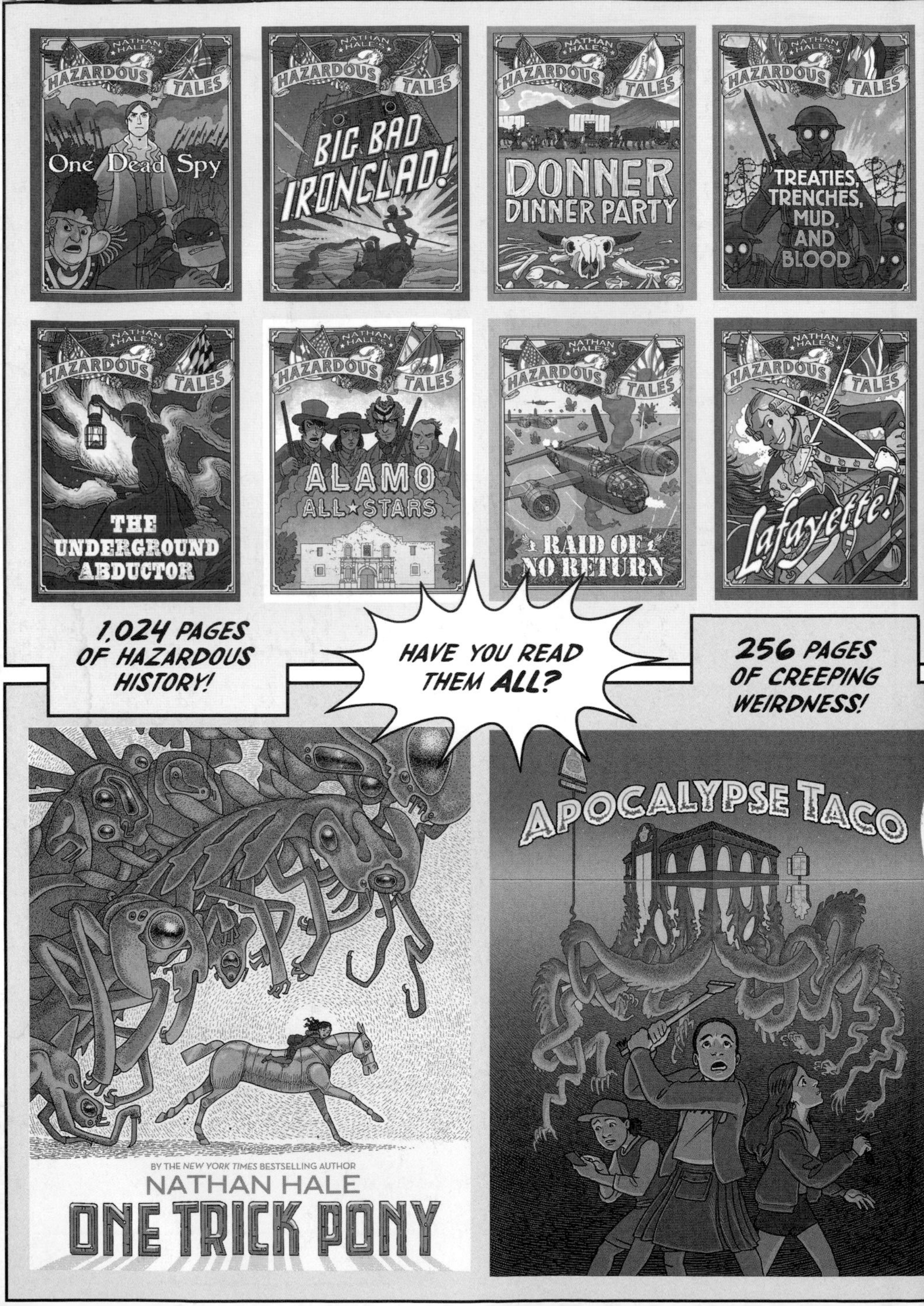
NATHAN HALE'S HAZARDOUS TALES
One Dead Spy
NATHAN HALE'S HAZARDOUS TALES
BIG BAD IRONCLAD!
NATHAN HALE'S HAZARDOUS TALES
DONNER DINNER PARTY
NATHAN HALE'S HAZARDOUS TALES
TREATIES, TRENCHES, MUD, AND BLOOD
NATHAN HALE'S HAZARDOUS TALES
THE UNDERGROUND ABDUCTOR
NATHAN HALE'S HAZARDOUS TALES
ALAMO ALL★STARS
NATHAN HALE'S HAZARDOUS TALES
RAID OF NO RETURN
NATHAN HALE'S HAZARDOUS TALES
Lafayette!
1,024 PAGES OF HAZARDOUS HISTORY!
HAVE YOU READ THEM ALL?
256 PAGES OF CREEPING WEIRDNESS!
BY THE NEW YORK TIMES BESTSELLING AUTHOR
NATHAN HALE
ONE TRICK PONY
APOCALYPSE TACO

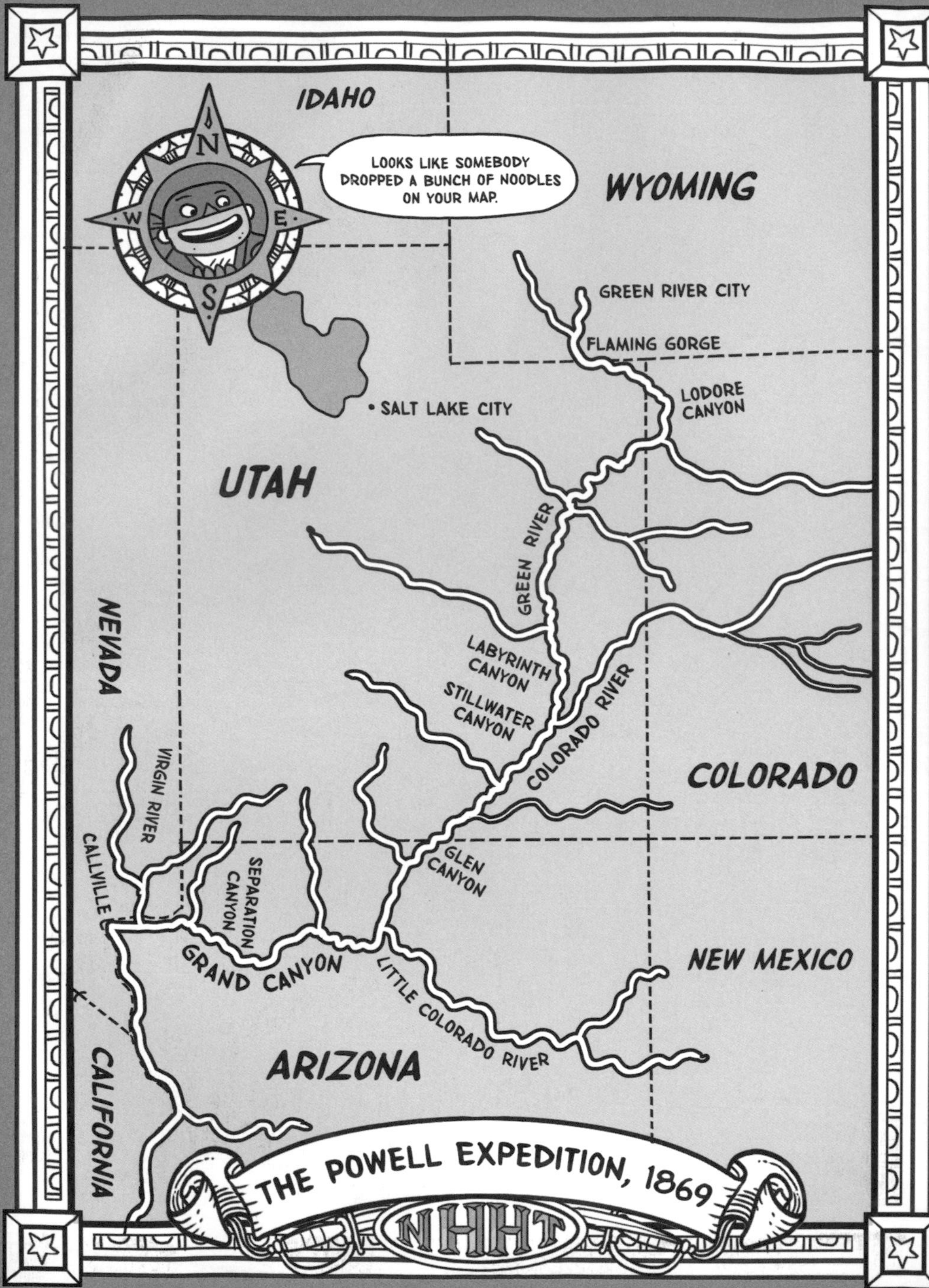

LOOKS LIKE SOMEBODY DROPPED A BUNCH OF NOODLES ON YOUR MAP.
N
E
S
W
IDAHO
WYOMING
GREEN RIVER CITY
FLAMING GORGE
LODORE CANYON
SALT LAKE CITY
UTAH
GREEN RIVER
LABYRINTH CANYON
STILLWATER CANYON
COLORADO RIVER
COLORADO
NEVADA
VIRGIN RIVER
CALLVILLE
SEPARATION CANYON
GLEN CANYON
GRAND CANYON
LITTLE COLORADO RIVER
NEW MEXICO
ARIZONA
CALIFORNIA
THE POWELL EXPEDITION, 1869
NHHT